THE YOUNGEST GIRL
IN THE FIFTH

A School Story

ANGELA BRAZIL

1ˢᵗ WORLD
LIBRARY
Literary Society

The Youngest Girl in the Fifth

Angela Brazil

© 1st World Library, 2007
PO Box 2211
Fairfield, IA 52556
www.1stworldlibrary.com
First Edition

LCCN: 2007934093

Softcover ISBN: 978-1-4218-9612-0
Hardcover ISBN: 978-1-4218-9712-7
eBook ISBN: 978-1-4218-9512-3

Purchase *"The Youngest Girl in the Fifth"*
as a traditional bound book at:
www.1stWorldLibrary.com/purchase.asp?ISBN=978-1-4218-9612-0

1ˢᵗ World Library Literary Society

Giving Back to the World

"If you want to work on the core problem, it's early school literacy."

- James Barksdale, former CEO of Netscape

"No skill is more crucial to the future of a child, or to a democratic and prosperous society, than literacy."

- Los Angeles Times

"Literacy... means far more than learning how to read and write... The aim is to transmit... knowledge and promote social participation."

- UNESCO

"Literacy is not a luxury, it is a right and a responsibility. If our world is to meet the challenges of the twenty-first century we must harness the energy and creativity of all our citizens."

- President Bill Clinton

"Parents should be encouraged to read to their children, and teachers should be equipped with all available techniques for teaching literacy, so the varying needs and capacities of individual kids can be taken into account."

- Hugh Mackay

CONTENTS

.

CHAPTER I

AN UNEXPECTED REMOVE

"Gwen! Gwen Gascoyne! Gwen! Anybody seen her? I say, have you all gone deaf? Don't you hear me? Where's Gwen? I—want—Gwen—Gascoyne!"

The speaker—Ida Bridge—a small, perky, spindle-legged Junior, jumped on to the nearest seat, and raising her shrill voice to its topmost pitch, twice shouted the "Gwen Gascoyne", with an aggressive energy calculated to make herself heard above the babel of general chatter that pervaded the schoolroom. Her effort, though far from musical, at any rate secured her the notice she desired.

"Hello, there! Stop that noise! It's like a dog howling!" irately commanded a girl in spectacles who was cleaning the blackboard.

"And get down from my desk this minute! Who said you might climb up there?"

"Look here, you kid, what are you doing in our classroom?"

"Take yourself off at once! Fly! Scoot!"

The "kid", however, stood her ground.

"Shan't move till you've answered my question," she replied with aggravating impudence. "I want Gwen Gascoyne."

"Why, there she is all the time!"

"Where?"

"Under your very nose, you stupid baby! Get down from my desk, I tell you!"

The Junior cast what was intended to be a withering glance before she descended.

"Gwen Gascoyne, why couldn't you answer when I called you?" she demanded abruptly.

Gwen paused in the act of sharpening a lead pencil, and eyed the intruder.

"Who asked you to come in here?" she retorted.

"You babes must keep to your own classrooms! Hey, presto! Vanish! And be quick about it!" interposed Myra Johnson.

"Shan't! Not till I've spoken to Gwen."

"Cheek!"

"Suppress that kid!"

"But I've got a message!" squeaked the babe, as sundry arms of justice thrust her summarily in the direction of the door. "Oh, I have really—a message for Gwen from Miss Roscoe! She's to go to the library—now!"

Angela Brazil

"Then why couldn't you say so at first?"

"You never gave me a chance!"

Gwen threw the half-sharpened pencil inside her desk and banged down the lid.

"What does Miss Roscoe want with me?" she asked in some consternation. "Are you sure she meant me?"

A summons from the headmistress rarely boded good fortune to the recipient, and the girls stared at Gwen with interested sympathy.

"What have you been doing?" murmured Eve Dawkins.

"Glad I'm not in your shoes!" proclaimed Daisy Hurst.

"Oh, Gwen, I am sorry for you!" bleated Alma Richardson.

"I've not been doing anything!" protested Gwen indignantly. "You've no need to look at me as if I were a cross between a criminal and a martyr! Here, you babe, what did Miss Roscoe say?"

"Only that you're to go to the library; and you'd better be quick, because she said: 'Tell her to come at once!' Said it in her snappiest way, too! I shouldn't be a month about going if I were you. Hello! There's the bell. Ta-ta, I'm off! I wish you luck!" and Ida Bridge fled to the region of her own classroom, with a grin on her impish face.

Though she might rail at the impudence of the small fry, Gwen was not above taking a hint—headmistresses do not lightly brook being kept waiting—so she started at a run up the passage, turning over in her mind every possible crime which she might unwittingly have committed.

"Can't remember using the front gate, or not changing my boots, or talking on the stairs, or—oh, wow! Here I am at the library! Well, whatever I've done, I suppose I'm in for it now! I hope she won't absolutely wither me up!"

So far from looking withering as Gwen entered the room, the Principal wore an unusually encouraging and benign expression. She was a handsome, large, imposing woman, with a stern cast of features, and was held in great awe by the whole school. As a rule, Seniors and Juniors quailed alike under the glance of her keen dark eyes.

"Come here, Gwen," she said blandly, as her pupil stood hesitating near the door. "I want to have a little talk with you. I've been looking over your reports for the last few weeks, and I find that you've done well—so well, that I consider the standard of the Upper Fourth is too easy for you. I think you ought to be able to manage the work of the Fifth Form, and I'm going to move you there."

Gwen stared at Miss Roscoe, too surprised to answer. Such a proposal as a change of Form was absolutely the last thing she could have expected. In the middle of a term it was surely an unprecedented happening. For the moment she scarcely knew whether to be alarmed or flattered at the honour thus thrust upon her.

"You may find the mathematics a little difficult," continued Miss Roscoe; "but Miss Woodville shall coach you until you've caught up the rest of the class. She can also go over the arrears of Latin translation with you. With that help you shouldn't be so far behind. I've spoken to both Miss Slade and Miss Douglas about it, and they fully agree with me. Do you think yourself you'll be able to manage the work?"

"I don't know, I'm sure," stammered Gwen. "I expect I'm behind in maths.—but—"

"But you must try your best. I shall trust you to make a great effort. I should be very sorry to have to put you down again. Come with me now, and I'll take you to your new Form."

Gwen followed the Principal with her head in a buzzing whirl. It seemed like a dream to be suddenly translated from the Lower School to the Upper. She wished she could have had a little time to get accustomed to the idea: she would have liked a day's preparation at least, so as to think the change over and discuss it at home. Miss Roscoe, however, always did things in a hurry; she never had a moment to waste, and at present she whisked her pupil along the corridor and into the Fifth Form room with almost breathless energy.

"Here's Gwen Gascoyne, Miss Douglas," she announced. "We'll try if she can manage the work, and I've arranged with Miss Woodville to give her the extra coaching we spoke about. She can bring her books from her old classroom at eleven."

Thus saying, she bustled away to take a history lecture, leaving the new member of the Fifth standing in much embarrassment. The eyes of every girl in the room naturally were glued upon Gwen, who felt herself twitching with nervousness under the scrutiny; but Miss Douglas motioned her to an empty desk in the back row, and went on with the lesson as if nothing had happened. I am afraid Gwen was too agitated to absorb much knowledge that morning. She had not brought notebook or pencil with her, and though at Miss Douglas's request her neighbour rather ungraciously lent her a sheet of paper and a stump of pencil, the notes which she took were scrappy and inadequate. She kept stealing peeps at the other girls, but turning away when she met the anything but friendly glances directed at her. The teacher asked her one or two questions, then, seeing that she did not quite grasp the subject, kindly ignored her.

"Talk of a fish out of water," thought Gwen; "I feel like an eel in a frying pan. I believe these girls are going to be detestable. I shall have to look out for squalls."

Nor was she mistaken. At eleven o'clock the storm broke. Directly Miss Douglas had left the room for the interval the seventeen members of the Fifth turned upon the newcomer.

"What are you doing here, Gwen Gascoyne, I'd like to know?" demanded Edith Arnold, opening the attack.

"We don't want any Fourth Form girls foisted on us!" proclaimed Rachel Hunter.

"You don't belong to the Upper School!" urged Charlotte Perry hotly.

"I didn't yesterday, but I do now," retorted Gwen. "Miss Roscoe's moved me up. Yes—and I mean to stay here, too!" she added, facing her opponents stubbornly.

"Miss Roscoe must be mad!"

"What can she be thinking of?"

"Better go and ask her yourself," said Gwen, "if you think she's likely to listen to you. She isn't generally very ready to enter into explanations."

"But this is monstrous! It's an unheard-of thing!" exclaimed Louise Mawson excitedly. "A chit like you to be brought into

Angela Brazil

the Fifth! Why, how old are you?"

"Exactly fourteen and a quarter—birthday on July 16th, if you want exact date," returned Gwen smartly.

"Oh!" "What a shame!" "We shan't stand it!" rose in such a chorus from all sides that Gwen took the opportunity to make her escape and go to the dressing-room for her lunch. The interval was only ten minutes, and she wished both to break the news to her old classmates and to fetch some necessary books from her former desk before the bell rang.

The other members of the Fifth lingered behind in perturbed consultation. They considered they had a just and most pressing grievance. In all the annals of the school such a case had never occurred before. It had been hitherto an inviolable though unwritten law that no one under the age of fifteen should be admitted to the Fifth Form, a law which they had believed as strict as that of the Medes and Persians, and here was the headmistress actually breaking it, and in favour of a girl only fourteen and a quarter. If Miss Roscoe had not brought her herself into the room they would not have credited it.

"It's abominably unfair!" broke out Rachel Hunter, a tall girl of sixteen. "Because my birthday comes on October 4th I had to stop a whole year longer in the Lower School. Yes— though my mother came and begged Miss Roscoe to let me go up!"

"Well, you couldn't get moved up on your work, at any rate, Rachel!" chirped Joan Masters. "It would have had to be favour in your case."

"That's not the point! It's a different question. If Miss Roscoe makes a rule she ought to stick to it. Why, half the girls in the Form might have come up sooner if it hadn't been for the age limit."

"You're right, and I can't see why Gwen Gascoyne should be so specially noticed."

"She's supposed to be clever, I believe."

"She doesn't look it! Besides, what do we care whether she's clever or not? It's the injustice of the thing that makes me angry. A kid like her amongst us seniors! The idea!"

"Miss Roscoe may send Gwen up," declared Louise Mawson, "but she can't make us accept her as one of ourselves. I vote we send her to Coventry."

"We will! She's nothing but a Lower School girl, and we won't tolerate her being imposed upon us!"

"She'll be so conceited at finding herself a Senior!"

"We'll soon take her pride down, then!"

"She'll meet with a few snubs here, I'll undertake to say!"

"If Miss Roscoe is going to bring up all the rank and file like that there's no credit in being in the Fifth!"

"It's a positive insult to the rest of us!"

So decided Gwen's new classmates, jealous for the prestige of their Form, and annoyed at the indignity which they considered they were made to suffer in admitting a younger girl among their number. To Gwen or her feelings they gave not a thought. If she met with an unpleasant experience all the better; it might deter Miss Roscoe from repeating the experiment. That the remove was not Gwen's fault, and therefore that it was scarcely fair to visit the headmistress's act upon her innocent head, did not enter into their calculations. Where they consider their rights are concerned schoolgirls rarely hold mercy before justice.

Meantime Gwen, who had gone to break the important tidings to the Upper Fourth, did not find her old friends as responsive as she had expected. They received her communication with marked coldness.

"Why should you have been moved up, Gwen Gascoyne, and not Daisy, or Aileen, or I?" enquired Alma Richardson, with a distinctly aggrieved note in her voice.

"Miss Roscoe always favoured Gwen!" said Eve Dawkins enviously.

"You're six months younger than Viola Sutton, so it seems absurd you should be put above her."

"You'll be so grand now, I suppose you won't care to know us!"

"It's not fair to the rest of the Form!"

"Oh dear! I'm between two fires," thought Gwen, as she hastily cleared her possessions from her old desk. "The Fifth don't want me, and the Fourth are horribly jealous. You're going to have a bad time, Gwen Gascoyne, I'm afraid! I see breakers ahead! Never mind. It's a great honour to be moved up, and Father'll be glad and sympathize, if nobody else does. The work will be pretty stiff: I expect it'll be all I can do to manage it. But I mean to have a jolly good try. I'll show those girls I can do something, though I am the youngest! Oh, I say! I've only just remembered that Winnie'll be the under-mistress. I'll have to call her 'Miss Gascoyne' whenever I speak to her. How perfectly idiotic! I'm sure I shall laugh. I wonder if Miss Roscoe's told her yet? What a surprise it would be for her to come into the room and find me there!"

"I wish you'd be quick, Gwen Gascoyne," said Eve Dawkins; "I'm to have your desk as soon as you've moved out. It's a nicer seat than mine."

"Right-o!" answered Gwen, piling her books on top of her big atlas. "You're welcome to it, I'm sure. I think you might all have seemed a trifle more sorry to lose me! I don't see any display of pocket handkerchiefs. No, I can't say I'm shedding tears myself unless they're crocodile ones. Please to recollect in future, my dears, when you speak to me, that you're addressing a member of the Upper School! You're only little Junior girls! Ta-ta!" and with a mock curtsy, in process of which she nearly dropped her pile of books, Gwen retired laughing from the Fourth Form to take her place and try her luck among the Seniors.

CHAPTER II

THE GASCOYNE GIRLS

At fourteen and a quarter Gwen Gascoyne was at a particularly difficult and hobbledehoy stage of her development. She was tall for her age, and rather awkward in her manners, apt at present to be slapdash and independent, and decidedly lacking in "that repose which stamps the caste of Vere de Vere". Gwen could never keep still for five seconds, her restless hands were always fidgeting or her feet shuffling, or she was twisting in her chair, or shaking back a loose untidy lock that had escaped from her ribbon. Gwen often did her hair without the aid of a looking-glass, but when she happened to use one the reflection of her own face gave her little cause for satisfaction.

"I'm plain, and there's no blinking the fact," she confessed to herself. "Winnie says I'm variable, and I can look nice when I smile, but I'm afraid no one would trouble to look at me twice. If only I were Lesbia now, or even Beatrice! People talk about the flower of a family—well, I expect I'm the weed, as far as appearances go! I haven't had my fair share in the way of good looks."

It certainly seemed hard that Nature, which had been kind to the Gascoynes in that respect, should have dowered her brothers and sisters so liberally, and have left poor Gwen out in the cold. Her bright little face had an attraction all of its own, of which she was quite unconscious, but she was entirely accustomed to stand aside while strangers noticed and admired her younger sister Lesbia. To do Gwen justice, though she might lament her own plainness, it never struck her to be jealous of the others. She was intensely proud of the family reputation for beauty, and even if she could not include herself among "the handsome Gascoynes", it certainly gave her a reflected satisfaction to be aware of the epithet.

"I'm like Daddy," she said sometimes; "nobody ever calls him handsome, but he's a dear all the same—the dearest dear in the world!"

The Reverend Maurice Gascoyne was curate-in-charge of the church of St. John the Baptist in the little fishing village of Skelwick Bay, on the coast of the North Sea. He was rich in the possession of seven children, but there his luck ended, for his income, as is often the case, was in exactly inverse ratio to the size of his family.

"The fact is, we're as poor as church mice," said Beatrice one day. "Indeed, I think we're poorer, because the mouse we saw in church last Sunday, that scared Winnie so, was very fat and sleek and prosperous looking, and didn't bear out the old saying at all."

For the last four years, ever since pretty Mrs. Maurice Gascoyne had gently laid down the burden that had grown too heavy for her, Beatrice had been the clever, energetic "mother" of the establishment. She managed the house, and the children, and the one maid, and the parish, and her father, all included, with a business-like capacity far in advance of her twenty years. She was a fine-looking girl, tall and straight-limbed and ample, with blue eyes and dark brows, and a clear creamy skin, and that air of noble strength about her which the Greek sculptors gave to their statues of Artemis. Though she did her best both for home and hamlet, Beatrice often chafed against the narrowness of her limits. It was a sore point that she had been obliged to leave school at sixteen, and devote herself to domestic pursuits, and while not regretting the sacrifice, she often lamented the two years lopped off her education.

"I'm so behind, I never could go in even for the matric. now," she sighed sometimes. "If I could have realized my ambition, I'd have studied for a lady doctor."

Since the profession of medicine was utterly and entirely out of the question, Beatrice often consoled herself by planning that when the children were old enough to do without her, she would go as a nurse to a big London hospital, and rise to be a ward sister, or perhaps—who knew?—even a matron. In the meanwhile her talent for administration had to confine itself within the bounds of the Parsonage and the parish, where it was apt to become just a trifle dictatorial and overbearing. It is so hard for a young, keen, ardent nature, anxious to set the world right, to remember that infinite patience must go hand in hand with our best endeavours, and that the time of sowing is an utterly different season from that of harvest.

Between Gwen and Beatrice there was often friction. The former resented being ordered about by a sister of only twenty, and would prove rebellious on occasion. Really, the two girls' dispositions were much alike, but Beatrice's early position of responsibility had turned into strength of character what was at present mere manifestation of indepen-dence and often bravado in Gwen.

Winnie, a sweet-tempered, pretty girl of eighteen, had just

been made an under-mistress at "Rodenhurst", Miss Roscoe's school, which she and Gwen and Lesbia attended daily. Teaching was not at all Winnie's vocation, she hated it heartily, but as her services cancelled her sisters' school fees, she was obliged to accept the unwelcome drudgery for the sake of the help it gave to her father's narrow income. If it was Beatrice's ambition to go out into the world and carve a career for herself, it was certainly Winnie's ideal to stop at home. She was a born housekeeper, and loved sewing and cake-baking and jam-making, and dusting the best china, and gardening, and rearing poultry and ducks. It seemed a great pity that she could not have changed places with her elder sister, but Beatrice's education had been stopped too soon for her to be of any use as a teacher, while Winnie, though not clever, had been carefully trained in Rodenhurst methods. Fortunately she had a very cheerful, sunny disposition, that was prone to make the best of things, so she struggled along, taking Miss Roscoe's many suggestions and reproofs so amiably that the Principal, often irate at her lack of capacity, had not the heart to scold her too severely. Of her own choice, I am afraid, Winnie would never have opened a book, but she managed to get up her subjects for her classes, and was a conscientious, painstaking mistress, if not a brilliant one.

After Gwen came the beauty of the family, twelve-year-old Lesbia, a dear, delightful, smiling, lovable little lazybones, usually at the bottom of her Form. Lesbia never attempted to work hard at school. She scraped through her lessons somehow, generally with Gwen's help at home, and took life in a happy-go-lucky fashion, with as little trouble to herself as possible. Lesbia's chief virtue was an admirably calm and unruffled temper: she would laugh philosophically over things that made Gwen rage, and though she had not half the character of the latter, she was a far greater general favourite. She was much petted at school, both by her own Form and by the Seniors, for she had sweet, coaxing little ways, and a helpless, confiding look in her blue eyes that was rather fascinating, and her lovely fair flaxen hair gave her the appearance of a large wax doll, just new from a toy shop. Lesbia had one great advantage: she was always well dressed. She possessed a rich cousin of exactly her own age, whose clothes were passed on to her. Irene grew rapidly, so her handsome frocks and coats were scarcely worn when they reached Lesbia, and as Aunt Violet invariably sent them first to the cleaners, they would arrive wrapped in folds of dainty tissue paper, and looking like new. It seemed rather hard that Lesbia should always be the lucky recipient of the parcels, and Beatrice, with a strict sense of justice, had often tried to adapt some of the things for Gwen. It was quite impossible, however—Lesbia's neat, dainty little figure exactly fitted into the clothes, while Gwen, tall and big-boned even for her extra two and a half years, was so many sizes too large that she had to resign all hope of "fineries", and content herself with plain blouses and navy-blue serge skirts that could be lengthened easily. Not that Gwen troubled much about dress at this period of her existence; indeed she was apt to throw on her garments in a haphazard fashion that greatly excited Beatrice's wrath, and would raise a remonstrance even from Winnie. Life was so full of different things, and so many fresh interests and new plans were crowding continually into her brain, that she never had time to think whether her tie was neatly knotted or her belt properly fastened; it is a sad admission to make, no doubt, but then Gwen was no ideal heroine, only a very faulty, impetuous, headstrong, human girl.

Three little brothers completed the Gascoyne family—Giles, Basil, and Martin, aged respectively ten, nine, and five, bonny mischievous urchins, who were alternately Beatrice's pride and despair. By vigorous measures she managed to keep them in tolerably good order, but she could never be sure what pranks they would play next, and was generally prepared for emergencies. She always had supplies handy of arnica, sticking plaster, and rags for cut fingers, and would toil away patiently mending long rents in small knickerbockers or darning holes in stockings and jerseys. Giles and Basil went daily to a branch establishment of Rodenhurst, kept by Miss Roscoe for boys under twelve; and Martin learnt his letters at home, and trotted about the house and parish in Beatrice's wake. He was a sweet little scamp, and the apple of her eye, for she had brought him up from babyhood, but she sometimes felt it would be an intense relief when he was old enough to go to school with the others.

For seven years the Gascoynes had lived at the little parsonage at Skelwick Bay. It was a small, low, creeper-covered place, built behind a sheltering spur of hill, to protect it from the fierce winter gales and the driving spray of the sea. Four latticed bedroom windows caught the early morning sun, and a stone porch shielded the front door, which opened directly into the sitting-room. There was nothing at all grand about the house, but, thanks to Beatrice, it was neatly kept, and had an air of general comfort. All articles likely to be broken by small fingers were wisely put away, or placed in father's study, a sanctum where no one might intrude without express permission; but books, paint boxes, &c., were freely allowed, and each member of the family had a special shelf on which to keep his or her particular possessions. Beatrice had many excellent rules, and though in the enforcement of these she was strict to the verge of severity, in the main she was just, and had her father's full sanction for her authority.

The garden at the Parsonage was a great joy, with its thick hedge of fuchsias, and its beds of fragrant wallflowers, and its standard roses growing among the grass, and its clumps of Czar violets under the sheltered wall. Here Winnie toiled early

Angela Brazil

and late, getting up sometimes with the sun that she might put in an hour's work before breakfast, weeding, replanting, pruning, raking, and tying up. It was chiefly owing to her exertions that the show of flowers was so good, though Gwen was her ally in that respect, and even Lesbia gave a little desultory help. There was a thick, bowery lime tree under whose shade it was delightful to have tea in summer, or to lie reading books on hot Sundays; and there was a fascinating corner of the old wall, which the girls called "the rampart", from whence it was possible to command an excellent view of the main road—a great convenience sometimes to the younger ones, who would keep watch, and beat a hasty retreat if they saw an unwelcome visitor arriving, leaving Beatrice to offer hospitality alone.

Gwen was the worst sinner in this respect. She was bashful, and hated to have to say "How do you do?" to callers. In spite of Beatrice's efforts to train her in social ways, she would fly at the very approach of a flower-trimmed hat or a white parasol.

"You scuttle off like a rabbit into its burrow," said Beatrice indignantly on one occasion; "and if you're caught, you behave in such a silly, awkward way that I'm ashamed of you. People will think you haven't been properly brought up, and blame me. It's not my fault that you've got no manners."

"I feel as if I don't know where to look when people speak to me, and as if my hands and feet were too big," protested Gwen. "I can't help shuffling and wrinkling up my forehead—I can't indeed! You're awfully hard on me, Bee!"

"Perhaps she'll grow a little more accustomed to her hands and feet when she's older," suggested Winnie, the peacemaker.

"They're useful for catching chickens at present, and that

ought to be enough for you, Win," laughed Gwen. "You'd have lost those white Leghorns if I hadn't rescued them."

Winnie was considered chief "henwife" at the Parsonage. She could not give as much time to the poultry as she wished, and had to delegate many of her duties to Beatrice, or Nellie, the maid, but nevertheless held herself responsible for the welfare of her feathered flock. On Saturdays she delighted to array herself in an overall pinafore and carry out improvements in the hen-yard. Armed with hammer, nails, and pieces of wire netting, she would turn old packing-cases into chicken coops and nesting boxes, or make neat contrivances for separating various fussy matrons with rival broods of chicks. Winnie was really wonderfully handy and clever, and albeit her carpentry was naturally of a rather rough-and-ready description, it served the purpose for which she designed it, and saved calling in the services of the village joiner, an economy which her father much appreciated. Winnie was determined to run her poultry systematically. She kept strict accounts, balancing the bills for corn and meal against current market prices for eggs and chickens, and being tremendously proud if her book showed a profit. On the whole she did well, for the fowls had a free run on the common at the back of the house, and could thus pick up much for themselves. With the help of the poultry, and a good vegetable garden, Beatrice was able to make her small housekeeping allowance supply the needs of the family, but there were no luxuries at the Parsonage. The girls possessed few or none of the pretty trifles dear to their sex, their pocket money was scanty almost to vanishing point, and they had early learnt the stern lesson of "doing without things". Adversity may be a hard task-mistress, but she is an excellent teacher in the school of life, and their Spartan upbringing had given the Gascoynes a certain resourcefulness and grit of character that they might possibly have lacked in more affluent surroundings. They were not a

Angela Brazil

perfect family by any means, and had their squabbles and their cross moods like many another; but on the whole they were ready to give and take, make sacrifices for each other, and to try day by day to live a little nearer to that wonderful high standard that Father ever set before them, and which he himself followed so faithfully and truly.

CHAPTER III

A FALSE STEP

The morning following Gwen's promotion to the Fifth Form was wet, one of those hopelessly wet October days when the grey sky and the dripping trees and the sodden grass and the draggled flowers all seem to combine to remind us that summer, lovely, gracious summer, has gone with the swallows and left her fickle stepsister autumn in her stead. It had been raining heavily all night, and it was pouring hard when Nellie placed the coffee pot and the porridge on the table and rang the breakfast bell.

"It's an atrocious, abominable morning!" grunted Gwen, peering disconsolately through the window into the damp garden. "It's sheer cruelty to be expected to turn out and tramp two miles through the mud. We oughtn't to have to go to school when it rains."

"Wet at seven, fine at eleven!" chirped Beatrice at the coffee pot.

"It's all very well for you to be cheerful and quote proverbs— you haven't to go out yourself, Madam Bee!" grumbled Gwen. "I wonder how you'd like it if—"

"Oh, Gwen, don't whine! Come and get breakfast," interrupted Winnie. "It's five-and-twenty to eight, and I've a strong suspicion the clock's late."

"It is," remarked Lesbia calmly, pausing with her porridge spoon suspended midway between plate and mouth. "Stumps put it back ten minutes last night when Father wasn't looking. I saw him."

A chorus of united indignation followed her information, each member of the family trying to bolt breakfast and scold the offender at the same time.

"We've only five minutes. Oh, you naughty boy!" shrieked Winnie.

"I didn't want to go to bed—I meant to put it on again this morning first thing—I did, honest," protested Giles, otherwise known as "Stumps".

"Lesbia, why couldn't you say sooner?" fretted Gwen.

"Only just remembered."

"And the porridge is so hot I've burned my mouth!" wailed Basil.

"You haven't a moment to waste!" urged Beatrice. "Have you all got your boots on? I shall tell Father what you've done, Giles, as soon as he comes downstairs."

Even the loss of ten minutes was a serious consideration to those members of the Gascoyne family who were bound for school. Skelwick was such an out-of-the-way place that they had quite a journey to get to Stedburgh, the seaside town where Rodenhurst was situated. First they had to walk two miles along a very exposed country road to the village of North Ditton, where they could catch the motor omnibus that would take them the remaining four miles into Stedburgh, and then there was a further walk of at least ten minutes before they reached the school. The bus always started with the utmost promptitude, so it was a daily anxiety to leave home punctually and not be obliged to run the last half mile. On this particular morning there was more than the usual scramble to get off. At the last moment Gwen could not find her galoshes, and remembered that she had broken the rib of her umbrella some days before, and had forgotten to mention the fact and ask Beatrice to have it mended.

"You're the most tiresome girl!" scolded the harassed elder sister. "Why couldn't you tell me and I'd have sent it to Johnson's last night? Now I suppose I shall have to lend you mine, and very likely you'll go and break that too!"

"I don't want yours!" snapped Gwen, tucking her hair inside her mackintosh and putting on her "stormy-weather" cap. "I wouldn't risk smashing it for a five-pound note. I'll go without!" and snatching her satchel of books she rushed after the others, who had already started.

The rain was driving furiously, and the road was full of little running rivers of yellow mud. The strong wind made Gwen's eyes smart and water, and she was obliged to hurry to make up for lost time; so when she arrived at North Ditton she was a breathless, rather pitiful object, and most decidedly cross. The omnibus was so full that she was compelled to take Lesbia on her knee and to sit wedged between a very fat wheezy old farmer and a market gardener, who nursed a parcel of plants.

"It's rather fun, isn't it?" laughed Lesbia, graciously accepting the rose that her neighbour offered her. (Somehow people always gave things to Lesbia.)

"More fun for you than for me!" growled Gwen. "I wish you knew how heavy you are!"

A bad start does not make a good preparation for the rest of the day, and Gwen marched into the Fifth Form room that morning in no conciliatory frame of mind. She was quite prepared to be ill received, so she thought she would meet possible coldness by showing a defiant attitude. It was an extremely foolish move, for it brought about the very state of affairs she anticipated. Several of the nicer girls in the Form had half repented their wrath of yesterday, and were ready not only to treat her kindly, but to influence the others in her favour. When they saw her enter, however, with a "don't care" scowling air and walk to her desk, without even looking in their direction, they decided that she was an ill-conditioned, disagreeable girl, and that they would not trouble their heads about her. Instead, therefore, of going and speaking to her as they had intended, they let her severely alone. As a rule, if we go through life expecting slights and dislike, we get what we look for: the self-made martyr can find stake and faggots waiting round every corner. Gwen raged inwardly at the neglect of her classmates, but she did not realize in the least that it was partly her own fault. She sat all the morning with a thundercloud on her face, hurrying out of the room at the interval and eating her lunch alone in a corner of the gymnasium.

"How are you getting on in the Fifth?" whispered Lesbia, who ran up for a moment to sympathize.

"Badly," groaned Gwen. "They're boycotting me. Of course the Fourth won't have anything to do with me now; so I'm like Mahomet's coffin, swung between heaven and earth! It's not pleasant, I assure you."

"I should think not. I wish I could do anything."

"You can't. Go back and play basket-ball."

It was not Rodenhurst etiquette for Seniors to talk to Juniors, so Gwen, mindful even in her forlorn state of her new dignity as a member of the Upper School, could not indulge in the luxury of a chat with Lesbia. She wandered down the corridor, read the time sheets and the announcements on the notice boards, peeped into several empty classrooms, and was glad for once when the bell rang. At one o'clock things were no better. She was given a new place at the dinner-table and had to sit between Rachel Hunter and Edith Arnold, both of whom behaved as if unaware of her presence, and talked to each other across her as though she were non-existent. When she asked for the salt (rather shortly, certainly) Edith only stared and did not pass it. By the end of the meal Gwen began to feel the situation was getting on her nerves. She had been fairly popular in the Upper Fourth, so the change was the more unpleasant.

"I'm not going to give in, though," she thought. "I believe what they want is to make me ask Miss Roscoe to move me down again. Well, they'll find themselves mistaken, that's all! I'll stay in the Upper School if nobody speaks to me till next midsummer, and if I have to stop up half the night slogging away at my work!"

"How cross that Gwen Gascoyne looks!" whispered Hilda Browne to Iris Watson.

"Yes, she doesn't seem to want to know us, does she?"

"She needn't, I'm sure. I think she's horrid!"

It was still raining and impossible to go into the playground, so Gwen strolled into the empty classroom, and for lack of anything else to do began arranging and rearranging the contents of her desk. She had not been there more than five minutes when the door opened and Netta Goodwin, one of her new form-mates, entered, humming a tune. She glanced at Gwen, went to her own desk, made a pretence of trying to find a book, sat whistling for a moment or two, then finally turned towards Gwen.

"Well, how do you like being a Senior?" she asked half mockingly.

"Too soon to tell yet," replied Gwen cautiously. "I shall know better at the end of a week."

"You've not had a very charming reception so far, have you? I saw how Rachel and Edith were behaving at dinner."

"I don't care!" snapped Gwen. "I don't want to talk to them, thanks! The Form can please itself whether it's friendly or leaves me alone as far as I'm concerned."

Netta whistled softly. There was a rather inscrutable expression on her face.

"All the same I suppose you don't always want to go on being a kind of leper and outlaw? Not very interesting, I should say, to come to school every day and speak to nobody!"

Gwen was silent. She had no argument to advance.

"They're annoyed with you just at present for being moved into our Form, but they can't keep it up long. In a little while they'll feel accustomed to you and you'll get on all right. Then the question is, are you going to belong to the Saints or the Sinners?"

"What do you mean?" asked Gwen.

"We're all one or other here. We call Hilda Browne and Iris Watson and Louise Mawson and Rachel Hunter and Edith Arnold and a few more 'the Saints'."

"Nothing very saintly about them that I can see!" sniffed Gwen.

"Well, it depends on your standards. Perhaps they thought they behaved like saints at dinner."

"More like Pharisees! Which are you?"

Netta's brown eyes twinkled.

"I leave you to guess!" she replied sagely. "I'm not stiff and stand-off like some of them are, at any rate. If you'd care to take a walk down the corridor, I'll go with you."

A stroll with anyone was better than sitting alone in the classroom; it was still only two o'clock, and there was half an hour to get through before afternoon school began. Gwen was not averse to exploring the upper corridor, for as a Junior it had been forbidden ground to her. She and Netta went into the Sixth Form room, the Senior French and German room, and even looked inside the teachers' room, finding nobody there.

"Miss Roscoe's private sitting-room is at the end of the passage," said Netta. "She's down in the library, so if you like to take a peep, you can."

The spirit of curiosity strongly urged Gwen to see what a

Angela Brazil

headmistress's private study was like, and thinking themselves perfectly safe, the two girls entered, and began eagerly to scan the pictures, the ornaments, the photographs, and the various objects which were spread about on desk and tables. It was a pretty, tasteful room, with choice prints from the old masters in carved oak frames, and pots of ferns and flowers, and handsomely bound books, and curios from foreign lands. The girls moved softly about, examining first one thing and then another with increasing interest.

"Oh, do look at this exquisite little case of butterflies! I never saw anything so perfect!" said Netta.

Gwen was standing absorbed in contemplation of a stained-wood blotter. She wheeled round, and as she did so her elbow knocked a parcel that had been placed on the corner of the desk, and sent it flying on to the floor. There was a smashing sound like the breaking of china, and at that exact moment somebody entered the room. Hopelessly caught, the two girls turned to face the newcomer. It was not Miss Roscoe—that was one thing to be thankful for—but it was Emma, the housemaid, which was quite bad enough. She looked at them as if she knew herself to be mistress of the situation, then waxed eloquent.

"I should just like to know what you two's doing here?" she demanded. "You've no business in this room—none at all. And you've gone and smashed that parcel as is only come five minutes ago from the china shop. I could hear it break. My word! What will Miss Roscoe say to this?"

"She mustn't know!" gasped Netta. "Emma, you must promise us faithfully not to tell you've found us here."

"Me not tell? And what for, please? Why should I screen you?"

"We shall get into such an awful scrape!" pleaded Gwen.

"You should have thought of that before you came!"

"Oh, Emma!" urged Netta. "We can't, we daren't let Miss Roscoe know. She'd be so fearfully angry. She might even expel us!"

"And what am I to say about this parcel you've broken? You don't suppose I'm going to take the blame of that on my shoulders! No, thank you!"

"The cat," murmured Netta.

"Cat, indeed!" repeated Emma scornfully. "That's too old a story to take in Miss Roscoe; besides which, there's not a cat in the house. She hates 'em. You'll just have to own up, and serve you both right for meddling."

"Is it badly broken, I wonder?" sighed Gwen, feeling the unfortunate parcel carefully. "It seems to be a box."

"Yes, but what's inside the box is smashed. You can hear the bits rattle when you shake it," returned Emma smartly. "It's her new afternoon tea set, I'll be bound. She told me she was going to order one from Parker's."

"There's Parker's name on the label," agreed Gwen despondently.

"Yes, and if you think—"

"Look here, I've got an idea," interrupted Netta. "You said the box only arrived about five minutes ago, so Miss Roscoe can't possibly know that it's come yet. If we could get it taken back to the shop and ask Parker's to send some more,

Angela Brazil

and we pay for it, she need never know."

"A pretty idea!" snorted Emma.

"Oh, it would be grand!" exclaimed Gwen, grasping at any way out of the dreadful predicament.

"You'll help us, Emma, won't you?" entreated Netta.

"Not I! It's none of my business."

"But suppose it were worth your while? Wouldn't half a crown buy you something nice?"

"Nothing I'd care for."

"Five shillings, then?"

Emma's face showed signs of yielding.

"I don't want to get you into trouble if I can help it," she replied more gently. "I dare say Parker's would replace the things if you was willing to pay for them, and nothing need be said. I'm not one for wanting scenes, and a scene there'd be if Miss Roscoe found her set broken. She's a sharp tongue, as I know to my cost."

"Then, Emma, will you take away the box now, and hide it somewhere, and we'll meet you in the pantry at four o'clock, and you can give it to us, and we'll take it ourselves to Parker's, and ask them to send some more china to-night. We'll bring you the five shillings to-morrow morning. It shall be a present from us both, and thank you so much for helping us! You promise you won't tell? Well, that's a weight off our minds! Come, Gwen, we'll scoot!"

CHAPTER IV

A DELICATE TRANSACTION

Gwen had stood by, listening to Netta's proposals, and offered no opposition. She was thankful to find any means of escape from the terrible prospect of braving Miss Roscoe's wrath. The Principal was a stern, even a severe woman, who never made allowances or admitted excuses, and greatly resented any liberties. How would she regard such an extreme liberty as an unauthorized visit to her private sitting-room, to say nothing of the accident to the tea service? Gwen shivered at the bare idea. She was aware that she and her sisters were received on rather special terms at Rodenhurst. Winnie's teaching scarcely compensated for the two younger ones' school fees, and did not include the daily board for the three girls, which was given in by Miss Roscoe, who knew of Mr. Gascoyne's poor circumstances. For this reason Gwen had been urged to work her hardest, so as to be a credit to her Form, and in some degree repay Miss Roscoe's generosity. The Principal had shown an interest in her, particularly in relaxing an old-established rule in her favour, and moving her up right in the middle of a term. If she were detected in such a grave breach of discipline, Miss Roscoe might consider her unworthy of any further kindnesses, might even ask her father to take her away altogether from Rodenhurst. To take her away! Why, the world would come to an end! At

Angela Brazil

home she was already regarded as the troublesome one of the family, and if she suffered this disgrace, she could never hold up her head again. Father—dear, patient, self-sacrificing Father—would be grieved and worried beyond expression; he hoped great things, she knew, from her schooling, and how could she bear to disappoint him?

Then there was Beatrice, who always seemed ready to find fault, and think the worst of her. She would almost as soon let Miss Roscoe know as Beatrice! No, at all costs the episode of that afternoon must be kept a strict secret. She dared not confide it even to Winnie or Lesbia. She must take the burden on her own shoulders, and get out of the scrape as best she could alone. Netta had assumed the leadership of the affair, so to Netta she turned for counsel and comfort.

"What's the next move?" she asked.

"Why, we must go to Parker's directly school's over, and take the parcel with us."

"I shall miss the bus!"

"You can't help that; you must catch the next."

"I shall have to dodge Winnie and Lesbia."

"Dodge them, then, and make up some excuse for missing the bus. You can say I kept you."

"How much do you think the china will cost?"

"I haven't the least idea; it depends how much is broken."

"Netta, you won't tell a soul about this, will you?"

"Tell! Am I likely to tell? No, you and I are in the same boat, and we must shield each other. I wouldn't trust anybody in the school. One never knows how things are talked about and get round from the most unlikely quarters. Whatever happens, this mustn't reach Miss Roscoe's ears."

The motor omnibus started at 4.20, and as a rule the Gascoynes had quite a scramble to rush off and catch it. To-day Gwen managed to avoid Winnie and Lesbia, and waiting until they were safely off the premises, she went with Netta to the pantry. Emma was not there, but they found the parcel behind the door and appropriated it, Gwen hiding it carefully under her waterproof. Parker's china store was in the principal street of the town, nearly a quarter of an hour's walk from Rodenhurst. When the girls arrived there, several customers were in the shop, so that they had to wait a little before anyone could attend to them.

"You speak to him—I don't know what to say!" whispered Gwen, thrusting the parcel into Netta's hand, as an assistant at last came to serve them.

Netta had any amount of presence of mind, and did not at all object to be spokeswoman. She rapidly explained that they had had an accident, and were anxious to replace some broken articles at their own expense. The shopman opened the box, and pulling out the shavings in which the china was packed, laid the various pieces upon the counter. The girls were aghast at the extent of the damage. Several cups were smashed to atoms, the teapot had lost its lid, and the cream jug its handle.

"Have you any more like them?" asked Netta anxiously.

"Fortunately we have, miss," replied the assistant. "It is a pattern we usually keep in stock, and—yes, I can match them all. I can repack the box and send it out by the six-o'clock van."

Gwen heaved a great sigh of relief. Miss Roscoe would receive her parcel that night, and would be no wiser for what had happened.

"We shall be very glad if you will do that," she said. "And will you please tell us what we have to pay extra?"

The man took the bill which had been enclosed in the box and rapidly glanced over the items.

"Let me see—teapot, cream jug, three cups, four plates—the sugar basin is all right—ah! but this saucer is cracked! Sixteen and six, seventeen and nine—it will be exactly one pound two and sixpence, please."

Gwen felt ready to sink through the floor. She had very little notion of the value of things, and could hardly believe that china cost so much. She looked blankly and helplessly at Netta, who after a moment's pause met the emergency.

"We haven't the money with us this afternoon, I'm afraid, but we'll bring it to-morrow without fail. Will that do?"

"Yes, thank you, miss, I dare say it will be all right if you give me the name."

"Miss Gwen Gascoyne," said Netta promptly.

"At Rodenhurst, I suppose?"

"Yes."

That ended the transaction, so the two girls left the shop.

"Well, Gwen, my child, you've let yourself in for a nice little bill!" laughed Netta, when they found themselves in the street.

"It's impossible! I can't pay it!" gasped Gwen, with hot tears trickling down her cheeks. "What am I to do?"

"Turn along this quiet road immediately, and don't stand mopping your eyes in the middle of High Street! Everybody's staring at you. I believe the policeman's going to ask if you're lost!"

And seizing her schoolmate by the arm, Netta hustled her away from the unwelcome attention which she was attracting. The road led to the promenade, where the girls found an unoccupied bench, and sat down to talk matters over.

"One pound two and sixpence!" ejaculated Gwen, with a sob between the words.

"And five shillings we promised Emma, so that makes twenty-seven and six," agreed Netta briskly. "Of course it was you who broke the china, so it's your business to pay for it, but I'll go shares in squaring Emma."

"I can't—I can't ever pay it! Oh, I wish I was at the bottom of the sea!" wailed Gwen.

"Don't be an idiot! It must be managed somehow. How much have you got at home?"

"I've about fifteen shillings in my money-box."

"Well, look here, I'll lend you ten, and that will just do it. We'll each give Emma half a crown to make her hold her tongue, and we'll settle up Parker, and then the thing will be done with. You may pay me back as soon as you can."

"You're a white angel!"

"No, I'm not. I'm anything but a saintly person. I'm ready to help a chum out of a hole, though. I'll bring the money to school with me to-morrow morning. And now, for goodness sake, do wipe your eyes, and put your hat on straight, and try and make yourself look respectable enough to walk down the promenade. I want to go home."

"So do I," said Gwen. "What's the time? I mustn't miss the next bus."

"It's twenty past five."

"Oh, horrors! And the bus goes at half-past! Can I possibly catch it?"

"I'll say goodbye if you're going to pelt along the promenade. I hate rushing."

"Goodbye! And thank you a hundred thousand times!"

It was only as Gwen was scurrying along the asphalted walk that it struck her that, after all, Netta was getting rather easily out of the scrape. Of course she, Gwen, had knocked over the box of china, but it was Netta who had taken her into Miss Roscoe's room, and who was therefore in a sense responsible for the whole affair. Well, she was glad enough to find help on any terms; she did not know how she was going to repay Netta the money, but that might wait. It was sufficient for the present that the tea set could be replaced without any fear of discovery. She hurried breathlessly on, fearing to miss the omnibus; taking any short cuts she knew, and breaking into a run when she reached the Ditton Road.

She could see the omnibus standing at its starting-place, and hoped it might be just possible to arrive in time. As she tore along the footpath, she noticed a boy a few yards in front of her who was running equally quickly, or even faster.

"I wonder if he's trying to catch it too?" she thought, and envied his longer legs and freedom from hampering skirts. "Oh! it's actually going! What a shame!"

The boy made a spurt, and shouted and whistled after the retreating omnibus, but it was not of the slightest avail; neither the conductor nor the driver took any notice. Realizing the hopelessness of his efforts, the boy stopped and saw Gwen, who came panting up.

"No use, it's gone too far!" he exclaimed. "It's an atrocious swindle! Those men never look. I suppose you were trying to catch it too?"

"Yes. I always go by the 4.20."

"So do I; so it's a nuisance to miss this. We're out of luck to-day."

Gwen knew the boy quite well by sight, as for the last few weeks he had been a fellow passenger morning and evening in the omnibus. He was a jolly-looking fellow, about her own age or perhaps a little older, with a brown skin and very twinkling, brown eyes. He wore a grammar-school cap, and carried some books, so she could guess his occupation in Stedburgh.

"I believe the next goes at half-past six," he remarked ruefully. "But you won't catch me waiting for it I shall walk."

"So shall I," agreed Gwen. "Walking's better fun any time

Angela Brazil

than standing waiting," and she suited her action to her words. The boy kept by her side, evidently not unpleased to have a companion to talk to.

"You're one of the Gascoyne girls, aren't you?" he began. "I see the whole lot of you every day cramming into the bus. Aren't you the one they call Gwen?"

"I believe I am."

"It's you who's generally left something behind, or lost something, or got yourself into some kind of a pickle; then the one with her hair turned up scolds."

"That's Winnie," chuckled Gwen.

"Those two youngsters are cheeky imps. Tell them they'll get their heads smacked some day!"

"They often do at home."

"Serve 'em right. I'm glad to hear it. How many more are there of you at home?"

"Only two."

"Quite enough, I should think!"

"Thank you! You've asked all about my family, but you haven't told me who you are."

"Why, I thought you knew. My name is Dick Chambers. My father is Dr. Chambers, who's just taken Dr. Harrison's practice."

"At North Ditton?"

"Yes, we only came six weeks ago. Dr. Harrison has gone to London."

"I knew Dr. Harrison," said Gwen. "He came to see us when we had scarlatina, and gave us some loathly medicine!"

"Dad can do a little in that line!" laughed Dick. "He once made me drink asafoetida when I was a kid, to cure me of sampling bottles in the surgery."

"Is it nasty?"

"It smells like a defunct rat, so you can imagine the taste."

"Ugh!"

"He doesn't give such bad things to his patients, though. There's some quite decent stuff in the dispensary, and sometimes the bottles are coloured pink, especially if they're for girls. I'm going to be a doctor when I grow up."

"I suppose you'll help your father. Have you any brothers and sisters?"

"Not a single one."

"Oh, I should think that's rather slow!"

"I don't find it so. There's always plenty to do."

"Do you like North Ditton?"

"Oh, yes, pretty well! It's nicer than Essington, where we lived before."

"Do you like the Grammar School?"

"Fairly. The chaps are rather a rotten set, and the Head's unspeakable."

Chatting thus, Gwen found the four miles to North Ditton wonderfully short ones, but when she had said goodbye to her new friend, and was trudging along the road to Skelwick by herself, she had time for many unpleasant reflections. At one blow this afternoon, she had sacrificed not only all the money in her savings box, but had got into debt as well—a debt which she had no present prospect of paying. It was most aggravating to have to empty her private bank; the contents were the accumulation of several little gifts that had been sent by her uncles and aunts on her last birthday, and even so far back as last Christmas. How would she explain, if Beatrice asked what had become of her money? She groaned as she splashed, recklessly through the puddles left by the morning's rain. She could foresee many difficulties ahead, especially at Christmas time.

The family had finished tea when she reached home, and Beatrice, grown uneasy at her absence, greeted her with upbraidings.

"Where have you been, Gwen? Why didn't you come with the others? Winnie nearly lost the bus with going back to look for you. You know quite well you mustn't stay behind like this. Answer me at once! Where were you?"

"I went along the promenade with Netta Goodwin, then I missed the 5.30 and had to walk all the way home. That's where I've been, and you may scold as much as you like—I don't care."

"Oh, Gwen!" exclaimed Winnie.

"I don't. I'm not going to be ordered about by Beatrice, and treated as if I were a baby. I'm surely old enough to manage my own affairs!"

Gwen was tired out with her six-mile tramp, and hungry, and very miserable, or I think she would not have talked in so lawless and foolish a strain.

Beatrice gazed at her in amazement. Gwen had often been naughty, but had never before ventured thus to wave the flag of defiance.

"I shall have to get Father to speak to you," she replied gravely. "He's gone over to Hethersedge to take the temperance meeting. He started at five o'clock. You'd better have tea now. Nellie has made you some more, in the little blue pot, and we kept you a potato cake, though you don't deserve it. Father will be very astonished and sorry when I tell him what you've said."

Gwen ate her meal with a big lump in her throat. She had not meant to rebel openly, but she had lost her temper, and the words had flashed out. Beatrice's threat alarmed her. Through all the tangled skein of Gwen's character there ran, like a thread of pure gold, the intense passionate love for her father, and the desire to preserve his good opinion. She could not bear to see the grieved look that came into his eyes when he was forced to reprove her. What indeed would he think of her when he heard Beatrice's account? She pushed the potato cake away, feeling as if she could not swallow a morsel.

Beatrice was putting Martin to bed. Better follow her now, and try to patch up peace. She ran upstairs and met her sister coming out of the little fellow's bedroom, candle in hand.

"Bee! I'm awfully sorry for what I said just now! I didn't really mean it I can't think what possessed me!" gulped Gwen.

Angela Brazil

"I try to do my best for you all. It's hard work sometimes to be eldest," said Beatrice, and there was a quiver in her voice too. "If only Mother were here."

"Don't!" said Gwen huskily. "I miss her so dreadfully still. Oh, Bee! If only you wouldn't tell Father about this!"

"If I don't, will you promise faithfully always to come straight home from school with Winnie and Lesbia, and never go anywhere without asking?"

"On my honour!"

"Then I won't trouble him. He's enough worries, poor darling, without adding any more to them! I only wish I could save him some of those he already has!"

Early next morning, long before Lesbia was awake, Gwen got up very quietly, and unlocked her savings box. It seemed dreadfully hard to have to take her treasured fifteen shillings; pocket money was such a scarce article at the Parsonage that she did not know when she would have the chance of accumulating so much again. There were only two threepenny bits and a penny left to rattle when she shook the box, so she sighed ruefully as she locked it, and put it back in its place on the top shelf of the bookcase. She hoped Netta would not forget to bring the half-sovereign she had promised to lend, though how the loan was ever to be repaid she could not imagine. For to-day it seemed enough if she had avoided Miss Roscoe's anger, and spared casting an added worry on Father's already overburdened shoulders.

Netta was faithful to her word; she came to school with both the ten-shilling piece and the half-crown which was to be her share of the "hush money" for Emma. The two girls held a long whispered conference together during the interval.

"I can't possibly go and pay Parker's myself," said Gwen. "You've no idea what a row I got into last night for missing the bus. Winnie'll keep an eye on me to-day at four o'clock, I can assure you. Could you go?"

"Very sorry, but I've got to go straight home too. Some cousins are coming to tea, and I have to ask Miss Evans to let me out of the drawing class ten minutes earlier. Why not get Emma to go? We shall have to see her to give her her tip."

"A good idea," said Gwen. "Emma understands all about it."

They found the housemaid when she was helping to lay the tables for dinner, and managed to draw her aside for a private talk.

"Did the fresh china come last night?" they asked eagerly.

"Oh, yes! it came all right, and Miss Roscoe never said a word, so you may think yourselves lucky," replied Emma.

"Here's the little present we promised you," said Netta, slipping the five shillings into her hand.

"I hardly like taking it!" protested Emma, though she popped it hastily into her pocket all the same.

"Could you do something more for us?" begged Gwen. "Will you call at Parker's and pay for the broken china? Here's the money—it's one pound two and six. Neither Netta nor I can possibly go."

"Oh, yes, I don't mind doing that!" returned Emma. "It's my night out this evening, and I shall be down High Street, so I can easily call at Parker's on my road. They don't close till eight o'clock."

"And you promise you'll never breathe a single word to anybody about this?"

"Not likely!" declared Emma, as she turned away to finish laying her table.

"Well, I'm thankful that's done with," thought Gwen. "It might have been an awkward affair, and I've come out of it uncommonly well. I feel as if I'd laid a ghost, and popped a stone on its grave."

It was all very well for Gwen to congratulate herself, but she quite forgot that ghosts have an awkward habit sometimes of disregarding tombstones, and rising from their graves to haunt those who have interred them. The matter of the broken china was not to be so easily disposed of as she had imagined, and though for the present her secret seemed safe, there was trouble ahead for her in plenty.

CHAPTER V

TROUBLE IN THE FIFTH

The direct result of Gwen's transaction about the china was to fling her into the arms of Netta Goodwin. With such a secret between them it was impossible not to be friendly, and though Netta was hardly an ideal chum, there seemed no choice in the matter. Moreover, she was the only one in the Fifth who had offered advances; the other girls, still indignant at the promotion of a Junior, turned the cold shoulder. This unfortunate intimacy caused Gwen to be banned the more.

"I see Gwen Gascoyne has taken up with Netta Goodwin," said Hilda Browne.

"Then that stamps her," replied Edith Arnold. "I wouldn't touch Netta with a pair of tongs myself. I thought better of the Gascoynes!"

Netta was a type of girl that can be found in every school and almost every Form. Rather deficient in moral fibre, and badly trained at home, her influence was always on the wrong side. She was clever enough, as a rule, just to avoid getting into open trouble with the authorities, but under the surface she was a source of disturbance. She had a certain following of gigglers and slackers, who thought her escapades funny, and were ready to act chorus to her lead, and though she had never done anything specially outrageous, her reputation at headquarters was not good. Every teacher realized only too plainly that Netta was the firebrand of the Form, and that while she might preserve a smug exterior it was really she who was responsible for any outbreaks of lawlessness among the others.

As Junior Mistress of the Fifth no one had more reason to be aware of this than Winnie Gascoyne. Teaching was uphill work to Winnie. She had not Beatrice's commanding disposition and capacity for administration, consequently it was the more difficult for her to keep order and enforce rules. She did her conscientious best, but girls easily find out a governess's weak point, and at present Netta was trying how far she could go. "Ragging Miss Gascoyne" was a favourite pastime of hers, and one which afforded much sport to her applauders, if not to the victim of her jokes.

A few mornings after Gwen's introduction to the Fifth there was a class for memory map drawing with the assistant teacher. Each girl was supposed to come prepared to make a map of India, and to mark in a large number of places, a fairly difficult task, and one over which many of them grumbled in unison.

"It's not fair! It takes such heaps of time to go over it at home, one hasn't a second for anything else!" wailed Minna Jennings.

"I'd a raging headache last night, and my mother said she thought Rodenhurst was getting too much for me," bleated Millicent Cooper.

"Poor frail flower! You look as if you'd wither at a breath!

Better pack you off to a sanatorium!" laughed Netta.

"And you to a lunatic asylum, you mad thing! Don't you ever get headaches with all this over-swatting?"

"No, my child, for I know a dodge or two! N. G. is no infant in arms, I assure you."

"Deign to explain, O commander of the faithful!" begged Annie Edwards.

"Well, as I told you, I'm up to a thing or two, and I flatter myself I know just exactly how to tackle Grinnie."

"Who's Grinnie?" asked Gwen rather sharply.

The others roared.

"My sweet babe, my dear ex-Junior, let us initiate you into the shibboleths of the Fifth! Yes, Seniors indulge in their little nicknames as well as the Lower School, though perhaps we are rather more cultured in our choice of them. Be it known to you then that our respected Head, vulgarly called The Bogey by ill-trained Juniors, is among our elect set yclept Lemonade, partly owing to her habit of fizzing over, and partly to a certain acid quality in her temper, otherwise hard to define. Miss Douglas, our honoured Form mistress, being a canny Scot, goes by the familiar appellation of Thistles, intended also to subtly convey our appreciation—or shall I say depreciation?—of her prickly habit."

"And Grinnie?" continued Gwen.

"Your sister, by her perpetual smile, courted the title."

"It's no good exploding, Gwen!" said Annie Edwards. "If

you've got a sister who's a teacher you'll just have to hear her called nicknames. You don't suppose we're going to shut up on your account?"

"And you needn't go sneaking, either, or it'll be the worse for you," added Minna Jennings.

"We'd soon know who'd told tales," snapped Millicent Cooper.

"Peace, turbulent herd!" said Netta, holding up her hand. "Our friend Gwen, being of a sensible disposition, and a lover, like ourselves, of all wholesome jests, fully realizes the exigencies of her peculiar situation. Though in the seclusion of her home she may be bound by many natural ties, family obligations cease entirely in the classroom. If her sister is a mistress, she is a pupil, and therefore bound to side with her Form through all those trials of tact known as 'thick and thin'. Have I not put the thing in a nutshell, O Gwendolen mine?"

Gwen could not help laughing, for there was undoubted truth in Netta's argument. Winnie would, she knew, treat her with the utmost impartiality, probably even more strictly, owing to their relationship. It would certainly never do if she were to be regarded as a sneak in the Form, ready to report misdoings and make mischief; such a character would be intolerable to her. Winnie must fight her own battles, and she would throw in her luck with her peers.

"You needn't be afraid of me!" she protested. "I'd be the very last to blab; and I like fun as well as anybody."

"I knew it, oh, altogether-wise-in-judgment! Have I not proved thee?" returned Netta, with a meaning look in her eyes which only Gwen understood. "Now, having established thy reputation, I will return to my original thingumgigs."

"Oh, Netta, stop being a lunatic, and tell us how you mean to tackle Grinnie!" interposed Minna.

"Well, my little dears, it's extremely simple, but a work of genius all the same. Genius always is simple, I believe! Behold my mapping book with its virgin page. Behold also this spotless piece of blotting paper. I turn it over, and hey, presto! a transformation. Here's my map, nicely done in pencil, with all the names marked. Nothing to do but copy it, you see. At the least approach of danger I turn it with its most innocent side up."

The girls sniggered their admiration. Gwen could not approve, but she did not protest. It was not her business to preach, so she told herself. As long as she did her own work honestly, she could not begin her career in the Fifth by assuming the very character she had just denied. Minna and Annie, inspired by Netta's brilliant idea, were copying the map on to pieces of blotting paper as fast as they could.

"It wouldn't be a bad plan to trace it the wrong way, and then rub it off like a transfer," suggested Millicent.

"Just a little too clever, most astute one! Grinnie comes round to look, and she'd think you'd got on too quickly, and want to know the reason why. You're bright, Millicent Cooper, but you're not far-seeing."

"You'll get caught yourself some time," said Millicent.

"True, O Queen! But I'll have somewhat in the shape of a run first," laughed Netta.

Gwen felt rather indignant as she began her map drawing.

She hated cheating, and it seemed very unjust that Netta and the others should win credit for what was not fairly their own work.

"Winnie's not half sharp enough," she thought. "If it were Beatrice, now, there isn't a girl in the room would dare to try any tricks."

Possibly even Winnie had her suspicions. She kept a watchful eye on the Form, and made an occasional tour round the desks. Netta was extremely cautious, but all the same her attention to her blotting paper was rather conspicuous.

"Netta Goodwin, hand me your mapping book!"

Netta started in some confusion at the abrupt order, and dropped both mapbook and blotting paper on to the floor. Gwen, equally startled, moved her hand hastily and sent her book spinning after the other. It was a complete accident, but one by which Netta did not hesitate to profit. Under the shelter of the desk she rapidly substituted Gwen's piece of blotting paper for her own, then passed up the book with an air of sangfroid truly heroic in the eyes of Annie, Minna, and Millicent. Miss Gascoyne examined the pages carefully, but finding nothing incriminating, supposed she had been mistaken. Netta might be the chief sinner of the Form, certainly, but she was not invariably at fault.

"She thought I was as innocent as Mary's little lamb!" laughed that damsel afterwards. "You were a trump, Gwen, to help me. It was a smart notion of yours to drop your book too. You did it so promptly!" Then putting her arm round Gwen's neck she whispered: "I helped you when you were in a tight hole, and I'm glad to see you're going to stand by me. I shall always count upon you in future."

So thus it happened that almost in spite of herself Gwen became Netta's ally, pledged to support her on all occasions. She was afraid to risk a quarrel lest Netta should press for the return of the ten shillings she had lent. The debt felt a millstone round her neck, from which there was no immediate chance of relief. Netta's particular clique of friends, proving Gwen safe, included her in their special set, a compromising arrangement which seemed nevertheless inevitable. The girls did not really mean much harm, but they were silly and flippant, and enjoyed evading rules simply for the fun of the thing. Netta loved to show off before the others, and because she found Miss Gascoyne an easier victim than Miss Douglas, she kept most of her sallies for the junior teacher. She could estimate to a nicety the fine distinction between giving trouble and open defiance. She never actually overstepped the line, but she contrived to make matters very unpleasant for poor Winnie. It was her boast that she could always raise a spark out of Miss Gascoyne, and her admirers were ready to titter in sympathy.

Winnie, mindful of her position as teacher, never mentioned school affairs to Gwen; but one day Beatrice tackled the latter on the subject.

"I hear you've struck up a friendship with Netta Goodwin," she began. "I'm very surprised, for she doesn't seem a nice sort of girl."

"She's the only one who's been kind to me," returned Gwen, up in arms at once at Beatrice's tone.

"Indeed! Well, I wouldn't be too much with her if I were you. I'm afraid she's anything but desirable."

"Who said I was much with her? Has Winnie been telling tales about me?"

"Don't be nasty, Gwen. You know Winnie never tells."

"There's no particular harm in Netta," protested Gwen, taking up the cudgels for her schoolmate out of sheer contrariness. "She's only rather lively and funny. I suppose that's no great crime."

"Are you sure Father would like her?"

"Dad doesn't know her, so I can't pretend to say what he'd think of her," retorted Gwen, shuffling out of the matter with what she knew was a lame excuse.

CHAPTER VI

A CASTING VOTE

Gwen had not been prepared to find the Fifth exactly a bed of roses, therefore she was hardly surprised at the thorns which beset her new path. In spite of the extra teaching from Miss Woodville, she found the work of the Form extremely difficult, especially in mathematics. There was a whole book of Euclid theorem which she had not been through, and the consequence was that every other problem had some little point proved by a theorem of which she had never heard. It was a most decided stumblingblock. It is possible to sit and look at a problem for hours without getting any further if there is just one statement of whose existence one is not aware. More than once Gwen had to hand in a blank page, and felt very humiliated at the meaning glances which passed between Rachel Hunter and Edith Arnold. Neither of these was yet reconciled to Gwen's presence in the Form. Rachel, mindful of her own delayed promotion to the Upper School, persisted in regarding her as an "intruding kid", and Edith could not forgive her intimacy with Netta Goodwin. Manifold small slights and snubs fell to Gwen's share, and though she affected to make light of them, they hurt all the same. She knew that under happier auspices she might have been friendly with Hilda Browne, Iris Watson, Louise Mawson, and several others of whom Father would have approved, and whom, with his entire sanction, she might have invited occasionally to the Parsonage. She was aware that she was in the worst set in the Form, and that not one of her new chums would pass muster if judged according to her home standards.

"I can't ever ask them, that's all," she declared. "Annie's giggles would give Beatrice a fit, Millicent puts on side horribly, Minna would probably make fun of everything, Claire Harris is absolutely vulgar, and as for Netta—no! Dad mustn't see Netta on any account."

Another not unexpected trouble had fallen to Gwen's share. As a member of the Upper Fourth she had, at the beginning of the term, been chosen Junior Basket-ball Captain, to arrange Lower School team games and matches, and she had worked very hard to get things going. On her promotion, however, it had been a greatly discussed point whether she should resign or finish the season. Some of the Upper Fourth, knowing how much was due to Gwen's exertions, had been anxious for her to retain her post, but on the whole the popular verdict was against her. To Gwen's disgust, her old friends, Eve Dawkins and Alma Richardson, were the loudest in her disfavour, and it was chiefly owing to their eloquence that she was requested to resign. She had been proud of her captaincy, and to give it up was a wrench. There seemed nothing at all in her new Form to compensate for the loss, and sometimes she wished heartily that she had never been moved.

The present excitement in the Fifth was a "Literary and Dramatic Club", the members of which intended to act a piece at Christmas. It was a rather cliquish society, worked with more favour than fairness, and was principally among those girls whose homes lay near to the school.

"They stay behind at four o'clock to rehearse," explained Netta. "It's really only among about half a dozen."

"Are you in it?" queried Gwen.

"I, my dear child? Hardly! You don't imagine the high and mighty Iris Watson would ask yours truly? Saints and sinners don't mix in this Form, if you please!"

"Do you mean to tell me the whole thing is in the hands of Iris and a few others?"

"With your usual astuteness you've hit the nail on the head."

"But that's monstrously unfair!" exclaimed Gwen indignantly. "A Dramatic Club ought to be for the whole Form. Everybody ought to have an innings, in the name of common justice."

Netta shrugged her shoulders.

"I don't want to act with Iris and Edith and Louise, thank you! A pleasant performance it would be! They may keep their precious piece to themselves, so far as I'm concerned."

"But that's not the point," persisted Gwen. "It's the fairness of the thing I'm talking about. One set has no right to monopolize everything."

"It is sickening, certainly."

"It's worse than sickening, it's intolerable, and I'm going to make a stand against it."

"You can try if you like, but you needn't expect success."

When Gwen had a cause to champion, she was ready for a

fight, even on the losing side. One of her characteristics was a strong sense of justice, and here, she considered, was a distinct case of oppression. She thought over her plan of campaign, and decided that she would ask to be admitted to the Dramatic Club. Next morning, accordingly, she approached the five or six girls who constituted that society.

"Want to join our Dramatic Club!" exclaimed Louise Mawson almost incredulously. "I dare say you do!"

"But you won't!" said Hilda Browne quickly.

"Cheek!" ejaculated Rachel Hunter.

"Why shouldn't I join?"

"On the other hand, why should you?"

"Because a society ought to be open to the whole Form, and not just kept amongst a few. We didn't manage things like that in the Upper Fourth."

"How very kind of you, fresh from the Juniors, to come and give us Seniors a lesson in managing our affairs! Perhaps you'd like to be President? Would that content you?" enquired Hilda Browne sarcastically.

"I don't want to be President, but I claim the right to have some say in the matter. The thing ought to be properly constituted, and every girl in the Form ought to vote for officers."

"Well, of all cool proposals!"

"Look here, Gwen Gascoyne, you need suppressing!"

"She's not worth noticing!"

It was only what Gwen had expected, but she felt she had at any rate opened fire. She did not mean to retire vanquished after a first attempt. She now directed her energies to another quarter. She canvassed the entire Form, asking each girl separately if she did not consider the Dramatic Club ought to be put upon a general basis. Everybody, except those who were already members, agreed. Many had thought the present arrangement unfair, and had grumbled loudly, though nobody had had the initiative to start a revolt. Now Joan Masters and Elspeth Frazer took the matter in hand seriously, tackled the clique, and argued the question.

"You may run a private club if you like for your own amusement," said Elspeth, "but if you're going to call it 'The Fifth Form Dramatic', and give a performance before the other Forms at Christmas, then it must be a fair and open thing. Everyone must be eligible for membership, and officers should be chosen by ballot."

"Half of you wouldn't be able to join," declared Hilda Browne.

"That's our own lookout. The point is that we ought to be able to do so if we want. If you persist in keeping it all to yourselves, you may act without an audience, for none of us will come to see you, and we'll tell the other Forms what the quarrel is."

"I know they'd back us up," said Joan Masters.

Very unwillingly the clique gave way. They knew they had no just ground for their position, but they had hoped it would not be called in question.

Angela Brazil

"It's all the fault of Gwen Gascoyne, with her Lower School notions," said Rachel Hunter.

"She needn't think she's going to act!" asserted Edith Arnold.

"Don't want to!" rapped out Gwen, who happened to overhear. "I should miss the bus if I stayed behind after four. I only wanted to see things made fair and square."

Though the new arrangements were really owing to Gwen's enterprise, nobody was willing to accord her any thanks. Joan Masters and Elspeth Frazer received all the credit for having righted the wrong; and though a few might remember that Gwen had started the movement, they were almost ready to agree with Rachel Hunter that it was rather pushing of an ex-Junior to have taken so much upon herself. They had not yet forgiven her translation to the Fifth, and only the utmost humility on her part would have reconciled them. Humility was certainly not Gwen's characteristic, so she still went by the epithet of "that cheeky kid" in the Form.

"So much for their gratitude," confided Gwen to Lesbia. "I don't want to act, but some of those who have got into the play might at least acknowledge what I've done for them."

"They seem a hateful set!" sympathized Lesbia.

"Detestable!" said Gwen with unction.

One thing had not been settled by the Dramatic Society, and that was their choice of a President. Names were canvassed freely in the Form, and finally Hilda Browne and Elspeth Frazer were put up as candidates. Voting was to be by ballot during the interval, but while the papers were being given out Gwen bolted. She was feeling cross and forlorn, and sick of the whole affair.

"I don't mind who's chosen President," she thought "It makes no difference to me. They may elect whom they like."

So she went a solitary little walk round the playground, whistling a tune, and trying to look as if she didn't care about anything. She had not been there very long before she saw Betty Brierley and Ida Young signalling to her from the gymnasium door. She took no notice of their beckonings, whereupon they ran after her, and seizing her one by each arm, began to drag her towards the house.

"You're wanted most particularly, Gwen Gascoyne!" said Betty excitedly.

"We've been sent to fetch you quick!" chimed in Ida.

"Hello! Hands off!" cried Gwen, dragging herself from their grasp. "What do you want with me, I should like to know?"

"It's the others who want you."

"What for? Didn't know I was so popular!"

"You've not voted for a President yet."

"No, and I don't mean to, either."

"But, Gwen, you must! We've taken the ballot, and the votes are exactly even. You've got the casting vote!"

"Have I, indeed? No, thank you! It's rather too great an honour!"

"But look here, Gwen, it's the only way to decide it. We've got to choose either Elspeth or Hilda."

"Then you may fight it out amongst you. You don't suppose, when you've all voted by ballot, that I'm going to take the responsibility of a casting vote. It's a most unfair proposal. Why, the rejected candidate and all on her side would never forgive me!"

"We might have the ballot again," suggested Betty. "Then you need only put your cross."

"As if everybody wouldn't know who was responsible for the extra cross! I might as well write Gwen Gascoyne on my paper at once! It's no use pulling my arm; I'm not coming in to be made a cat's paw. You may go and tell the others so if you like."

Betty and Ida departed, grumbling loudly at Gwen's "unaccommodatingness", as they called it, and Gwen stayed in the playground until the bell rang, fuming with indignation. Every fresh little episode seemed to serve to make her more of an alien in the Form than ever. But here her decision was absolutely justifiable; not one of the girls would have cared to accept the unenviable role which they had wished to thrust upon her. Perhaps for that very reason they were all the more annoyed at her action. She was received with black looks when she re-entered the classroom. Elspeth Frazer whispered something to a friend, and turned away. Gwen could not quite hear, but it sounded painfully like "beast!"

"Have they settled it?" she asked Netta.

"Yes; Elspeth and Hilda drew lots, and Hilda won. I'm fearfully sorry she did. Elspeth says it's all your fault, and that you ought to have voted for her when you'd made such a fuss about the clique."

"Would you have given a casting vote yourself?"

"Well, no; but if you'd only stayed and voted by ballot like everyone else, then nobody would have known who'd given the odd one. It was most stupid of you to rush away. You're rather an idiot, Gwen Gascoyne!"

"'*Et tu, Brute!* Then fall, Caesar!' I'm like the old man and his ass in AEsop; I seem to end by pleasing nobody."

"Do you wish to compare yourself with the old man or the quadruped, my child? The latter's the more apt, certainly!"

"Oh, good night!" said Gwen, who was getting the worst of it "I wish sometimes I'd never come into your wretched Form."

"You'd be far more at home among the Juniors!" snapped Netta, rather out of temper.

A few days after this was the Rodenhurst Annual Distribution of Prizes. It was always held in the beginning of November, rather an unusual date, to be sure, but Miss Roscoe found it convenient in many ways to have it in the middle of the autumn term. It gave plenty of time to receive examiners' reports, and to chronicle successes in the July examinations, but on the other hand it did not interfere with Christmas celebrations.

The function took place in the Town Hall at Stedburgh, and there was invariably a large gathering of parents and friends. To the whole school it seemed an important occasion, and both Gwen and Lesbia were full of excitement when the afternoon arrived.

"Not that I need alarm myself that I shall be called upon to walk up and receive a prize!" said Lesbia. "Never got one in my life, and never shall!"

"You might get the Sewing or the Holiday Competitions," said Gwen, trying to be encouraging.

"No fear! One genius is enough in a family! I'll go prepared to clap you!"

All the girls wore white dresses and blue hair ribbons, and made quite an imposing array as they sat in the central aisle of the large room at the Town Hall.

"There seem to be far more of us when we're in white!" said Gwen. "We don't look half so many in the lecture hall at school. Have a few little angels crept in unawares?"

"You're not one of them, at any rate," laughed Netta, who was sitting next to her.

To Gwen the great feature of the occasion was that Father was seated on the platform, in company with several other clergymen and the Mayor, who was to distribute the prizes. Beatrice was amongst the audience, and had brought Martin with her, and Giles and Basil had come with the Boys' contingent. All her family were present, and if she were to get a prize, how pleased they would be!

The proceedings began with the usual speeches from the chairman and others. Gwen had heard these every year, and they were always pretty much on the same theme. It is hard to be original at prize-givings, and the gentlemen who had been asked to "say a few words" might be forgiven if their remarks were somewhat hackneyed. Miss Roscoe read the examiners' report on the school, and the successes in the Matriculation and the Senior and Junior Oxfords. These the girls knew already, so, though they clapped heartily, it did not cause much excitement. Everyone was waiting in suspense for the prize list.

Miss Roscoe always began with the lowest Form, so the first to walk up to the platform was a small kindergarten child, who had won honours for "general improvement". Neither Giles nor Basil had any luck; they were too erratic to be serious students, but when it came to the turn of the Middle Second, Lesbia Gascoyne was awarded the prize for plain sewing. A perfect storm of clapping greeted pretty Lesbia as she returned down the hall to her place. She was a tremendous favourite at Rodenhurst, and Seniors and Juniors alike applauded. It was the first time she had ever distinguished herself in any way, and though it was only for plain sewing, the girls were ready to give her an ovation. At last the Upper Fourth was reached, and Gwen knew that as she had taken her exams with her old Form (the Middle Fourth it had been in July) her name would be still on that list.

"First prize for Mathematics, Gwen Gascoyne," read Miss Roscoe.

Gwen's heart thumped, for a moment she did not move, till Netta gave her an admonishing push, then she walked up the hall. The Mayor handed her a volume of Coleridge's poems, handsomely bound in calf, and emblazoned with the school arms; he smiled pleasantly as he did so, and added a word of compliment. Gwen murmured "Thank you", and turned away. Father was clapping his loudest on the platform, and there was a nervous little applause from the rest of the family and from Netta, but that was all. Not a single girl in either Gwen's old Form or her new one gave her the least sign of appreciation. The colour flamed into her face as she made her way back to her seat. It is hard at any time to be unpopular, but it is a cruel thing when the lack of favour is displayed before a public audience. Gwen stuck her nose in the air, and put on the most defiant, don't care expression she could assume, but she felt the slight deeply, especially when she heard the hearty reception given to Iris Watson, who had won the Languages medal.

"Never mind, childie!" said Mr. Gascoyne, when at "good night" time that evening, in the safe sanctuary of Father's study, she broke down, and burst out crying; "you did your best, and you deserved your prize. That's the main thing!"

"I shall hate the prize now!" sobbed Gwen. "I can't bear to look at it; it will always remind me of this horrid afternoon. Why should they have been so nasty to me? They clapped Lesbia!"

"Gwen, you're not jealous?" Father's voice was just a trifle anxious.

"No, no!" gulped Gwen emphatically. "Lesbia's a darling; I don't wonder people are fond of her. But oh, Dad, it is hard sometimes to be left out in the cold!"

"Very hard. Many older and wiser people than you have felt that. Yet to bear neglect well is one of the bravest things in life. Don't worry about not being appreciated; your own self-respect is worth more to you than the opinion of other people. If you're quite sure you're doing your duty, you can afford to ignore what the world thinks."

"I don't know why I should be so unpopular," sighed Gwen, squeezing Father's hand tightly, and rubbing her cheek against his coat sleeve, as if there were something comforting in the very feel of the cloth.

"You must live it down. It may take a long time, and a great deal of patience, but I'm sure you'll win, and the girls will be proud of you yet."

"Proud! They may get to tolerate me, but I don't believe I'll ever make them like me, Daddy!"

"Courage! We never know what we can do till we try. If you want to be liked, make yourself wanted. Good night, childie! Cheer up! The world's not such a bad place, after all."

"Not while you're in it!" said Gwen, kissing the dear, plain face that was so like her own.

Angela Brazil

CHAPTER VII

DICK CHAMBERS

Since the afternoon when Gwen had stopped behind in Stedburgh to arrange about the broken china, and had been obliged to walk home, she had seen nothing more of Dick Chambers. She looked out for him every morning on the bus, but he was not there, and she was just wondering what had become of him when he turned up in the most unexpected quarter. It was the Saturday morning after the prize-giving. Saturday was a whole holiday, and therefore a blissful day, every moment of which was appreciated. Gwen was returning about ten o'clock from an errand she had been sent to do in the village, and as she opened the Parsonage gate she saw in the middle of the front walk a boyish figure that looked familiar.

"Hello! What are you doing here?" she exclaimed.

"Come on business of a rather particular character," grinned Dick. "Didn't you know your Father's coaching me?"

"He never said so!"

"He is, though. I'm to come three days a week, from nine to ten, and I've just made a start this morning. I say, he's a ripping chap!"

"I agree with you there," remarked Gwen. "But why aren't you going to school?"

"Thereby hangs a tale! I happened to do an idiotic thing one afternoon—fainted in the lab, and had to be picked up in the midst of fragments of glass that I'd smashed to smithereens. Then Dad got some wretched specialist to come down and see me, and the fellow said I must stop school for this term at any rate."

"Oh, I'm so sorry! Do you feel ill?"

"No. I'm all right—but it's rather rotten, for I'm knocked off 'footer'."

"How sickening for you! I know how wild I should be if I mightn't play hockey. What may you do?"

"Only just loaf about—not even golf."

"May you go walks?"

"Oh, yes! but it's rather slow mooning about on the moors by oneself."

"Have you been to see Stack Head, where the sea-birds build? Or the chasms? Oh! you ought to go there! I'll show you the way if you like!"

"I wish you would!"

"There'd be heaps of time this morning—that's to say if I may go," added Gwen, suddenly recollecting that she had promised Beatrice on her honour not to go anywhere without leave. "Oh, here's Dad, so I can ask him."

"Yes, by all means take Dick to Stack Head, the walk will do him good," replied Mr. Gascoyne. "Be careful, and don't scramble about too much, that's all—those cliffs are dangerous, remember!"

"We'll go as cautiously as two pussy-cats," said Gwen.

"Hardly an apt simile!" laughed Mr. Gascoyne, pointing to Pluto, the black Persian, that was careering madly up a tree at the moment. "However, you're used to Skelwick rocks, and Dick will have to learn his footing. Only please don't learn it at the expense of your neck, Dick! We haven't gone far enough with the Latin prose yet!"

"You needn't be afraid for me, sir, though I came a cropper over old Cicero this morning," laughed Dick.

It was a beautiful, sunny day in early November; one of those late autumn days when a little crisp hoar frost lingers in the hollows, but in the full sunshine it is almost as warm as summer. Gwen fetched a favourite stick, her indispensable companion on the moors, and, discarding her jacket, set forth joyously for a five-mile tramp. She loved the great bare headland that rose behind the Parsonage; there was a sense of freedom in leaving the houses of the village, and seeing only sea and sky around, and feeling the short, fine grass under her feet. It was a stiff climb to the top of the plateau, but once up there was a tolerably flat walk of about a couple of miles to the jagged rocks that formed the end of the promontory.

"Isn't it glorious?" said Gwen, when, the scrambling part finished, they sat for a moment or two on a rock to take breath. Below lay the clear, grey, even, shimmering surface of the sea, a little hazy at the horizon, and changing to deepest green as it neared the cliffs, where the sea-birds wheeled round screaming in sheer joy of life. "Don't you feel as if you could take a jump from the edge and just go sailing down like a gull, and land gently on the water, and float off?"

"Better not try the experiment unless you provide yourself with a parachute! An aeroplane could make a good start up here. Do you ever get any guillemots' eggs? Or puffins'?"

"Not often; though sometimes the lighthouse men bring us a few. Are you collecting eggs?"

"Rather! I've got nearly five hundred. I could do with a razor-bill's or a puffin's."

"You'll have to wait till next summer. June and July are the best months. I can show you where the birds sit, though. They haven't proper nests, they just squat on the rocks, packed as close together as sardines. It's wonderful to see them. And the noise they make! No, it isn't here, it's over by the chasms; we shall get there soon."

Half an hour's brisk walking brought them to what must have seemed to the ancient inhabitants of these islands the end of the world. The headland descended in a sheer precipice into the water, while wicked-looking rocks showed a black point here and there among the surf as a warning to any vessel to give them a wide berth. The cliff was hardly less dangerous than the rocks below, for its surface was torn into great rugged chasms, each as deep as the sea level, though often only a few feet in breadth. These curious natural rents wound in tortuous course to the edge of the precipice, sometimes crossing one another, and thus leaving islands stranded between, or long promontories, from the ends of which there

Angela Brazil

would be no escape except by a jump. Gwen and Dick picked their way carefully along. There was scarcely need for Mr. Gascoyne's warning; each felt the entire necessity for extreme caution. Peeping over the edges of the chasms they could see green ferns growing in splendid clumps in clefts of the rock, and farther down darkness or a glint of water.

"Ugh! It would be horrible to tumble there!" declared Gwen, shivering as she gazed into the dim depths. "You don't feel as if you'd ever come up again, do you? Why, what's that? Did you hear?"

"Nothing but the gulls."

"It's like someone shouting. There it is again—behind us."

"By Jove! it is someone calling. Has anybody slipped down one of these holes? We'd best go and see, but do be careful. Hello, there! We're coming!"

Walking, as Gwen had said, like cautious cats, they threaded their way along the narrow strips of land till they reached the particular chasm whence the shouts issued. Looking over, they could see on a ledge about six feet down a little corduroyed, blue-jerseyed figure, and a frightened, freckled face that peered upwards. Gwen recognized the urchin in a moment: it was Johnnie Cass, the scapegrace of a family of fisher folk who lived in the village, and the naughtiest boy in Winnie's Sunday School class. He was in no immediate danger, for the ledge was wide, but the wall of rock above him was too steep to admit of his climbing up.

"Johnnie, what are you doing down there?" she called.

"Oh! boo-hoo-hoo!" wailed the scared voice from below. "I were reachin' after a sea-gurt with a broke wing and down

I cooms!"

"Serve you right, too! How do you intend getting back?"

"I don't know—I wish my mother was 'ere!" and again he broke into a howl of woe.

"I'm glad she's not—she'd make a worse noise than you, from my experience of her," murmured Gwen. "Look here!" she continued, turning to Dick, "I suppose we've got to fish this little wretch up somehow."

"If I reach down can you catch hold of my hand and let me pull you?" shouted Dick to the snivelling Johnnie.

"Nay! I durstn't stir an inch—oh! where's my mother?"

"He's lost his nerve—that's what's the damage. If I go down for him could you give me a haul back?"

Gwen shook her head.

"You're too heavy. Better do it the other way. I'll go down, hand up the kid, and then you shall pull me back. Nonsense! I'm not bothered with nerves. Shan't mind in the least!"

It seemed the more feasible plan, for the six feet of rock that sheered down to the ledge was so steep and smooth of surface as to render it impossible for anyone to climb it without assistance; and it would be comparatively easy for Dick to drag Gwen's lighter weight to the top, though a difficult matter for her to pull him. If her heart went into her mouth as she let herself over the edge, Gwen did not show it. She was not given to exhibiting the white feather, and both at school and at home kept up a well-deserved reputation for pluck. Five seconds landed her by Johnnie's side, and once there she tried not to look into the gulf below. After some amount of cajoling, she persuaded the young rascal to take his dirty little fists out of his eyes, and allow himself to be hoisted up within reach of Dick's firm grip; then a successful heave did the rest. Johnnie was soon in safety, but it was much harder work for Gwen to follow; there was nobody to boost her, and not an inch of ledge on the rock to make a foothold.

"It's good practice for Alpine climbing!" she gasped, as with dishevelled hair and grazed face she at last scrambled back. "I thought my arms were being dislocated."

Dick was rubbing his own arms ruefully, but he did not complain. He had turned very white. Perhaps the effort of pulling up two people had been rather too much for him. Gwen suddenly remembered with compunction that he was ill, and not even allowed the exertion of golf, much less "footer". She wished she had thought of it before and gone to the lighthouse for help.

"I'm an idiot," she told herself. "It was I who suggested he should do the hauling part. I hope he hasn't done himself any harm."

Meantime Johnnie Cass stood surveying Gwen with the grin of Puck.

"Yer face is bleedin', and yer hair's all over yer eyes. Aye, yer do look a sight!" he volunteered.

Gwen shook him! She really couldn't help it; it relieved her feelings so very much. After all, it is rather nervy work to go down a chasm; and though she wouldn't own that she had minded in the least, her legs seemed weak and queer, and her hands were hot and trembling, and there was a funny buzzing sound in her head. She was rather ashamed of herself for losing her temper, however, and tried suddenly to be dignified.

"Johnnie Cass," she protested solemnly, "you ought to be grateful to me for saving your life instead of making impertinent remarks!"

Dick burst out laughing.

"Bravo!" he said. "Look here, you kid, if you don't want your head punched as well you'd best obliterate yourself."

Johnnie took the hint and fled away over the moor, bolting for home with all possible speed and lifting up his voice as he went in a melancholy howl. Dick and Gwen sat down on a rock to recover themselves.

"You've got some pluck—for a girl," said Dick, throwing a pebble into the chasm. "I didn't expect you'd really go down there and fetch him. Girls generally stand by and shriek."

"Not modern girls," affirmed Gwen. "They used to do the shrieking business in oldfashioned novels. It's gone out of fashion since hockey came in."

"I thought ladies were supposed to scream and wring their slim, fair hands!"

"Shows you haven't got any sisters! Do my hands look slim and fair?"

"Well, no, they're a good deal more like a boy's," admitted Dick.

"I often wish I were a boy," sighed Gwen regretfully.

Angela Brazil

"Don't! You're a jolly sight nicer as you are," returned Dick, getting up to go.

The pair did not reach the Parsonage until after one o'clock, and Beatrice and Mr. Gascoyne were beginning to wonder what had become of them.

"I hope Dick's none the worse," said Father rather anxiously when Gwen poured out the tale of their adventure. "I'm afraid it's been a tiring morning for him. He had better stop to lunch and have a good rest afterwards before he attempts to walk home. I'll go and telephone to his father from the post office and say we're keeping him. Perhaps Dr. Chambers will say he mustn't come here again if we let him do rash things!"

The family laughed at the humorous account of the rescue of Johnnie Cass which Dick and Gwen gave at the dinner table.

"You needn't have expected gratitude from that imp!" said Winnie, who had suffered many hard experiences in Sunday School. "Possibly his mother may thank you, but I doubt even that."

"All the same Gwen did her best, and that's a satisfaction," said Father. "Johnnie's a clever little lad in spite of his naughtiness, and may turn out better than we expect Some day he may even thank you for having saved his life. Gwen must keep her eye on him. He owes her so much it ought to make a bond between them."

"Well, I wish her joy of her protege," said Winnie, with a dubious shake of her head.

After that Dick spent many Saturday mornings at the Parsonage. His father would not allow him to invite his own friends as they always proved rather too much for him, but the boy was lonely, and found the Gascoynes pleasant companions. Gwen especially, who was nearest his own age, became his particular chum, and the two carried out many experiments together in the way of photography, amateur bookbinding, and one or two other hobbies in which they were mutually interested. Dick's lessons with Mr. Gascoyne were over by ten o'clock, and he generally stayed an hour or two longer, adapting himself so well to the household that he soon seemed to be almost one of the family. Giles and Basil adored him, and haunted his footsteps as much as they were allowed, but their mischievous young fingers generally worked such havoc among slides and specimens that Gwen was often forced to turn them out and lock the door upon them.

"Monkeys from the zoo are tame and well-behaved compared with Stumps and Bazzie," she declared. "If one wants one's things ruined commend me to two small brothers!"

Gwen was delighted to have found so congenial a friend. Beatrice and Winnie, being both older, were naturally companions for one another and were inclined to treat her entirely as one of the younger ones, forgetting how fast she was growing up, and it was difficult to make childish little Lesbia interested in anything. Here at last was somebody who appreciated birds' eggs, and butterflies, and collections of shells, and pressed flowers; someone who did pen-and-ink drawings a great deal better than herself, and who knew exactly how to make lantern slides, and could even manage to mend the toy printing press that Giles had broken.

Dick was clever with his fingers, and as he was not allowed to read very much he spent long hours at home constructing wonderful boxes for birds' eggs, or stretchers for butterflies and moths, or preparing slides for the microscope.

"I'm going to be a doctor when I grow up," he confided to Gwen, "so microscopic work will be a help to me. Dad's teaching me a little scrap of dispensing now, just to amuse me."

"I hope he doesn't let you make up the bottles of medicine!" laughed Gwen. "I pity the patients."

"Rather not, but I see what goes in them. If you'll come over to the surgery some day I'll make you taste something for laughing!"

"We should be lost without Dick now," said Gwen one day at tea. "What shall we do when he goes back to school?"

"I'm afraid that won't be just yet," said Mr. Gascoyne. "He doesn't get strong as fast as his father hoped. He's a nice lad, not brilliant, but very painstaking over his work. It's quite a pleasure to teach him."

CHAPTER VIII

GWEN RECEIVES A LETTER

After her talk with Father on the evening of the prize-giving Gwen went back to school determined, if she could not feel cordial just at present towards her classmates, she would at least bury the hatchet and take no notice of the unkindness they had exhibited. It seemed much the most dignified course, for Gwen was far too proud to look injured, or to show even to Netta that she had felt hurt. Perhaps the girls were a little ashamed of themselves. Iris Watson and one or two others spoke to her with quite an approach to friendliness, and Elspeth Frazer asked her opinion about the costumes for the play. Gwen was not taking a part, so she was rather a free lance in that respect, and her advice was likely to be disinterested. Each Form got up its own particular act with a secrecy worthy of the Freemasons. It was a point of honour not to betray the least tiny hint of what was going to happen, in order that the performance should be a complete surprise to the rest of the school.

Now the Fifth had decided to give the trial scene from the *Merchant of Venice*—rather an ambitious and decidedly a hackneyed piece to select. The Dramatic Society was influenced in its choice, however, by several considerations; the Form was studying *The Merchant*, and had learnt the principal speeches for recitations, which would save a great deal of trouble to the performers in the matter of studying parts. Then Hilda Browne's father was a barrister and would lend his wig for the occasion, and Louise Mawson could bring a gown that would do excellently for Shylock's gaberdine, also two sets of tights and doublets and feathered caps, all of which were invaluable assets in the way of stage properties.

"We must manage the rest of the costumes as best we can," said Elspeth. "Charlotte Perry knows of a dressmaker who makes fancy dresses very cheaply. She does them for other schools. The chief question is the scheme of colour: Hilda wants us to copy exactly from some celebrated picture, and Louise says it doesn't matter as long as everything looks very bright and gay. Here's a book of costumes. Tell me what you think."

As Gwen turned over the pages of the little volume, with its illustrations of Bassanio, Jessica, &c., a horrible suspicion suddenly shot into her mind. Where had she seen that book before? And just lately too! Why, at home, of course! She had come into the sitting-room suddenly and found Winnie and Beatrice discussing it over the fire. Winnie had suppressed it instantly, but not before she had caught a glimpse both of the illustrations and the title. She remembered them perfectly. Now Winnie, as well as being Junior Mistress for the Fifth, was a member of a class for higher mathematics composed of a few Senior girls and taught by a professor who came weekly from the University at Radchester. On the strength of this class she considered herself still one of the Sixth for special purposes, and licensed to take part in school performances. Was the Sixth going to act in the *Merchant of Venice*? It looked uncommonly like it. Why else should Winnie be studying that particular book of costumes?

Gwen was in a dilemma. She did not know what to do. Not only did the Rodenhurst code of honour regard Form secrets as being inviolable as those of the confessional, but further she had been continually warned by Father and Beatrice that, now Winnie was a mistress, she and Lesbia must be particularly careful never to repeat anything they heard at home which might be likely to compromise their sister at school. It was clearly impossible to betray the least hint of her suspicion, but on the other hand it would be an exceedingly stupid *denouement* if both Forms were to act the same play. She decided to try finesse.

"Have you absolutely decided on *The Merchant*?" she said. "Don't you think it's rather stale to choose our Form subject? It's been done before too."

"Not for three years," objected Elspeth. "That's quite time enough for most of the girls to have forgotten it. Besides, I know the speeches."

"You could learn some fresh ones."

"Oh, I dare say! It sounds easy enough when you haven't to do it yourself. One's homework is quite enough just now without learning pages of blank verse. Then there are the costumes."

"Wouldn't they come in for *The Rivals*? You might do some scenes from that. We've never had it at school before, and it's simply ripping. Or part of *She Stoops to Conquer* would be gorgeously funny."

"You couldn't put Sir Anthony Absolute into Shylock's gaberdine, or Tony Lumpkin into a Venetian doublet and tights! And what about the wig? Hilda's had hard work to persuade her father to lend it, and she'd be fearfully offended if it wasn't used."

These arguments were so conclusive that Gwen sighed. Nevertheless she made a last appeal.

"Well, I think you're very silly to act *The Merchant*," she said. "You might choose something far more original and interesting. It's an opportunity wasted—and, if you'll only believe me, I'm quite sure you'll be sorry for it."

"It's you that's silly, Gwen Gascoyne!" retorted the indignant Elspeth. "We've chosen *The Merchant*, so why need you go trying to upset everything. I was asking you about the costumes, not the play."

"Like Gwen's cheek!" murmured Louise Mawson. "We don't want ex-Juniors interfering with our Dramatic!"

Gwen turned sharply away. It seemed most unfortunate that she always got across the rest of the Form. In this instance her motive was the purest, but as she could not explain, the girls naturally thought it was only her love of putting herself forward which caused her to suggest such a drastic measure as a change of programme.

"They never will understand me!" she thought bitterly. "Father said they would be proud of me yet, but oh, dear! the more I try to do, the more I seem disliked. They'll be fearfully sold when it comes to the performance. I wonder if I ought to give them just a hint! It's really too idiotic to have two *Merchants*. No, I won't! They'd probably only slang me for letting out Form secrets. I'm glad I'm not acting, at any rate. School's not exactly a terrestrial paradise at present. I wonder what other troubles are coming to me? I believe I'm one of those people who are born under an unlucky star!"

Gwen's words might almost have been prophetic, for the very next day something happened—something so unprecedented and overwhelming that she could never have anticipated it, even if she had been expecting general ill luck.

At the interval she received a summons to Miss Roscoe's study. She went at once, wondering why she had been sent for.

"Hope the Head's not going to put me into the Sixth!" she laughed to herself. "That would be rather too good a joke. I'm willing to be a prefect or even proctor if I'm asked!"

Gwen's reception at her last visit to the study had been so favourable, that this time she tapped lightly at the door, and entered confidently. One glance at Miss Roscoe's face, however, showed her that she was in dire disgrace. The Principal's rather handsome, heavy features seemed to cast themselves in a Roman mould when she was annoyed; her brows would knit, and her mouth assume a set, dogged expression of authority. All these storm signals being visible, Gwen quaked in her shoes. Miss Roscoe had an unopened envelope in her hand, and to this at once drew her pupil's attention.

"Gwen Gascoyne, a letter arrived this morning addressed to you at Rodenhurst. Now, it is one of our principal rules that no girls are allowed to have letters sent to them at the school. Tell your correspondent on no account to write to you here again. If I find anything further addressed to you, I shall enclose it in an envelope, and post it to your father. I will not have Rodenhurst made a vehicle for clandestine correspondence. You may go, but understand clearly this is never to happen again."

Gwen took the letter, and left the room in silence. She was

too much astonished to defend herself. She could not imagine who had written to her and put the school address. As soon as she was in the corridor she tore open the envelope. It contained a bill from "Messrs. John Parker & Sons, Glass and China Merchants" for

"Replacing 10 articles in broken
Tea Service ...   L1   2   6"

And at the bottom was written in a business hand:—

"Messrs. Parker beg respectfully to request Miss Gascoyne's settlement of above. Should she prefer it, they will send the account to her father. They beg to assure her of their best attention at all times."

Gwen gasped.

"Why, I paid it!" she said almost aloud. "At least, I sent the money by Emma. Is it possible she can have pocketed it? Oh, the deceiving wretch! Where's Netta? I must tell her at once!"

She rushed into the gymnasium, and calling Netta aside, showed her the fatal document. The two talked it over, aghast.

"Whew! This is a bad job!" exclaimed Netta. "Certainly it looks as if Emma had decamped with the one pound two and six. She's left the school, you know."

"I didn't know," sighed Gwen.

"Yes, she went ten days ago. Haven't you noticed there's a new housemaid waiting at dinner? You must be as blind as a bat!"

"I'm afraid I am done for," said Gwen dramatically.

"Oh, I shouldn't give up too soon if I were you! I suppose, by the by, you wouldn't care to tell your father?"

"I'd rather die!"

"Then you'll have to go somehow to Parker's, and ask if they've made a mistake. If, as I strongly suspect, Emma really didn't pay it, then you might get them to take part on account now, and leave the rest till after Christmas. What could you give them?"

"I don't possess more than sixpence. I'm bankrupt, and in debt to you, too."

"But you're sure to get something at Christmas, aren't you?"

"I expect so."

"Well, I'll tell you what I'll do: I'll lend you another ten shillings. That will make a sovereign altogether, and you can pay me back when you've had your Christmas presents."

"Oh, Netta, how good of you!"

"Not so particularly. It's only a loan, and I expect you to give it back."

"Of course."

"You'd better go to Parker's this afternoon at four."

"I daren't!" said Gwen, who felt that she was floundering deeper and deeper into a morass of trouble. "You don't know what a scrape I got into at home for stopping behind that other time. Beatrice made me promise absolutely always to come home with Winnie and Lesbia. I should have to give all kinds of explanations."

"I'm supposed to go straight home too, on these dark afternoons. My mother's rather particular about it."

"Then what's to be done?"

"You'll have to make a bolt in the dinner hour. There's nothing else for it."

"Umph! It's risky."

"You must risk something, O my cautious philosopher! Nobody but Thistles is about just then, and I think we can outwit Thistles. I'll bring the half-sovereign to school with me to-morrow, and you can take it to Parker's, in case it's wanted. I'm afraid you'll find you'll need it."

"I should like to prosecute Emma—she richly deserves it!"

"Couldn't do that without giving ourselves away, so you'll have to restrain your righteous wrath, my child!"

Gwen spent the rest of the day feeling as if a black shadow had suddenly fallen over her life. She had believed the episode of the china was completely finished with, and here it had cropped up again like some horrible bogey prepared to haunt her. It was worse than ever, for she had lost her own fifteen shillings as well as the ten which Netta had previously lent her. Between Parker's and Netta she now owed thirty-two and sixpence. The largeness of the debt appalled her. How was she ever to refund it? She hoped she might get a little money at Christmas. Her grandmother and Aunt Violet generally sent postal orders for presents, telling the girls to buy what they liked; it was these welcome gifts that constituted most of her contributions to her savings box.

The hint which Parker's had given about sending the account to her father frightened her greatly. Father must not know. He would have quite enough Christmas bills to pay without adding an extra one. Besides, what would he think of her? Gwen liked to stand high in her father's estimation. Beatrice, too, would hear of it, and would not spare her.

"I'm always the black sheep of the family," thought Gwen. "None of them have ever done anything so dreadful as this. No! I simply shouldn't dare to tell at home."

Netta turned up next morning with the half-sovereign, according to her promise. She was not an ungenerous girl, and she had plenty of pocket money, for her father was well off, and liberal to his only daughter. She was willing to help Gwen out of a difficulty for which she knew she herself was partly responsible, and perhaps also she rather appreciated the sense of power that the debt gave her over her schoolfellow. Netta dearly loved to lead: she would have liked to be of importance in the Form, and was often annoyed that Hilda Browne, Iris Watson, and some of the others looked down upon her. It was pleasant therefore to feel that she had one satellite who was bound to revolve in her orbit, and could be reckoned upon to support her on all occasions.

Gwen had decided to commit a breach of school rules, and to rush out between dinner and afternoon school to pay her visit to the china shop. As she had said, it was a risky performance. If she were caught, she would be reported to Miss Roscoe, and the penalty would be severe. It seemed sailing 'twixt Scylla and Charybdis, but it was worth trying. The first difficulty was how to put on her outdoor things without anybody noticing. Girls kept strolling in and out of the dressing-room in the most tiresome manner and after waiting as long as she dared for the room to be empty, she was finally obliged to smuggle her hat and coat into the passage, and garb herself there.

"I've barely time," she said to Netta, who was acting scout. "For goodness sake tell me if you see Thistles about! Is the coast clear? Then I'll scoot."

At the end of the passage, however, she encountered danger. Winnie was standing by the gymnasium door, and Gwen only just drew back in time to avoid her. Chafing with impatience, she waited while Winnie leisurely examined some papers on the notice board. Was she going to stay there all the afternoon? At last she moved, and went inside the gymnasium, and Gwen plucked up courage to make a dash for the street door. She hurried along with such enormous strides that passers-by turned to look at her and smiled, but careless of the notice she was attracting, she even broke into a run as she caught sight of the Market Hall clock. She was panting and altogether out of breath by the time she reached the china shop, and not at all sure what she ought to say. She marched up to the counter, and produced the bill which she had received.

"Look here! You've sent me this," she began, "and I want to know whether it was really paid or not."

"I'll just enquire, miss," said the assistant, referring to his superior; then returning, after a whispered colloquy, he continued: "No, miss. Mr. Evans says it certainly never has been paid. You've no receipt for it?"

"I gave the money to the housemaid at school, and told her to take it," faltered Gwen.

"Have you asked her about it, miss?"

"She's left, and I don't know where she's gone."

The assistant shook his head.

"I'm afraid, in that case, she won't want to be found, though perhaps the police could trace her if you cared to prosecute."

"Would it not be simpler if we sent the account to your father, missy?" suggested the shopwalker, coming to join the assistant at the counter. "Ah! I forget whether we have your home address? Always best to refer bills to one's father, isn't it? Then there's no trouble."

His tone verged on the familiar and impertinent. Gwen drew herself up very straight.

"I prefer to manage it myself, thank you," she replied icily. "If you will take ten shillings on account now, I will pay you the balance after Christmas. Will you let it remain till then?"

"I dare say Mr. Parker wouldn't object—that's to say, if you don't mind giving me your home address as a reference."

"You can put 'c/o Miss Goodwin, The Thorns, Manor Road, Stedburgh'," said Gwen, who wished at any cost to avoid the chance of a letter being sent to her at her own home. She got a receipt for the ten shillings on account, and put it carefully away in her purse. She thought both the shopmen looked at her very inquisitively, but she took no notice. She did not mean to gratify their curiosity by explaining the details of how she had incurred the expense. She wished Netta were with her; it was so much harder to keep up her dignity alone. With a curt "Good afternoon!" she left the china stores and hurried back to school. She was only just in time, for the

Angela Brazil

second bell was already ringing. Fortunately the dressing-room was empty, except for one agitated Junior, who was in too great haste to notice anything. Gwen scuttled into the Fifth exactly five seconds before Miss Douglas, and sat down at her desk, exhausted but congratulating herself. She contrived to write a surreptitious note to Netta, and to pass it, neatly rolled into a ball, on the waste-paper tray. Its tenor was calculated to be ambiguous to outsiders, but intelligible to the initiated.

"All hail, Protector of the Poor! This is to inform you that the deed is done—successfully. I thought I was within an ace of exposure, but things righted themselves, and lo! I triumphed. For the present the supplier of brittle goods is satisfied, and for the future—well, I leave it to luck. I feel like a warrior who has been through a campaign—I'm not sure if I haven't acquired some wounds. My head is swimming, and I'm a broken flower for the afternoon. Expect me to collapse in maths. My brains are capable of nothing more arduous than the three R's. I am living till four, when I can have the exhilaration of reciting my breathless experiences to your sympathetic ear.

"Yours in abject gratitude,

"G.G."

CHAPTER IX

KEEPING CHRISTMAS

The end of the term seemed to arrive very rapidly—too quickly for the amount of work that had to be done, yet too slowly in the estimation of the three hundred and eleven girls who were looking forward to the holidays. Exam week came and went, leaving inkstained fingers and a crop of headaches; mistresses were busy correcting papers; "swatters" were daring to congratulate themselves, and "slackers" were bewailing the difficulty of the questions. Gwen, who had done pretty well on the whole, considering her handicaps, ventured to think she must be through in most subjects, and not such a disgrace to the Fifth as to necessitate her dismissal to the Lower School again, a consummation at which one or two of her detractors had occasionally hinted in times of irritation.

The few days left were chiefly occupied with what the girls called "scratch lessons", just something to keep them employed until the lists were out. A good deal of latitude was allowed to those rehearsing for the various performances, and though Gwen could not claim that excuse for exemption, she managed to make a little work spin out a long way without incurring reproof.

She was tired with the strain of the term; it had needed much

Angela Brazil

effort to keep up with the rest of the Form, and the daily bus journey and walk to and from home were all extra exertion. She had grown enormously in the last few months—"grown out of all conscience", said Beatrice, who sighed ruefully over boots too small and skirts too short—and she had become so pale and lanky and angular in the process that Winnie unfeelingly compared her to a plant raised in a cellar. Her unlucky hands and feet seemed bigger than ever, and more inclined to fidget and shuffle, and to her bad habit of wrinkling up her forehead she had added a nervous blink of her eyes.

"Winnie Gascoyne is charming," confided Miss Douglas to a fellow mistress, "and Lesbia is about the loveliest child I've ever seen. I can't imagine why Gwen should vary from pretty to plain continually. But she does."

Unfortunately, Gwen's temper suffered in exact proportion to her increased inches. She was snappy at school and snarly at home, difficult to please, and ready to take offence at everything. Probably a week's rest in bed, on a feeding diet and a good tonic, was what her tired body and irritable nerves required, but nobody had the hardihood to make such a suggestion. Except in cases of dire necessity, the Gascoynes did not indulge in the luxury of medical advice or chemist's bills, so Gwen perforce did without a doctor, and the medicine he would most undoubtedly have prescribed for her. So far from thinking of rest, she was making plans sufficient to fill five holidays instead of one; even she herself laughed sometimes at the largeness of her projects compared with the brief month in which she was to carry them out.

Meantime the two days of the dramatic performances had arrived. The Seniors always had the first afternoon and the Juniors the second, the audience being composed of the rest of the school together with the mistresses. The outside public was not invited, as the little plays were only intended to be acted among the girls themselves. The Sixth naturally led off, and Gwen quaked as she sat with her Form in front of the heavy red curtains. She was afraid an unpleasant surprise awaited her comrades, and she wondered how they would take it. Exactly what she expected happened. The bell rang, the curtains were drawn aside to reveal—alas, alas, for the Fifth!—a very excellently got up trial scene from the *Merchant of Venice*. Bessie Manners, the head of the school, was a majestic Portia in a handsome scarlet robe; Winnie made an attractive Nerissa; while all the other characters were arrayed in slightly more sumptuous costumes than Elspeth and Hilda had been able to collect.

A shudder of cold horror ran through the unfortunate Fifth, the dramatic representatives of which listened with a kind of fascination to their own speeches, tripped off lightly and easily by their Seniors. It was more particularly galling as all realized that the whole thing was on a rather higher scale than theirs; it was better staged, much prompter, the actions were more appropriate, and the players less stiff and self-conscious, to say nothing of the superior dresses. In gloomy resignation they sat the scene out, and had the magnanimity to applaud heartily at the end. Then came the crisis.

"We can't possibly give the very same thing all over again," whispered Hilda to Elspeth. "We shall just have to announce that ours is 'off'."

Deeply humiliated and disgusted, the Fifth retired to its own classroom to discuss the untoward event.

"It's too sickening—when I'd borrowed the wig on purpose!" wailed Hilda. "You can't think how I had to pester Dad to lend it."

"And my Bassanio doublet and tights were made at a dressmaker's!" lamented Louise Mawson.

"Who'd have thought of the Sixth choosing that very scene?"

"Well, I tried to persuade you to take something else instead," declared Gwen, offering Job's comfort to the disappointed ones.

"Gwen Gascoyne, I verily believe you knew all the time what the Sixth were going to have."

"You must have known when your sister was in it."

"I wasn't sure, but I had an inkling," confessed Gwen.

"Then why didn't you tell?" howled the girls in chorus.

"Why? Because it didn't seem fair. Winnie hadn't said a word—I only guessed. You know we're all supposed to keep our own secrets."

"In this case you ought to have warned us properly. It was too bad to let us rehearse all that time, and get all the costumes together—for this!"

"We've made ourselves ridiculous, and it's your fault entirely."

"Couldn't you act it here, just among ourselves?" suggested Gwen humbly; but her proposal was squashed by an indignant and scornful majority.

"Act it here indeed! Who'd care to do that, I wonder? Don't be so idiotic. You've spoilt our performance, Gwen Gascoyne, when you might have saved it. Why couldn't you stay in the Lower School? You haven't sense enough to be a Senior."

It was not a very satisfactory ending to a first term, even though Gwen had done better in the exams than she expected, so that her place in her new Form was well assured. She still felt an outcast, and as she shut her desk for the last time on breaking-up day, she gave a sigh of intense relief to think that she was going to enjoy a whole month's freedom from the society of her classmates.

Home at present was the *summum bonum* of her wishes. She almost danced along the road from school, and behaved so jubilantly in the bus that Winnie had to interfere, and give her a hint to restrain her hilarity before the other passengers. She rushed into the Parsonage like a cyclone, and flung her satchel under the bookcase.

"There! That's done with! Hurrah! No more horrid, hateful, scrambly, early breakfasts, and tramping off through the mud. Every day's a Saturday, and I'm just going to have a glorious time."

"There's plenty for you to do," said Beatrice, fishing out the satchel and putting it tidily away on Gwen's special shelf. "I haven't finished those texts I was making for the church yet, and—"

"Oh, wow! Don't set me to work too soon! I've a heap of things of my own that want doing first. Winnie is far cleverer at cutting texts than I am."

"She's more to be depended upon, certainly," said Beatrice dryly.

Each member of the family was mysteriously occupied with

special secrets. There were still five days before Christmas, time for an energetic person to get through a great deal, and Gwen hoped to accomplish wonders. She was in a sad quandary about her Christmas gifts. Her savings box, which ought to have contained over fifteen shillings, only held a threepennybit and two halfpennies; and she shook her head dismally as she reviewed her pauper condition.

"I must make presents, that's the long and short of it," she told herself. "They can't be handsome ones. And, oh dear! they'll all think me so horribly stingy and mean. Well, they'll have to, for I can't explain! It's absolutely sickening, but it's inevitable."

So Gwen shut herself up in her bedroom, locked out the injured Lesbia, who had plans of her own which she wished to pursue in privacy, put on a thick jacket and a pair of mittens to keep herself warm, and set to work bravely. It is rather hard to make bricks without straw, and her supply of materials, mostly purloined from Beatrice's piece-box, was decidedly scanty. She held a review of the articles when she had finished, and screwed up her face over them in expressive dissatisfaction.

"They're a shabby little lot, that's flat!" she decided.

She turned them over disconsolately—the needle-book for Beatrice, not too tidily sewn; the blotter for Winnie, with its brown paper cover, hastily painted with a spray of roses, and its one sheet of blotting paper begged from Father's writing-table; the pincushion for Lesbia, trimmed with a piece of washed ribbon; and the two postcard albums for Basil and Giles, made out of pieces of cardboard with slits cut in the corners.

"I can afford to spend the threepennybit on Father and

Martin," she thought; "but I must leave the halfpennies to rattle in my box, so that it doesn't sound empty."

The village shop did not offer a very large selection of goods for an expenditure of threepence. Gwen was almost at her wits' end what to choose, and finally came away with a cake of oatmeal soap and a large red chalk pencil. Walking back up the village she met Beatrice.

"I've just been to see the Casses," said the latter. "They're in awful trouble. Thomas Cass has sprained his wrist and can't go out in his boat, and Mrs. Cass is in bed with bronchitis. Johnnie's running about with his toes all through his boots, and says he can't come to church or Sunday School because he hasn't another pair."

"Haven't you an old pair of Lesbia's or Stumps's?" suggested Gwen.

"Not one. We sold them all at the Rummage Sale."

"Then he'll have to go barefoot, I suppose."

"I was wondering," said Beatrice tentatively, "if we could manage to get him a pair ourselves. Winnie would give something, I'm sure, and so would I, and so would Father."

Gwen was silent.

"I thought perhaps as you'd rescued him you might feel interested in him, and you'd care—"

Beatrice did not finish the sentence, but looked at her sister hopefully.

Gwen stared at the ground and went very red, but she said

Angela Brazil

nothing, and Beatrice, after waiting a moment, turned away and entered the post office.

"Of all absolute frauds, I feel the meanest!" groaned Gwen. "Beatrice will think me a perfect miser, hoarding up my money and not willing to spend a farthing on anybody! If she only knew the bankruptcy of my box! Was any wretched girl ever in such a fix? Oh! Gwen Gascoyne, you've got yourself into an atrocious mess altogether, and I don't see how you're ever going to climb out of it."

Gwen's one sheet anchor of hope, to which she clung in a kind of desperation, was the thought of the postal orders that Grannie and Aunt Violet almost invariably sent at Christmas. If these did not arrive, she could not pay Netta, and then— well, any kind of catastrophe might be expected to follow. She went about with a load of lead on her heart, and a consequent shortness of temper highly trying to the rest of the family. She was grumpy with the little boys, impatient with Lesbia, and so unaccommodating over doing the decorations in church that Beatrice finally begged her to go home, saying she and Winnie could finish alone.

"You two always want to get rid of me!" flared out Gwen as she stumped defiantly away.

It was not a very happy preparation for Christmas, and Gwen stood rather forlornly in the church porch, her hands in her pockets, watching a few snowflakes that were beginning to fall silently from the heavy grey sky and to whiten the tops of the gravestones and the outlines of the crooked yew trees near the gate. The peace and goodwill that ought to have been present everywhere to-day seemed to have vanished.

"Beatrice was just horrid," thought Gwen, quite oblivious of the fact that the quarrel was of her own making. We are so apt to forget that the world is like a mirror, and if we insist upon frowning into it, it will probably frown back. We sometimes expect other people to do all the forbearing, and then are astonished if our much-tried friends fail in the very point in which we ourselves are so deficient.

"Why, Gwen, what a woebegone face!" exclaimed Father, who hurried in for a moment to speak to the parish clerk. "You'd make a grand model for an artist who wanted to paint a picture of 'Misery'. Are the decorations finished?"

"Almost; at least my part of them."

"Then go home and open that parcel of Parish Magazines you'll find on my study table, and deliver those that belong to the village. You know where to find the list. Be sure to tick the names off. And don't go farther down the road than Marriott's farm; it's getting dark."

Gwen cheered visibly. She was always glad to do something for Father, if it were only distributing Parish Magazines, so she strode off with a swinging step, humming the carol that the school children had been practising with Winnie that afternoon.

> "Show us, dear Christ-Child, Thy Christmas light,
> Teach us the song of the Angels bright,
> And the love of the Mother blest.
> And help us this Christmas to learn of Thee
> All we should do, and all we should be,
> And how we can please Thee best."

Fortunately the Gascoynes were a forgiving family, and when they all met at tea-time nobody seemed to remember Gwen's ill humour. The evening was a busy one, for there were holly and ivy to be put up in the Parsonage now the church was finished, and the usual mirth over a bough of mistletoe which old Mr. Hodson, who owned the big farm by the mill, always cut off every year from an apple tree in his orchard and brought to them with his own hands. Gwen forgot her troubles and romped with the rest, accepting Martin's sticky kisses in the spirit in which they were intended. The Gascoynes did not hang up their stockings, but laid their presents on the breakfast-table, so that they could have the gratification of opening all their parcels together. It was a point of honour not to take the tiniest peep inside even the most tempting-looking package until the whole family was assembled. Gwen had tried to make up for the poverty of her offerings by the warmth of the greetings she wrote outside, but she did not feel proud of her collection as she carried it downstairs. She was the last, so she hastily made her distribution, and turned to her own plate. She had been well remembered: a book from Father; a nightdress case, beautifully embroidered, from Beatrice; a new purse from Winnie; a big bottle of scent from dear little Lesbia, who to buy it must certainly have gone without the blue-handled penknife she had coveted so much in Bayne's window; some pencils from Giles and Basil; and a piece of indiarubber from Martin, who had compassed seven presents on a capital of eightpence-halfpenny. Gwen looked rather anxiously as the others opened the packets she had addressed to them; but whatever they thought, they all had the niceness to hide their feelings, and thanked her as if she had given them the most expensive objects obtainable.

Father's humour, however, could not help twinkling out at the cake of soap: "To Darling Dad, with dearest and best love, from Gwen".

"I hope it isn't a hint I need washing," he said with mock seriousness.

"I thought you liked oatmeal soap!" protested Gwen, nearly crying.

"So I do, my dear; and I haven't had any for a long time. Like the man in Pears's advertisement, I shall now use no other."

"Here's the postman!" shouted Giles, rushing excitedly to the door, where that much-burdened official, with an extra man to help him, was sorting out what belonged to the Parsonage.

"Six letters for you, Gwen, and two parcels," said Beatrice, assuming command of the correspondence, and distributing it among the eager family.

Gwen snatched her share nervously. Would any of the letters contain the longed-for postal orders? No, they all had halfpenny stamps, and were clearly only Christmas cards.

Then she fell upon the parcels. The first contained a handsome knitted coat, and cap to match, "with love from Grannie", and the second, a beautiful little set of Wordsworth's poems in a cloth case, "with Aunt Violet's best wishes".

Gwen sat down on the sofa, feeling as if she had received a rude shock. That both Grannie and Aunt Violet should have sent presents instead of money was worse than she had calculated upon. She tried to pull herself together, and not show her disappointment too plainly, but the thought of what she owed was paramount. It only made it worse that the gifts were really acceptable, and that the rest of the family persisted in considering her extremely lucky.

"It was kind of Grannie to send that lovely coat: dark green will just suit you. Try it on, and the cap too," said Winnie.

"It looks swank!" declared the boys.

"They'll go with your dark green skirt," affirmed Beatrice.

"The Wordsworths are scrumptious!" said Lesbia. "You've done awfully well this Christmas!"

"Yes, but how am I going to pay my debts?" thought Gwen, as she ran upstairs to get ready for church.

CHAPTER X

A PRODIGAL

As the next term seemed likely to bring its own crop of troubles, Gwen, with a kind of grim philosophy, determined to enjoy herself while she could, and make the most of the holidays. She helped vigorously at the schools, where tea parties for children and grownups, concerts and other entertainments were in full swing, and she even wrung a few words of appreciation from Beatrice for her active services in the way of slicing up cake, cutting ham sandwiches, and pouring out innumerable cups of tea. Gwen liked the village festivities, she knew everybody in the place, and found it all fun, from listening to the comic songs of the local grocer, to playing Oranges and Lemons with the babies in the Infant School.

"We've three real parties too," she said on December 30th, "as well as going to the Chambers' this afternoon."

"I hardly think Mrs. Chambers will expect you," declared Beatrice, looking out of the window at the dark sky. "It's beginning to snow already, and I believe we shall have a heavy fall."

"Then it must keep off till to-morrow, for we've got to get to

North Ditton somehow!" announced Gwen.

Dick's mother had asked the younger Gascoynes to tea, and amongst their various invitations it was to this that Gwen looked forward the most. She wanted to see Dick's home, and the collection of birds' eggs and butterflies which he had promised to show her, and his magic lantern, and his microscope, and all the Natural History books of which he had so often spoken. She watched the weather impatiently, and when the snow fell faster and faster, and Beatrice decided emphatically that the visit was impossible, she broke into open mutiny.

"It's too bad! We shouldn't take any harm. What an old mollycoddle you are, Beatrice!"

"I've a little more sense in my head than you have! With this wind the roads will be deep in drifts. It's quite unfit to go out, especially for you with that nasty cough. I should have you laid up with bronchitis."

"My cold's better," affirmed Gwen, trying not to sound hoarse; "snow doesn't hurt people. Father's gone out in it!"

"Father was obliged to go—it's quite a different thing for him. I'm sorry you're disappointed, but really, Gwen, don't be so childish! Look at Lesbia, she isn't making such a dreadful fuss!"

"Lesbia never worries about anything, so it's no virtue at all!" snarled Gwen, knowing perfectly well that she was unfair, for Lesbia undoubtedly added self-control to her naturally sweet disposition. "You always hold up Lesbia! You've no right to say we must stop at home, just because you're the eldest!"

Beatrice sighed. Sometimes she thought this turbulent cuckoo of a younger sister was the cross of her life.

"It's no use talking in this way, Gwen! Somebody must be in authority, and you'll have to do as you're told."

"I shan't! I don't care! You're only six years older than I am!"

And Gwen flounced out of the room in a rage. She ran upstairs, her eyes smarting with hot tears of temper. She was disgusted with the others for not taking the matter more to heart. How could Lesbia sit reading so calmly, or the boys amuse themselves with their absurd engine?

"They don't care like I do! I wish I could go without them!" she said aloud.

The idea was an excellent one. What fun it would be to go alone, and have Dick all to herself—no tiresome youngsters to claim his attention, finger his books, and perhaps break his birds' eggs; not even Lesbia to ask stupid questions about things any ordinary person ought to know. She could easily tell Mrs. Chambers that her sister had thought it too stormy for the little ones to venture, and probably Dr. Chambers would drive her back in the gig.

"After all, Father never told me not to go!" she thought, "and Beatrice is getting a perfect tyrant; I can't be expected to obey her as if I were an infant. A girl in the Fifth is quite old enough to decide things for herself, especially when she's as tall as I am!"

Gwen changed her dress, put on her best hair ribbon, her brooch, and her locket, then peeped cautiously down the stairs. Although she felt full of self-assertion, she had no wish to risk a further encounter with Beatrice. All seemed

Angela Brazil

quiet, so, donning hat and coat, she crept to the cupboard where mackintoshes and galoshes were kept, and armed herself to defy the weather. It was quite an easy matter to slip out by the back door, and in less than ten seconds she was hurrying through the village, chuckling at her own daring and cleverness. Thick flakes were whirling everywhere: when she looked upwards they showed as little dark patches against the neutral-tinted sky, but when they passed the line of vision, each soft lump of crystals gleamed purest white as it joined the ever-deepening mass below. Every gate and stump and rubbish heap was a thing of beauty, glorified by the ethereal covering of the snow; the dead clumps of ragwort by the road side, the withered branches of oak, the shrivelled trails of bramble all seemed transformed by the feathery particles into a species of fairyland.

As Gwen left the village, and took the path that led across the moor, she seemed to walk into a cloud of whiteness that enclosed her and shut her out from all before or behind. She stood still for a moment, and drew in her breath with a sense of intense exhilaration. She was all by herself in the midst of this new-found world of snow, and the very solitude had a fascination. It is good sometimes for the spirit to be alone; strange vague thoughts, half memories, half imaginings, fill the brain like a full high tide; strong impressions, unfelt and unknowable in the distraction of human company, force themselves silently yet persistently upon us; the corporal and the tangible lose their hard outlines and begin to merge into the in visible—in such moments the soul grows. It is perhaps one of the disadvantages of a large family that the members are apt to lack what one might call spiritual elbow room, the constant close companionship, the fridging and rubbing of the continual, daily, hourly intercourse, though an excellent discipline for the temper, leaves scant opportunity for the development of the individuality. Gwen could not have explained this in the least, but as she stood in the still quiet of the falling snow, she felt as if all the little fretting cares and worries and squabbles and anxieties dropped away into a subordinate place, and she were viewing life with another range of vision, where the proportions of things were quite changed.

She walked on, almost as if she were in a dream, without even the sound of a footstep to break the intense silence. She was now on the open wold, where there were neither hedges nor walls, but only a few stones to mark the road from the sedgy, heathery expanse of moor that stretched on either side. Gwen knew the way so thoroughly that she thought she could have followed it blindfold. Every rock and boulder and bush were familiar, and as a rule were so many points along the daily path to school. Now, however, all the well-known landmarks seemed to have a strange similarity, and to be merging into one great white waste, in which tree stump was indistinguishable from stone or gorse clump. The light was fading rapidly, for the clouds went on gathering, and the flakes came down ever thicker and faster. So far Gwen had gone on with the utmost confidence, but now she stopped and entertained a doubt. She did not recognize the boulder on her right, and the juniper bush on her left was surely strange.

"I verily believe I've come wrong somehow," she muttered. "There's nothing for it but to turn back."

She could see her own footsteps in the snow behind, and for some hundreds of yards she traced them; then they began to get fainter and fainter, and presently they were hidden entirely by the new-fallen flakes. The road was completely obliterated, there was nothing round her but shapeless indefinite whiteness. Then it dawned upon Gwen's soul that she was lost, lost hopelessly on the bare wold, where she might wander for miles without seeing the gleam of a farmhouse window or hearing even the bark of a shepherd's dog. The solitude that before had seemed so inspiring, suddenly became oppressive loneliness. What was she to do? Tramp on and on, perhaps in a circle, till she could go no farther? Already it was heavy walking, and under the rocks and bushes the drifts were deepening. Yet it would never do to sit down in the snow. Tired as she was, she must keep moving, and while the faintest gleam of daylight lasted she must try and find some guide-post to civilization.

"I wish I'd brought Jingles. I never thought of him," she sighed, longing regretfully for the shaggy Irish terrier that acted watchdog at the Parsonage. "I wonder how soon they'll miss me at home? Not till tea-time, I expect, and then they'll probably think I'm at the Chambers'. Beatrice would guess where I'd gone. How furiously angry she'll be!"

For the first time a little awkward uncomfortable inward suggestion began to croak that elder sisters are occasionally right, and may even be wiser in their generation than tall girls who have entered the Fifth. Gwen's cough, which had been hacking all day, came on much worse, and began to hurt her chest: she wished she had brought her *thick* muffler. It was a subject of perennial dispute between herself and Beatrice, and she often discarded it simply because the latter told her to put it on. She hated to appear mollycoddlish, and sometimes indeed did very silly things out of sheer foolhardiness. At present she was bitterly cold. The snow had sifted inside her galoshes, and made her feet wet, and the chilly wind was creeping down her neck and up her sleeves, and whirling frozen flakes at her face. No cheery tea in the Chambers' drawing-room, and no delightful chat with Dick afterwards about photography and magic lanterns.

"The fact of the matter is that I've been an idiot!" she confessed to herself. "Anybody with an ounce of sense would have known it was too snowy to cross the wold. I ought to have gone round by the high road. I seemed to turn across here just out of habit."

Gwen could not tell how long she stumbled about. It felt like interminable hours as she wearily dragged herself along, watching the sky grow darker, and the landscape more and more blurred, till she could scarcely distinguish which was snow and which was sky. At last her aching limbs absolutely refused to carry her any farther, and she crouched under the shelter of a big juniper bush that overhung a piece of rock. Here at least she was out of the biting, freezing wind. The comparative warmth made her feel sleepy. She roused herself with an effort. To sleep in the snow, she knew, was fatal, so she fell to rubbing her hands and feet to try and restore the circulation. All at once she started up and shouted aloud.

In the distance she had heard a short, sharp yelp, and she reasoned that where there was a dog, a man might possibly be following. Again and again she called, till, to her intense relief, a "Hallo!" came in answer, and she made out a snowy form moving in her direction. The dog found her first; it bounded at her, whining and sniffing at her skirts, then rushed away barking loudly to inform its master of her whereabouts.

"Can you tell me where I am? I've got lost!" cried Gwen, wading through a drift in her eagerness to meet her rescuer.

"Why, you're close to our house—Rawlins' farm. Who is it? I can't see in the dark. Miss Gascoyne? Why, whatever are you doing here all alone?"

He might well ask, Gwen thought, but she ignored the question. She knew the man, for he was a parishioner, and two of his boys sang in the choir at church.

"Can you tell me how to get home?" she said, with chattering teeth and watering eyes.

"Better come and have a sup o' tea first; you look clemmed wi' the cold," he returned. "We'll tak' you back after wi' the lantern. It's nobbut a step to the farm."

He whistled to the dog and moved on, and Gwen stumbled after him, wondering how she had missed seeing the house when it was so near. She scarcely knew whether to pose in the light of a heroine or a culprit as she walked into Mrs. Rawlins' kitchen, but decided to give as guarded an account of the matter as she could. There would be explanations in plenty when she returned to the Parsonage. She was very glad to sit and thaw by the fire and drink hot tea, despite the difficulty of fencing with Mrs. Rawlins' questions, that good dame being consumed with curiosity, and not restrained by any feelings of delicacy from catechizing her guest.

"Yes. No, I wasn't coming back from school, it's the holidays—yes, I'm generally with one of my sisters—no, I wasn't delivering Parish Magazines, we sent yours by Charlie—yes, I expect my father will be missing me. Thanks very much for the tea; I think I must be going now," said Gwen, gulping her second cup and making a move.

"Here's the lantern, Jim," said Mrs. Rawlins to her husband, "and take Miss Gascoyne round by the road; 'tain't fit to venture over the moor. It's scarce a night for a Christian to be out—and her with that churchyard cough, too! Goodness, gracious, how it's blowing!"

Gwen reached home so spent and exhausted with her long tramp through the snow, that she had only wits enough left wearily to thank Mr. Rawlins for his escort, and to stumble in at the front door. Winnie ran forward with a cry of relief, and shouted to Beatrice the welcome news of the arrival.

"Don't ask me anything! Oh, I just want to go to bed; I'm done!" wailed Gwen, subsiding on to the nearest chair.

Beatrice took the hint, and refrained from any reproaches till she had tucked up the prodigal in warmed blankets, with a hot bottle at her feet, and seen her consume a basin full of steaming bread and milk. Then she observed:

"I suppose you know Father and half the village are out hunting for you with lanterns? They raised the Boy Scouts and broke up the Band of Hope meeting. They telephoned to the Police Station at North Ditton too. I expect you're rather proud of yourself!"

And Gwen turned her face to the wall and sobbed and coughed till she nearly choked.

Next afternoon a very miserable-looking object, with watering eyes and a swollen cheek sat wrapped in a shawl by the fire in Father's study. Gwen had made her peace with Beatrice and had been forgiven, but she was still "eating the husks" of her escapade in the shape of a thoroughly bad cold and a touch of toothache. She refused to stay in bed, yet the noise of the family sitting-room made her head throb, so finally Father had taken pity upon her, and allowed her to bring her troubles into his sanctum. He had said very little about the events of the day before, but Gwen knew exactly what he must be thinking. She mopped her eyes with her handkerchief, and tried to believe it was her toothache that was making her cry. After a long time she said huskily, a propos of nothing in particular:

"Things always go so hardly with me, somehow, Dad! I don't know how it is. I generally seem unlucky, both at school and at home. I suppose it's partly me, but if things were easier, I'd be better. I should, really."

Father did not reply: he was busy addressing the motto-cards that he was sending to his parishioners for the New Year. He handed one to her silently.

And Gwen read:

> "O do not pray for easy lives. Pray to be stronger men. Do not pray for tasks equal to your powers; pray for powers equal to your tasks. Then the doing of your work shall be no miracle. But you shall be a miracle. Every day you shall wonder at yourself, at the richness of life which has come to you by the Grace of God."
>
> —*Phillips Brooks.*

Gwen sat staring hard into the fire.

"I'll hang this up in my bedroom, Dad," she said presently.

"Do; you'll find it worth thinking about," replied Father, as he blotted the thirty-fourth envelope.

CHAPTER XI

A PRIZE ESSAY

Gwen went back to school feeling rather tamed and sober. The bad cold and face-ache, subsequent on her adventure in the snow, had seriously interfered with her plans for the holidays, and she had not accomplished half she intended to do in the time. Dick Chambers had been laid up in bed with an attack of rheumatism, so she had scarcely seen anything of him, and altogether the much-longed-for month had held its disappointments. She returned to her desk in the Fifth almost glad to begin a fresh term, though she knew many difficulties awaited her. First and foremost was the horrible fact that she owed a whole sovereign to Netta Goodwin, and had absolutely no prospect of paying it. She tried to avoid any private conversation with her chum, but the ruse was not successful for long. Netta was a girl who was accustomed to get her own way, and she followed Gwen round the school until she caught her alone.

"I say, you old slacker, what about that sov.?" she began. "I suppose you got your Christmas presents all right?"

"Oh, yes, I got my presents!" said Gwen, trying to pass things off airily. "Not quite what I expected, though."

"But you can pay me back?"

"I'm afraid I can't just yet."

Netta's rather pretty face changed its expression considerably.

"When can you, then?" she asked sharply. "I want to know."

"Could you wait a fortnight?"

"It's inconvenient, but I might."

Netta was still scowling. "Will you promise faithfully to bring it by the 1st of February?"

"I'll do my best," agreed Gwen, escaping from what was to both a very unpleasant interview.

She had mentioned a fortnight simply on the spur of the moment to put Netta off, but she knew that the 1st of February would bring no way out of her entanglement. It was something, however, to have even a respite of two weeks; it gave her time to think and to lay plans. She wondered what Netta would do if, as seemed most likely, the debt still remained owing. She did not suppose Netta would turn informer to Miss Roscoe, but she might very possibly mention the matter to Winnie, who would tell Beatrice, who would promptly tell Father.

"Only a fortnight!" groaned Gwen, feeling like a criminal in a condemned cell. "Unless 'something turns up', as Mr. Micawber says in *David Copperfield*. If I were the heroine of a novel, a forgotten uncle in America would suddenly die, and leave me a million just at the opportune moment. But I'm only a very unromantic, every-day kind of person, not the forget-me-not-eyed, spun-gold-haired, wild-rose-petal-complexioned, pearly-toothed sort of girl who gets fortunes; I'm solid fact, not fiction. Most things are nowadays, I suppose."

Certainly the Fifth Form did not offer scope for romance or sentiment. Its daily doings were most prosaic, a round in which Latin, mathematics, and chemistry were chiefly to the fore, and the only appeal to the imagination was the weekly lecture on English literature from the Principal. Gwen liked these; Miss Roscoe had the knack of making historical dry bones live, and encouraged the girls to read for themselves. All her lessons were interesting, but in this she was inspiring. She was accustomed to give themes for fortnightly exercises, and at the first lecture of this new term she announced as a special subject: "An Essay on any one of the Great Writers of the Victorian Era", promising a volume of Browning's poems as a prize.

"I had intended to offer it for Christmas," she said, "but I thought you were too busy preparing for examinations to be able to give time to such an essay. I hope you'll do justice to the subject now."

It was a large order, thought Gwen, when already their homework had about reached its outside limit. Miss Roscoe was quite unconscionable in her demands on their time and brains. She fixed the standard of the Form so high that only the very bright girls could possibly keep up to it. Many slacked off entirely, but Gwen could not, dared not slack. She knew Miss Roscoe was watching her work, and that very much depended upon her reports for the next year or two. Father had thrown out a few hints that had stirred her ambition and raised wild hopes for the future. She was aware that there were several good scholarships from Rodenhurst, and visions of College began to dawn on her horizon.

"'Gwen Gascoyne, B.A.', sounds no end. It would be worth the grind. I mayn't be the beauty of the family, but I believe I've got the best share of the brains. Beatrice would be proud of me if I took my degree. I must make something of this essay if I 'burn the midnight'. Miss Roscoe will expect me to turn up trumps. I'll toil like a navvy!"

So Gwen decided, and stuck to her resolution. She had an undoubted capacity for work, a power of application and of steady plodding that were of immense service, as well as more brilliant gifts. She attacked the question at once. The Victorian writers offered a fairly wide choice of subject. She hesitated at first between George Eliot and Dickens, and finally selected Thomas Carlyle. Something about the rugged old prophet attracted her, and she thought he would be a congenial theme for her pen. She spent every spare moment in reading his biographies or his works, till she felt she had him at her fingers' ends. Then, with a mass of notes as a foundation, she began her essay.

Most young writers undergo the same first agonies of composition: the vainly sought simile, the sentence that will not turn nicely, the tiresome word that crops up too often, yet for which there seems no adequate substitute; the sudden lack of ideas, or the non-ability to clothe those one has in suitable language.

Gwen wrote and burnt, and wrote and burnt again, till at last she managed something, not at all up to the ideal of her imagination, but the best her limited literary experience could produce. She refused to show it to anybody at home, and bore it off to school to read over and correct during the dinner hour. She was sitting at her desk, busy altering sentences and erasing words, when Netta came into the room.

"Hello, you old solitary hermit!" she exclaimed. "What are you doing here, with your nose buried in an exercise book? There's no getting at you nowadays. You'll grow old before your time, Gwen, my child! Come out this instant, and play basket-ball."

"Can't, so that's flat," responded Gwen. "Netta, if you love me, if you've any humanity in you, leave me alone. Basket-ball's off till I've finished this."

"Well, you've got to tell me what you're doing, at any rate. Let me look! No, Miss Modesty, you're not going to hide your light under a bushel. I insist! Oho! What have we got here now?"

Netta dragged the book from Gwen's reluctant hands, and sitting on a neighbouring desk, began hastily to skim through the essay, giving grunts of approval as she read.

"First rate! I say, this is immense! Gwen, my hearty, I didn't think you'd got it in you!"

"Will it do?" demanded Gwen anxiously. She had sat on metaphorical pins to hear Netta's verdict.

"Do? I should rather think it would! If Lemonade doesn't mark it A1, First Prize, I shall say she doesn't know her business, that's all! You're pretty safe for that book of Browning, in my opinion."

"Wish it were cash instead! But I shan't get it in any case," sighed Gwen. "If I did, I'd trade it for anything I could."

"You mercenary wretch!"

"I'm so hard up. I'm no nearer paying what I owe you, Netta.

Angela Brazil

I literally haven't a penny in my pocket I wish you'd take it in kind instead of money."

Netta sat silent, drumming with her fingers on the desk.

"I've a rather decent locket, if you'd care for that—" continued Gwen.

"Hush! Be quiet! You've given me an idea, Gwen Gascoyne."

"Or I've a really jolly writing case—almost new—"

"I don't want your lockets or your writing cases; I've heaps of my own. I know one thing I do want, though, and if you like to trade, you can."

"Done! Only name it, and it's yours with my blessing."

"Well, I want this essay—"

"My essay! What do you mean?"

Gwen snatched back her exercise book as a mother clutches her first-born.

"I mean what I say. If you like to hand over 'Thomas Carlyle' to me, I'll take it instead of the sov., and call us quits. It would be a new experience to win a prize. How amazed everyone would be!"

"You surely wouldn't pass it off as your own?"

"Why not?"

"Why, Netta! That would be rather strong, even for you!"

"I told you long ago I was no saint. Besides, what's the harm? It's a business arrangement. You offered to pay me in kind, and this happens to be the 'pound of flesh', I fancy. It's perfectly fair."

"Um! Don't quite see the fairness myself."

"But it is!" protested Netta rather huffily. "I believe lots of popular authors don't do all their own writing themselves. They engage secretaries to help them. I've even heard of clergymen buying their sermons."

"Oh, oh! Father doesn't!" Gwen's tone was warm.

"Well, I didn't say he did, but I believe it's done all the same. And if a vicar can read somebody else's sermon in the pulpit as if it were his own, I may hand in somebody else's essay. *Quod est demonstrandum*, my child."

"Can't see it!" grunted Gwen.

"Look here, Gwen Gascoyne, you've got to see it! I've been uncommonly patient with you, but I don't quite appreciate the joke of being done out of that sov. I must either have it or its equivalent. You can please yourself which."

Netta's eyes were flashing, and her mouth was twitching ominously. She was a jolly enough fair-weather comrade, but she could be uncommonly nasty if things went wrong.

"I suppose you don't consider it unfair to keep me waiting all this time?" she added scathingly.

Gwen kicked the desk and groaned.

"Well, it just amounts to this: if you don't choose to come to terms, I'll tell Lemonade. Yes, I will! I don't care a scrap if I went into her room as well as you. You broke the china, and you'd get into the worst row. It wouldn't be pleasant for you. I think you'd better hand over Mr. Thomas Carlyle to me, my dear."

"And what am I to do, I should like to know?"

"Write another on a different author."

"There isn't time."

"Yes there is, heaps! I don't want it to be as good as this, naturally. Well, are you going to trade, or are you not? I can't wait here all day!"

For answer, Gwen held out the exercise book. She was in a desperately tight corner; everything seemed to have conspired against her. She knew Netta and her mad, reckless moods quite well enough to appreciate the fact that her threat to tell Miss Roscoe was no idle one. When her temper was roused, Netta was capable of anything.

"It's her fault more than mine if it's not fair. I really can't help it," thought Gwen, trying to find excuses for herself.

"Oh! Glad you've come to your senses at last!" sneered Netta, as she clutched the precious manuscript and stalked away, slamming the door behind her. There was no one else in the room, so Gwen laid her head down on the desk, and indulged in an altogether early Victorian exhibition of feeling. Her essay—her cherished essay, over which she had taken such superhuman pains, to be torn away from her like this! It was to have brought her such credit from Miss Roscoe, for even if it did not win the prize, it would surely be highly commended. And she had made herself a party to a fraud, for however much she might try to whitewash her act, she knew she had no right to allow Netta to use her work.

"Dad would despise me! Oh, what an abominable mix and muddle it all is! And I was going to start the New Year so straight!" wailed Gwen.

Netta in the meantime had put the essay away in her locker with the utmost satisfaction. She felt she had decidedly scored. Neither brilliant nor a hard worker, she had no opportunity of distinguishing herself in the Form under ordinary circumstances: here chance had flung into her hand the very thing she wanted. It would not take long to copy the sixteen pages of rather sprawling writing, then "Thomas Carlyle" would be her own.

"And a surprise for everyone!" she chuckled complacently. "Of course, it's rather dear—a whole pound! But—yes, most undoubtedly it's worth it!"

To Gwen, not the lightest part of the business was that she was faced with the horrible necessity of writing another essay. Only two days remained, so time pressed. It was impossible to look up any subject adequately, so she chose Dickens, as being an author whose books she knew fairly well, and by dint of much brain racking and real hard labour contrived to give some slight sketch of his life and an appreciation of his genius. She was painfully conscious, however, that the result was poor, the style slipshod, and the general composition lacking both in unity and finish. She pulled a long face as she signed her name to it.

"That isn't going to do much for you, Gwen Gascoyne," she said to herself. "It won't even get 'commended'. Bah! I'm sick of the whole thing!"

She felt more sick still on the day when Miss Roscoe returned the essays.

"I had hoped the average standard would be higher," commented the Principal. "Very few girls have treated the subject in any really critical spirit. There is only one paper worthy of notice—that on Thomas Carlyle by Netta Goodwin, and it is so excellent that it stands head and shoulders above all the others. I am very pleased, Netta, very pleased indeed, that you should have done so well. Your essay is carefully thought out and nicely expressed, and is evidently the result of much painstaking work. You thoroughly deserve the prize which I offered, and I have written your name in the book."

The Fifth Form gasped as Netta, with a smile of infinite triumph, marched jauntily up the room to receive her copy of Browning's Poems. Each girl looked at her neighbour in almost incredulous astonishment. Netta Goodwin, of all people in the world, to have won such praise!

Gwen drew her breath hard, and clenched her fists till her nails hurt her palms. At that moment, I am afraid, she hated Netta.

"Who was your author, Gwen? I chose Thackeray," said Louise Mawson afterwards.

"Dickens—and I only got 'fairly creditable'," responded Gwen. "It's just rotten!"

Which was a word utterly tabooed both at Rodenhurst and at home, but the sole one that seemed bad enough for the occasion.

"So I hear Netta Goodwin's was the prize essay," remarked

Father that evening. "Well, we can't all of us win prizes, can we? It was a strange coincidence that she should have written on Thomas Carlyle too!"

"Most remarkably strange, and very unfortunate for me," admitted Gwen, drinking her cup of bitterness to the dregs.

CHAPTER XII

GWEN TURNS HENWIFE

To Gwen the spring term seemed to pass much more rapidly than the autumn one had done. She was growing used to the Fifth Form; and the work, though certainly not easy, was now, thanks to the extra coaching that she had received, well within her compass. She did not feel so terribly harassed over her preparation, and instead of, as formerly, spending the whole evening until bedtime at her books, she was able to spare a chance hour or two occasionally for other things. The change of thoughts and the extra interests did her good; she lost her worried expression, and though she still could not help wrinkling up her forehead when trying to answer a question, some of her other bad habits began to drop away. Beatrice had not to correct her nearly so often, consequently there was less fridging of tempers between the two sisters, and a great increase of calm in the home atmosphere. It was a matter of tacit understanding at the Parsonage that Gwen raised most of the household storms. Winnie and Lesbia had peace-loving dispositions, and jogged along very evenly; and the boys, though apt to be mischievous, were always good-humoured little fellows, not much given to quarrelling unless they were teased. At present such a blessed tranquillity reigned at the breakfast and tea-tables that Beatrice really began to hope that the family volcano was quieting down, and that her eruptions and explosions would be things of the past.

Perhaps it was partly the pleasant spring weather that had such a beneficial effect on Gwen's temper. She loved the early growing season of the year, when every day was a little longer and lighter than the last, and the bulbs were pushing up in the garden, and the hazel catkins showering clouds of pollen in the lane, and the rooks cawing and building in the clump of elms near the mill, and great flights of screaming white sea-gulls, noisy, chattering jackdaws, and cheery, whistling starlings flew all together in mixed flocks to feed on the wolds. The morning walk to North Ditton across the heath, so bleak and wretched in December, was a daily delight now the sun was glinting over the sea and the gorse was in bud, and the stonechats, which had vanished during the cold weather, were back among the boulders, darting from stone to stone in short, jerky flight, with that sharp, jarring cry which is the prelude to their sweeter spring note. The moorland air at 8 a.m. was so fresh and pure and exhilarating that it seemed to blow away all the cobwebs, and Gwen often felt inclined to dance along the path for sheer joy of the sun and the wind, and the birds and the countless green things that were rapidly showing their heads through the brown skeletons of last autumn's heather and bilberry. The thrill of springtime is a totally different sensation from what we experience on even the most gorgeous day in October; there is a message of hope in the air, a foretaste of the coming summer, a glow of reawakened vitality, an exaltation half physical and half spiritual, as every year nature tells us afresh in her own fashion the miracle of the Resurrection.

Life was a busy round at the Parsonage. Winnie devoted each moment she could spare to the garden and the hen-yard, and Gwen, who at present had a craving for out-of-doors, lent a hand as often as she could. She whistled and sang over her work as she transplanted forget-me-nots, sowed seeds, or tidied up the rockery, and her stalwart arms made the lawn mower fly.

"There's some advantage in growing!" she declared, as she trundled away the wheelbarrow full of weeds. "My muscles have hardened since last year. I'll wheel you back up the garden, Martin, if you like. Tumble in!"

Gwen and Winnie had a great scheme between them of building a summer house, and every Saturday they managed to get on a little with their operations. There was a large pile of young felled trees in the yard which Mr. Gascoyne had bought for firewood, and some of these were admirable for the purpose. With considerable toil they dragged out half a dozen, dug holes in the ground, and planted them as posts to make a framework. Smaller boughs were nailed across and across, and then bunches of heather were tucked and tied securely into all the interstices. The roof was at first a terrible problem, till Winnie conceived the brilliant idea of using an old worn-out gate that lay in the orchard. It was heavy to lift, but with the aid of Father, Beatrice, and Nellie the maid, they managed to heave it up so that it rested securely upon the six posts. Then they thatched it neatly with heather and fir boughs.

"I don't suppose for a moment that it will be watertight," said Winnie; "but we shan't use it in wet weather. What I want is a nice shady place to sit in at the end of the tennis lawn. It will be perfectly lovely to have tea here. I believe I can make seats with some of those stumps."

"I'd back you to do anything in the joinering line," laughed Dick, who still came for lessons on Saturday mornings, and generally stayed to chat and help the gardeners, though he was yet debarred from any very violent exertions, greatly to his indignation. "You ought to be a Colonial. I believe you'd be equal to running up a shanty on your own and making the furniture out of old boxes."

"Perhaps I'll emigrate some day," nodded Winnie. "It would be more in my line than teaching. I'll leave University honours to Gwen, and try my luck in another hemisphere. Women are wanted in Canada if they're domesticated—and I flatter myself I'm that."

"Don't know that I won't join you when I've got my degree!" declared Gwen. "I've yearned to go to Canada ever since I saw those ripping pictures on the kinematograph—only Father'd have to promise to come and see me every fortnight."

"How particularly possible! Gwen, you're a rotter!" chirped Dick, throwing a piece of stick at her. "I thought your last idea was to study medicine and go to College with me."

"Perhaps I shan't be able to do either: scholarships don't grow on every bush like blackberries. Probably I'll just have to stay at home and 'wash dishes and feed the swine'. By the by, we haven't shown you our eleven little pigs! They're absolute darlings, as sweet as the Duchess's baby in *Alice in Wonderland*. Come along this instant, and I'll catch one for you to nurse. We've never had a pet pig before, but I declare I mean to tame one of these. They're the sharpest, cutest little scaramouches you ever saw: as funny as kittens, and twice as intelligent as puppies. Yes; I'm a pig enthusiast at present, and if you laugh I'll make you buy one for yourself!"

There was plenty of scope for Gwen's energy as spring came on and added hatch after hatch of fluffy chickens and downy ducklings to Winnie's hen-yard. She helped to arrange the coops, to make wired enclosures for the tiny chicks, and, hardest task of all, to collect the young pullets and cockerels that were allowed to roam on the common, and lock them up safely for the night.

"No one who hasn't tried henkeeping could possibly conceive the difficulty of getting in those wretched long-legged, half-fledged fowls," declared Gwen. "They know I'm going to shut them up, and they're so clever they come for the Indian corn when I call 'chuck, chuck', and eat it with one eye upon me. Then when I try to cajole them into the henhouse they fly all ways. Lesbia, you may come and act guard, but I won't have the boys; they only rush about and frighten the chickens. The last time I took Stumps the Buff Orpington with the black feather in its tail flew over the hedge into the turnip field. I didn't get him back till it was moonlight, then I caught him perching on a stump, and carried him round."

The particular pride of Winnie's heart was a clutch of little Partridge Wyandottes, mothered by a comfortable old Plymouth Rock hen. The setting of eggs had been given her by a farmer's wife in the neighbourhood; they were from a particularly good strain, and ten out of the dozen had hatched and thrived. She watched over them with more than ordinary zeal, leaving manifold instructions with Nellie for their diet during her absence at school, and visiting them the very first after her return each afternoon. On the evenings when she took the choir practice at church she entrusted them solely to Gwen's charge.

"Give them a last feed of 'Chikko', and see that they've got clean water, and don't let Jingles go near them, because the old hen gets excited, and stamps about and treads on them," urged Winnie one Wednesday as she started off with a roll of music in her hand. "Be sure you shut them up early, because

Nellie says she saw a rat last night, and I noticed something had been burrowing near the shed."

Gwen promised complete accordance with all directions, and then went off to finish her Latin translation. It was a particularly stiff piece of Virgil, and she puzzled over it so long that she utterly forgot all about the chickens, and it was only the call of an owl waking up on the ivy-covered ash tree at the bottom of the garden that reminded her of her henwife's duties.

"Gracious! It's nearly dark!" she exclaimed, flinging down Virgil and making a rush for the hen-yard. "I hope to goodness those chicks are all right! What an idiot I am! Winnie will be ready to slay me if anything's happened to them."

It was growing very dusk indeed, and though none of the doors were yet shut, the feathered flock had all gone to roost. As Gwen crossed the hen-yard she suddenly saw something dark and shadowy creep from behind the shed and dart stealthily in the direction of the coops. It disappeared inside the very one where the cherished Partridge Wyandottes were cuddling under their foster-mother's wings. Gwen's heart almost stood still. She well knew the cunning and daring of rats, and how they would snatch the chicks or young ducklings from the wariest and most warlike hen. To leave this in the coop for even a minute while she went to call help would certainly result in the loss of one or more of Winnie's favourites.

Very cautiously she peered inside. The hen, who knew her well, clucked softly, and the chickens popped their little speckly heads out from the mass of encircling feathers and "peeped" gently. They were not yet aware of danger. Where was the rat? It appeared to have vanished into thin air. It

Angela Brazil

certainly could not have left the coop. At the opposite end from where the hen was sitting there was a billet of wood, and on looking at this closely she saw a long tail dangling out underneath. Without doubt her enemy had taken refuge there and was hiding in the corner.

"These precious chicks have got to be saved somehow or Winnie'll never forgive me," muttered Gwen, clenching her teeth to brace her nerves.

Then she did a thing from which her whole spirit shrank. She took her handkerchief in her hand to give her a firmer grip and seized hold of the tail. She dragged the rat out of the coop and bore it off, hanging head downwards and whirling round and round in vain effort to escape, while it squeaked with wrath and indignation. Fortunately it could not raise its head sufficiently to bite her or she might have suffered a nasty wound. Gwen rushed towards the back door, shouting loudly for Nellie, but when that worthy domestic saw what she carried she uttered a yell of terror instead of offering help.

"Throw it down, Miss Gwen, it'll bite you!" she shrieked. "Oh! gracious goodness! throw it down!"

"Bring the poker! Where's Jingles?" screamed Gwen. Then, realizing that she could hold her wriggling burden no longer, she dropped the rat into the water-butt, and catching up the yard brush which lay handily near, held down the victim till it was drowned.

"Miss Gwen! How did you dare!" shivered Nellie.

"Ugh! It's a hateful, horrid, barbarous thing to have to do. I feel as if I'd committed a murder. It's made me quite sick," said Gwen. "Nellie, do go and shut up those chickens before any more rats get into the coop. I don't feel equal to catching another." Then she sat down on the pump-trough to recover.

"You're a heroine!" declared Winnie when she came back from the choir practice and viewed the interesting corpse. "I shouldn't have dared! No, nothing in this world would have induced me to seize the creature by its tail. It's a huge one too, with such wicked-looking teeth. What a wonder you weren't bitten! You shall have one of those Partridge Wyandottes for your very own. Choose whichever you like and I'll call it yours."

"I wish you'd help me to finish my Virgil," said Gwen. "I'm only halfway through and it's almost bedtime!"

"You're as good as a terrier, Gwen!" said Dick, when he heard the exciting story the next Saturday. "I wish you'd come ratting in our stable at home. I'd undertake to find you some sport."

"Don't be detestable! You talk as if I'd enjoyed it. I had to bury the thing afterwards, for Winnie wouldn't touch it. I made a mull of my Virgil in class next day, and I couldn't tell Miss Douglas the reason."

"You might have put the episode into Latin. It sounds quite Homeric. Did you keep the tail as a trophy? If we want to excite you we'll just say 'Rats'. Please let us know when you're on the warpath again and we'll come to see the fun;" and Dick dodged round an apple tree and fled.

"You've got to be here early next Saturday, mind, and help us to take things to the Agricultural Show!" Gwen shouted after him. "You may come to breakfast if you'll behave yourself."

"Right-o! I'll act beast of burden provided it's hens I'm to carry—not rats! Ta-ta!"

The Agricultural Show was the great event in the year at Skelwick. It was held in the big field beside the mill, and all the villagers for miles round made holiday to attend it. For days beforehand men were busy putting up pens and erecting a tent where eggs and butter and dressed fowls could be exhibited, while a few travelling caravans arrived with shooting galleries or cheap bazaars and set up a kind of fair in an opposite field.

There were many classes for poultry, so Winnie decided to send some of her best cockerels, a selection of Buff Orpington chickens, and a pair of big white Aylesbury ducks. She and Gwen got up very early on the Saturday morning to take a final review of their exhibits. They were determined to give the ducks a washing in order that they might show them with their plumage in an absolutely spotless condition. Armed with a tin bath, a can of warm water, some soap and a sponge, they shut themselves in a disused pig sty and commenced operations. It is no easy task to wash a large, struggling, flapping, protesting duck, and though Gwen held their wings down while Winnie did the scrubbing, both girls were splashed all over and drenched with water before they had finished.

"But the Aylesburys look gorgeous," said Gwen, flinging her dishevelled hair from her hot face. "They're clean to the very tips of their beaks. The drake looks as if you'd curled his tail feather with the curling tongs. They're fearfully upset and angry, poor dears; they think they've been half killed. Winnie, how are we going to get them to the Show?"

"That's what's puzzling me. We don't possess a basket big enough for them. I believe we shall have to carry them."

"In our arms? Yes, that'll be by far the best way. They'd knock their feathers about in a hamper and get dirty again. They've had one breakfast already, but I think they deserve a little scrap of Indian corn as a reward for what they've gone through."

All exhibits had to be delivered at the Show field by nine o'clock, and precisely at half-past eight a procession set off from the Parsonage: Lesbia carefully carrying a dozen beautiful brown eggs in a basket, the three boys with small hampers of chickens, Dick holding a little wooden crate containing Black Minorca cockerels, and finally Winnie and Gwen, each clasping a huge white Aylesbury in her arms. Dick had offered gallantly to be duck bearer, but the girls preferred to transport their own pets.

"They know us so well, you see," said Gwen, "so they won't struggle like they would with a stranger. Besides, we know just the dodge of holding down their wings so that they can't flap."

They decided to take the short cut to the mill, through two meadows, across a small stream, and over a stile that led them direct into the Show ground. Gwen and Winnie got on very well with Dick and the boys to open gates: it was rather perilous work crossing the stream on a single plank, but they accomplished that in safety, and Winnie, with infinite caution, climbed over the stile into the mill meadow, still hugging her burden. Gwen essayed to follow with equal skill, but the stile was a very steep and awkward one, and she needed both hands to hold the drake. She was stepping carefully over the top bar when somehow her foot caught and she stumbled; she put out one hand to save herself, and the cunning drake, quick to seize his opportunity, wriggled himself free and made a dash for liberty.

Off he went over the Show ground, flapping and fluttering like a white whirlwind and quacking his loudest, and the Gascoyne family, popping down hampers and baskets, followed hard behind; Winnie, much encumbered by her duck, shouting frantic directions. It was Dick who caught the runaway, and pinioned him cleverly until Gwen secured him, then with much triumph they shut him up with his agitated mate in the wire pen marked "No. 207".

"I thought we'd lost him," panted Winnie. "Oh, dear! It's no joke bringing one's beasties to a show. I'm glad we decided not to exhibit the pigs! Martin, you're not to open that hamper. We shall be having the chickens escaping next! Stop him, Stumps! I feel like the 'Old Woman who lived in a Shoe'. Gwen, you take charge of the cockerels while I find where the Black Minorcas have to go to."

The public was not allowed in the field while the judging was in process; so until twelve o'clock the Gascoynes were obliged to wait with what patience they could muster. As soon as the gates were opened they trooped into the Show.

"Hurrah! First Prize for White Aylesburys!" exclaimed Winnie ecstatically, gazing with rapture at the large pink card that decorated No. 207 pen. "It was worth washing them. The darlings! How nice they look!"

"And the chickens have got a third!" yelled the boys, who had taken a hasty round of the exhibits.

"The eggs haven't won anything, but the cockerels have 'commended'. Mrs. Hodges' have got the first."

"We haven't done badly," said Winnie, "considering I can't devote all my time to it like the farmers' wives. Gwen, you've helped loyally, and I'm going to give you half a crown out of the prize money. I shall save the rest to buy some really good White Leghorns; Mrs. Hodges says they lay better than any others in the winter. Oh, here's Father! We must go and tell him of our success."

Angela Brazil

CHAPTER XIII

THE SHOE PINCHES

The very first thing which Gwen did, when Winnie had given her the promised half-crown out of the prize money, was to go straight to the post office and buy a postal order for that amount and a penny stamp. She possessed a few odd coppers, but otherwise no funds had come her way for a long time, and she had been growing very uneasy about the bill which she still owed to Parker's for the broken china. She now sent them the postal order, with a note saying that she hoped very soon to settle the remainder of the account, and begging them to wait a little longer. She also asked them to return her a receipt addressed "c/o Miss Netta Goodwin, The Thorns, Manor Road, Stedburgh".

"I dare say Netta'll be angry, and call it cheek on my part, but I can't help it," thought Gwen. "I daren't get another letter sent to school after the rowing Miss Roscoe gave me, and if it comes home, Beatrice will want to know who's been writing to me. It's only fair that Netta should take a little of the bother on her own shoulders. She's certainly had the best of it in this affair. Oh, dear, I still owe Parker's ten shillings. I haven't the ghost of a notion how I'm to pay it!"

Gwen could not forgive Netta for appropriating her prize

essay. She still felt indignant whenever she thought about it, especially as there was always an uneasy sensation of guilt on her own part. She knew it was not a straight transaction, and poor Gwen, with all her faults, loved straightness. For lack of other friendships at school she was forced into companionship with Netta, but she never whole-heartedly liked her. Lately, especially, Netta had taken a rather high-handed tone, and was apt to order her chum about in a manner that Gwen's independent spirit greatly resented. The friction between the two was sometimes hot, but neither cared to risk a quarrel, for each knew that the other, if turned into an enemy, might come out with some decidedly awkward revelations. So they went on in the old way, squabbling continually over trifles and making it up again, but on the whole ready to stand up for each other against the rest of the Form. Yes, alack!—the rest of the Form, for Gwen, in spite of her well-meant efforts, had not yet won popularity in the Fifth. She had tried to be genial and sociable, but nobody seemed to want her. If she joined in a conversation, Rachel Hunter or Edith Arnold would stare at her as if they thought it great impertinence on her part to intrude herself into their concerns. They never asked her opinion, or consulted her about anything, but simply ignored her, and left her to her own devices. Nearly all the girls lived in Stedburgh, and their talk was often of Stedburgh affairs, concerts, amateur dramatic performances, and entertainments in which Gwen, living far away at Skelwick, could have no possible part. Though she sometimes got in a word about school matters, her remarks were never well received, and she was always more or less conscious of being an alien and an outsider in her Form.

She tried to pretend that she did not care about the opinion of the others, but it was hard, all the same. Most of us like popularity, especially when we believe we have done nothing to deserve the reverse.

"If I'd been as pretty as Lesbia, they'd have made ever such a fuss over me," thought Gwen. "She's the pet of her form, and the darling of all the big girls. I'd have been a beauty if I could! They never even give me a chance to be nice to them—they just leave me alone. Yes, it's hard!"

But all the while, Father's New Year motto hung over the dressing table in her bedroom, and every morning she could not help looking at it. It seemed a stern gospel to pray for strength instead of ease, and yet it attracted her. After all, was it not a nobler conception of life to work away and not mind what people thought of you, than to be always caring whether you were popular? There was a certain joy in overcoming difficulties, and surmounting obstacles. She was already succeeding in mastering the lessons that had baffled her at first. Could she ever win a place for herself in the Form? It would undoubtedly seem almost a miracle if she did.

"I wonder if I should be happier at another school?" she sometimes thought. "Dad spoke once of the possibility of sending me to one of the Clergy Daughters' Schools; he said I might get a scholarship. But oh, dear! That would mean leaving home, and being a boarder! Suppose I didn't like it any better than Rodenhurst; then it would be perfectly awful to have to spend the whole term without once seeing Dad or any of the others. No, I won't suggest it. I'd better stick where I am, and peg along as best I can."

Gwen was a great home-bird. On the few occasions in her childhood, when she had paid visits at relations' houses, she had, after a few days, grown so intolerably homesick, and wept so hopelessly and inconsolably, that she had had to be packed back, rather in disgrace; and though she was now old enough to behave herself, she had not been asked again, nor was she very enthusiastic to receive invitations. She felt bashful, awkward, and badly dressed under the critical eyes of Aunt Violet or Aunt Christina, and much preferred the atmosphere of the Parsonage, and the society of her own family. To come back every evening from school, and spend Saturday and Sunday at home, seemed indispensable at present, though she supposed if she went to College later on, she would have to get used to being away.

Eastertide came, and brought welcome holidays. Gwen helped to deck the church with daffodils, and great boughs of pink almond blossom, and bunches of sweet-smelling wallflowers. She loved the Easter decorations far more than those at Christmas, and this time she had rather a free hand, for Beatrice was too busy to come, and Gwen was allowed to do the lectern and reading desk all by herself, while Winnie undertook the pulpit. She gave infinite pains to her work, and Father praised the result, which was a tremendous satisfaction. To do anything for Father was a joy. Gwen often wished she could play the organ like Winnie, but she was not clever at music. Beatrice had made a great effort to teach her the piano, with poor success, for she was not a docile or attentive pupil, and the lessons generally involved a wrangle between the two sisters, Beatrice losing her patience, and Gwen arguing hotly. Finally Father had put a stop to the lessons altogether, on the ground that it was sheer waste of time, and Gwen was better employed at something else. Lesbia, however, played rather nicely; she could manage the harmonium at the Sunday School, and was just beginning to practise the organ under Winnie's instructions. It was the one thing Lesbia did pretty well, for she did not distinguish herself at school. She was not a remarkably bright girl, and was very childish for her age. Though Gwen was fond of her younger sister, and petted her like everybody else, the two were not in any sense companions. Lesbia was far more on a level with the little boys, and generally amused herself with Giles or Basil; Gwen's schemes and projects were miles above her head.

The holidays, though very enjoyable, were quite uneventful. They slipped away much too swiftly, and the ordinary round of school and home work began again. It was the summer term, however, and to Gwen that meant a great deal. She took up tennis with hot enthusiasm, practising both at home and at school in any time she could spare. Her long arms and strong wrists stood her in good stead, and it began to be said in the Form that "Gwen Gascoyne's play was quite decent". She mowed and rolled the little lawn at the Parsonage vigorously, marked out the courts with a brush, and persuaded either Beatrice or Winnie to have a game every evening before bedtime, and Father whenever she could catch him.

"If only I'd a better racket!" she sighed one night, "it's impossible to do very much with a wretched old thing that's half sprung. You should have seen my serves when Netta lent me hers yesterday!"

"Why don't you buy a new one, then?" suggested Lesbia. "You're the Croesus of the family. Your money box must be bursting, for you've been hoarding up for ages. How much have you got in it?"

"Ah! Wouldn't you like to know!" returned Gwen, suddenly desirous of changing the subject.

"You really might get a new racket, Gwen," agreed Winnie. "It's a good idea of Lesbia's. We'd all borrow it on occasion."

"Oh, I dare say! Very nice for you all, no doubt. Rackets are rather expensive little luxuries, my dear girl. Otherwise I'd be happy to accommodate you."

"You're a perfect old miser! What are you going to do with your wealth? Invest it in an annuity?"

"Probably speculate on the Stock Exchange, or take up Mexican mines!" declared Gwen, trying to turn things off with a laugh.

"Well, you're the only member of the family who keeps any money."

"A good example in thrift to the rest of you, then!"

Gwen did not dare to complain again about the poorness of her racket, though it was a serious handicap in her games at school, where most of the girls came supplied with the very best. In spite of this impediment her play improved steadily, and she several times beat Louise Mawson, though she could not vanquish Hilda Brown or Charlotte Perry, the champions at present of the Form.

"I suppose you're going to take swimming, Gwen?" said Netta one day. "Miss Trent says we begin this afternoon."

"Haven't heard anything about it. Please condescend to enlighten my ignorance."

"Why, don't you know? We're going to the baths every Wednesday. It's clean-water day, and the whole school's to go in relays. They've a ripping teacher of swimming there now, a Miss Morris, who swam the Channel halfway, or did something else marvellous, I forget exactly what. Anyway, it's arranged we're to have a proper course of lessons. I expect every girl in the Form will join."

"It sounds—well, just idyllic!" said Gwen. "Whether I can take it or not is another question. I shall have to ask at home first."

"Oh, Mr. Gascoyne's sure to say 'yes'. Why shouldn't he? All girls ought to learn to swim."

It was impossible to explain to Netta that the fee for the course might prove an insurmountable barrier. Gwen was always too proud to plead poverty, and hid her father's narrow circumstances from her schoolmates as well as she could.

"You won't have time to ask before this afternoon," said Netta. "I advise you to go to the baths, though. I believe the lessons don't begin till next week, and this is only what you might call a trial trip, so you could see how you like it. Miss Trent says we can get bathing dresses there to-day, and bring our own afterwards."

The Rodenhurst girls had not before been taken to the public baths at Stedburgh, and the swimming course was a new departure of Miss Roscoe's. The idea proved extremely popular, and almost everybody wanted at least to sample the experiment.

"Oh, yes, you might go to-day," said Winnie, whom Gwen caught and consulted in the passage. "There's no great damage in that. You don't pledge yourself to take the course. Lesbia can go too. Miss Roscoe said it was to be a special afternoon."

"That's all right, then," said Gwen, rushing jubilantly away.

She was immensely anxious to learn to swim. The bay at Skelwick was so dangerous that Father would not allow any of them to bathe there, so as yet she had had no chance of testing her skill in natation. She loved all kinds of physical sports, they seemed a necessity of her active, fast-growing young body, and the prospect of trying a new element was alluring. In the very highest of spirits she joined the procession of Fifth Form girls that filed off at three o'clock, in charge of Miss Douglas.

The baths at Stedburgh had only lately been enlarged and re-opened, and in their improved shape were now quite a feature of the town. They were supplied with salt water, and could boast great conveniences in the matter of dressing-rooms, hair-drying apparatus, and plentiful hot towels. Gwen had never been inside before, so she gazed with delighted admiration, at the ladies' large bath, with its pale-green tiles, its flights of steps, and its diving board at the deep end. There was a cord across the middle, with a big notice that non-swimmers were to venture no farther, and must confine themselves to the shallow end; also that water wings could be hired.

"I hear Miss Morris won't let her pupils use those, though," said Netta. "She calls it an amateurish dodge. I should think we shall have to hold each other up while we practise our strokes!"

Gwen secured a bathing costume that fitted quite tolerably. She had no mackintosh cap, but she plaited her hair very tightly instead. She did not much care whether it got wet or not. It was most exciting to run down the steps and slip into the lovely clear green water. She had undressed with such record speed that she was actually the first, but she was very soon joined by a bevy of laughing, squealing maidens. It was an amusing, but not a picturesque sight. The Fifth Form attired in bathing costumes were about as different from the academy pictures of classical nymphs as a man in the street from a statue of Apollo. Instead of floating about in graceful attitudes, with the "amber dropping hair" of Milton's Sabrina, they "larked" like a school of porpoises, splashing each other and playing tricks. There was no attempt at a lesson that afternoon. The girls just enjoyed themselves in their own way, with many cautions from Miss Douglas not to trespass beyond the danger line. Gwen, held up by Netta, made frantic efforts to try her strokes, though her attempts invariably ended in a plunge from which she came up spluttering. Netta, with a very little help from Gwen, got on much better, for she had been to the baths before, and had had some practice. Several of the girls were already good swimmers, and after showing their prowess, were allowed to disport themselves at the deep end.

"I shan't be content till I can dive," declared Gwen, watching enviously as Elspeth Frazer took a header. "I shouldn't think it's difficult when you get the knack. It will be just having the pluck to try. I can float the least little scrap already, so I've learnt something this afternoon, and so have you."

"We shall both get on grandly at the lessons," assented Netta.

The whole Form agreed unanimously that the experiment was "ripping", and everyone was extremely anxious to come again. Gwen went home mad with enthusiasm, and Lesbia, whose Form had preceded the Fifth, was in equal ecstasies. Both besieged their father with wild entreaties to be allowed to take the course.

"You haven't told me the fees, and that's a very important point," said Mr. Gascoyne.

"I quite forgot to ask," admitted Gwen, brought down to the mundane side of the question. "Lesbia, do you know?"

Lesbia shook her head. She rarely knew anything; as a rule other people were ready to manage her affairs for her.

"Miss Douglas says the swimming course is to be half a

guinea each, and admission to the baths threepence a time. There is a special arrangement for schools," said Winnie, supplying the needed information.

"Then I must think it over," returned Father. "Times are bad just now, chicks, and I don't know whether I can afford it. A curacy is not a fat living, remember, and there are seven of you!"

Very much sobered, the enthusiastic bathers betook themselves to their preparation.

"I wish everything nice didn't cost money!" sighed Gwen.

She broached the subject to Beatrice during the evening.

"I've been talking about it to Father," said the latter. "I'm afraid he can't manage it for you both, but he might possibly for one. It will be a choice between you and Lesbia."

"I'm the eldest!" urged Gwen quickly.

"Yes, I know you are, but on the other hand, it really is Lesbia's turn, because you took the St. John's Ambulance last winter at the Parish Room, and Lesbia didn't."

"Swimming's a million times nicer than ambulance!"

"It's not any more useful. Don't be selfish, Gwen! You know how hard up we are. We can't all of us do everything, and I think this time it certainly ought to be Lesbia."

Gwen kicked the orchard gate against which they were leaning, and tried to keep down a lump that rose in her throat. Beatrice's arguments were unanswerable.

Angela Brazil

"It'll be sickening to be the only one in the Form who doesn't take swimming," she said at last. "Every single girl will join except me. I shall have to stop behind and do prep. instead. I'll feel more utterly out of things than ever."

"You could pay for the course yourself, if you like," suggested Beatrice. "What have you done with all your money?"

Gwen's restless hands were hacking notches on the top bar of the gate. Her penknife slipped suddenly, and cut her finger.

"Your own fault, if you will be so clumsy!" said Beatrice. "Come indoors, and I'll tie it up for you. You'd better hold it under the cold-water tap first."

Gwen groaned in spirit as she went to bed that night.

"I shall never hear the last of that wretched fifteen shillings!" she thought "I feel like Mr. Caudle in the *Curtain Lectures*, when he'd lent a five-pound note to a friend. That money of mine was to have bought Christmas presents, and boots for Johnnie Cass, and a new tennis racket, and paid for the swimming, and I don't know what else, according to my family's ideas. Oh, dear! Being poor's a hateful business! I wish Dad were Archbishop of Canterbury, instead of only Curate-in-charge of Skelwick Bay!"

CHAPTER XIV

GWEN MEETS TROUBLE

"There's a sickening author called Virgil,
Don't I wish I were chanting his dirge—ill!
As a door-nail he's dead
Yet his works live instead,
And to me they're a regular scourge—ill!"

So sang Netta, banging down her copy of *AEneid I* and *II* with a force that almost dissevered its cover and made the desk ring.

"I call it absolute sickening nonsense," she continued energetically. "Why in the name of all common sense should we girls in this modern twentieth century be expected to bother our precious heads over antiquated old rubbish that would be far better consigned to decent burial? What's the use of it, I want to know?"

"'An admirable training for the intellect', my dear! to quote Thistles," said Annie Edwards. "According to her theory you ought to feel your mind sprouting at every fresh page, and sending out shoots of wisdom."

"Sprouting, indeed! Just the other way!" grunted Netta.

Angela Brazil

"Latin has a paralysing effect upon my brain. Instead of sharpening me it deadens my faculties. When I've been trying to construe a page of Virgil, my intellect feels a pulp."

"Then the obvious moral is, don't try!" yawned Millicent Cooper.

"I don't."

"No more you do, you old slacker!"

"Why should one try when one can scrape through without?"

"Not an easy thing if Thistles puts you on a difficult bit! Have you made any sense out of this part? It's uncommonly stiff."

"Not I—I shall throw myself as usual on Gwen's mercy. Come here, Gwendolen mine, that's a sweet angelic cherub, and interpret these abominable lines!"

Gwen came rather reluctantly. Of late Netta had grown into the habit of applying to her for help with her extremely ill-prepared work, and the habit was assuming proportions that Gwen did not like. At first it had only been a word or two, then an odd sentence, but it was rapidly developing into a demand for a translation of the whole lesson.

"Oh, I say, Netta, you make me a regular henchman!" she objected. "Why should I act as providence to you continually?"

"Because you know the lesson, my hearty, and I don't. Ergo, it is your duty and privilege to impart your information to me."

"Don't always see my privileges."

"Then you ought. If you're helped, you ought to help others."

"I'm not helped!"

"Oh, Gwen! I'm sure Grinnie helps you at home!" broke out Millicent Cooper.

"She doesn't! She doesn't, indeed! I do all my prep, by myself."

"Can you actually swear on your honour she's never once helped you?" said Annie Edwards.

"On my hon—" began Gwen, then stopped and stammered lamely. "Well, at least, there was once—"

The recollection had struck her of the evening when she had caught the rat in the hen-coop. She had been so upset and flurried on that occasion that she had certainly applied to Winnie for assistance with a passage that she could not have otherwise prepared.

"Once!" sneered Annie. "Oh, no doubt! Everybody in the Form knows how it is you get on so well with your work!"

"I get no help at home!" declared Millicent self-righteously.

"Oh, drop drivelling, and let Gwen alone! She's got to tell me these lines," said Netta. "What do I care how she prepares her work? Come, Gwen, ma-vourneen, be a real friend!"

As Gwen translated the passage Netta wrote it rapidly down in pencil, and even Annie and Millicent, in spite of their condemnations of assisted preparations, seized their books and followed the words carefully.

"A particularly nasty bit—I could never do it if I tried half a year. Thanks awfully!" said Netta, slipping the paper inside her *AEneid*.

"Netta, you're not going to—"

"Never mind what I'm going to do. My concerns are my own," returned Netta airily. "I'm an unlucky person, and I'm sure to get the worst piece if there is one. It's Kismet."

Gwen's desk was close to Netta's, and when the Virgil class began she could not help noticing the latter pop the scrap of paper on her knee under cover of a pocket handkerchief.

Miss Douglas followed no fixed order in the Form; she called on any girl she wished to translate, choosing from back or front desks with strictest impartiality. As Netta had predicted, the difficult passage fell to her lot. To the surprise of almost the whole Form she came off with flying colours. Though Annie and Millicent had strong suspicions, only Gwen had seen the little piece of paper hidden under Netta's handkerchief. At lunch time she flew out on the subject.

"Look here, Netta," she began grimly, "helping you a little is one thing, but I'm not going to act crib for you again; so just don't think it."

"What do you mean?" gasped Netta sharply.

"What I say. You'd better prepare your own Virgil next time."

"Aren't you going to help me any more?" There was an unpleasant look in Netta's eyes.

"Not when you write it out and crib."

"It was only one scrap. Don't be horrid, Gwen!"

"I like things square, and they've not been quite straight lately. I'm going to put a stop to it, so I give you warning."

"Won't you tell me just the hard bits?"

"Not a single sentence."

"Then you're a mean, stingy thing, Gwen Gascoyne! I don't know why you should have taken it into your head all of a sudden to be so sanctimonious. You've not been so remarkably square before that you need turn saint now. You promised you'd stand by me, and this is how you keep your word, is it? I'll know better another time than to help you. You may get out of your own scrapes as best you can. I'll pay you for this, Gwen Gascoyne! I'll catch you tripping some time, see if I don't—and then—" and with a significant nod Netta turned away.

"You can do anything you like; I don't care," grunted Gwen.

She was out of temper that morning, for it was swimming day, and the thought of the rest of the Form jaunting off to the baths without her filled her with despair. She did not speak to Netta during the dinner hour, nor did the latter seek her company.

"What have those two quarrelled about? I thought they were ever so chummy," said Charlotte Perry to Elspeth Frazer.

"I'm sure I don't know. It would be a good thing for Gwen Gascoyne if she did quarrel with Netta, in my opinion."

Angela Brazil

"Then she'd be in a set by herself! Perhaps she thinks 'better Netta than nobody'."

"Better nobody than Netta, I should say. Do you know, Charlotte, I don't believe Gwen's half bad by herself, if only Netta would let her alone. It's when they get together they're so silly."

"Um—perhaps you're right. Gwen's straight, whatever else she is, and one can't say that for Netta."

"Hardly! I vote we watch them, and if they really are out of friends, we'll see if we can do anything with Gwen. It's rather rough on her to be such an outcast."

"Pity she's not as nice as Lesbia."

"Do you know," said Elspeth reflectively, "I'm not sure that she mayn't be at bottom. Of course Lesbia's awfully sweet-tempered, but then she's made such a fuss of, and there's really nothing in her. Now, I think there is something in Gwen, if she were taken the right way. I didn't like her at all at first, I don't know that I even do very much now, but I fancy she's one of those girls whom one might get to like if one saw the other side of her—I'm certain she has another side, only it never comes out at school."

"It isn't nice of her to rag her own sister, though."

"That's Netta's fault; she starts all the ragging and throws it on to Gwen."

"I'd be glad if I could really think so," returned Charlotte, and there for the moment the matter ended.

That afternoon a joyful, jubilant, rejoicing crew of Fifth

Formers set off for the baths, duly armed with their costumes and mackintosh caps, and from the window of the classroom one dejected, miserable girl watched them depart. Gwen thought she had never felt quite so forlorn in her life before. She was aggrieved with Fate, and kept muttering, "Hard luck! hard luck!" to herself as the last school hat whisked round the corner.

"I didn't see Netta," she thought, and then turned, for she heard Netta's indignant, protesting voice in the passage outside in loud altercation with Miss Trent.

"It's no use, Netta, I can't allow it," the mistress was saying. "With that sniffly cold in your head it would be folly to bathe, and as you say your mother is away from home, and you could not ask her permission this morning, I must be the judge, and I say most emphatically no."

"But, Miss Trent! If I just—"

"Not another word, Netta! Go into your own Form room at once, and do some preparation. Do you want me to report you to Miss Roscoe? Then go, this instant!"

A very sulky, angry, rebellious, disconsolate Netta flung herself through the doorway and flounced to her desk. She gave one stare at Gwen, and, frowning, began to get out her books.

"We're companions in misfortune!" ventured Gwen, but Netta took not the very slightest notice.

"Oh, very well, madam; if you're going to cut me I'll cut you!" thought Gwen, and she turned to the window again.

There was no mistress in the room, and Gwen knew that for

the next hour she could practically do as she liked. She would begin her preparation soon and finish some of it before she went home, but there was no particular hurry. The window commanded a view of a side street and just a peep into the main street, and it amused her at present to stand watching the passers-by. They were not remarkably enthralling—an old gentleman in a Bath chair, a nursemaid wheeling two babies in a perambulator, a baker's boy, a young woman with a large parcel, a vendor of boot laces, and a man delivering circulars. Gwen looked at them with languid attention, drumming her fingers idly on the window sill; then quite suddenly an expression of keen interest flashed across her face and she leaned out over the protecting iron bars.

"Dick!" she called loudly and impulsively, "Dick!"

The boy on the pavement below stopped and gazed up.

"Hello! Why, Gwen, by all that's wonderful!"

"What are you doing in Stedburgh, Dick?"

"Come in to have my hair cut, Miss Inquisitive, if you must know!"

"Oh, what a shame! I like it curly best. Have you had it done?"

"The fatal operation has been performed," said Dick, uncovering his closely-cropped head for a moment.

"And what are you going to do now?"

"Go home again."

"I wish I could," sighed Gwen.

"Are you supposed to be in school?" queried Dick.

"Of course I am, silly! I'm in my own Form room."

"Must be a queer sort of school, then, if they let you talk at the window."

"They don't as a rule. But the others have all gone to the baths to-day and I'm left here to do prep."

"Hard luck!"

"Just what I've been saying to myself. It's simply sickening. You know what it feels like to be out of things."

"Don't I, rather!"

"I feel like a captive in a tower or a nun in a convent," continued Gwen plaintively.

"Not much of the nun about you!" grinned Dick. "I'd be sorry for the convent you were in. Look here, if I got you some sweets and chucked up the bag would you catch it or muff it?"

"Try me."

"If you muff it I'll expect you to throw it down again."

"Right-o!"

"Then wait half a mo. and I'll cut round the corner to Sherrard's and see what I can fish up for you. You really look like an object for charity."

"You philanthropist!"

"Better wait till you've caught your catch before you bless me!" chuckled Dick.

He was certainly not gone long; he returned almost immediately with a most interesting-looking paper bag in his hand.

"Oh, do tell me, is it chocolate or caramels?" asked Gwen eagerly.

"Find out, madam! Now we'll see if I'm a good shot and if you're a butter-fingers. Are you ready? All right then, here goes! Oh, I say, well caught! Good old girl!"

"Told you I'd do it. Thanks most awfully! Have you kept any for yourself? Then take—"

"Gwen Gascoyne!" said a stern voice suddenly at her elbow.

Gwen jumped as if she had been shot, and turning guiltily, found herself face to face with Miss Trent. By the door stood Netta in visible triumph.

"Gwen Gascoyne," said Miss Trent again, "is this the way you conduct yourself when you're left to do your preparation? You're a disgrace to the school—an absolute disgrace! We had thought our Rodenhurst girls could be trusted to behave themselves."

"I was only talking to Dick," urged Gwen in self-defence.

"Is Dick your brother?"

"No—but—"

"Then you ought to be utterly ashamed of yourself. Such an affair has never happened at Rodenhurst before. I sincerely hope nobody in the street or in the houses opposite noticed the occurrence. It would be enough to spoil the reputation of the school."

"I didn't know I was doing anything so dreadful!" retorted Gwen.

"Then it's time you learnt. Miss Roscoe will have to hear about this. Report yourself in the study at four o'clock, and go at once to your desk and begin your preparation. Put that paper bag on the mantelpiece, I can't allow you to keep it."

Miss Trent sat down on Miss Douglas's vacant chair, evidently with the intention of staying in the room to act Gorgon. Gwen walked to her desk in the depths of humiliation. She caught Netta's glance as she went by, and it seemed to add insult to injury.

"I know who sneaked," she thought. "Very well, Netta Goodwin, I've done with you. You may tell any tales of me you like now; nothing would ever induce me to be friends with you again. In for a penny in for a pound. I expect you'll cut up nasty about that china business, but I feel as if I don't care. I'm booked for an awful row with Miss Roscoe! Oh, Dick, your sweets were well meant, but you little know what they're going to cost me!"

Gwen had a very hazy remembrance of how she did her preparation that afternoon. She wrote a French exercise almost automatically, feeling the mistress's eye upon her the whole time. At four o'clock, with her heart somewhere in the region of her shoes, she reported herself in the study. Miss Trent had been beforehand; so when she entered Miss Roscoe was already aware of the nature and extent of her crime. The headmistress was not disposed to make light of the affair; like Miss Trent, she considered that the reputation of the school might be seriously compromised by Gwen's behaviour, and she did not spare the culprit. Gwen did not often cry at school, but on this occasion she left the Principal's room weeping like Niobe, and poor Winnie, who had been called in to hear the tail end of the lecture, followed blinking a little on her own account.

"You do such lunatic things, Gwen," said Winnie on the way home.

"I meant no harm," protested the still tearful Niobe.

"I dare say you don't, but they're stupid things all the same. You might have known you'd get into trouble. I shall scold Dick about it."

"It wasn't his fault."

"Well, it's been a silly business all round, and why Miss Roscoe should send for me and talk as if I were partly responsible I can't imagine," said the aggrieved Winnie. "It's bad enough to have to teach in class without being blamed for what no person in her senses could consider my fault."

"That's Miss Roscoe all over," gulped Gwen. "If she's angry she must fizz whether there's justice in it or not. I'm fearfully sorry, Win! It's too bad you were dragged in."

"Well, I suppose it can't be helped now," said Winnie, somewhat mollified. "Miss Roscoe's storms are soon over, that's one blessing. I expect by to-morrow she'll have calmed down. You'll be in disgrace for a while, but she'll forget about it."

"What became of the sweets?" asked Lesbia.

"Left them on the chimneypiece and I expect the housemaid will commandeer them. I daren't ask for them, I can tell you."

Next morning the lower sashes of the Fifth Form room windows were found firmly screwed down, and the glass had received a coat of white paint put on the outside, so that not even a peephole could be scratched from within. The girls whose desks had formerly commanded a view were savage; even Miss Douglas wore an air of plaintive resignation.

"Might have known it would be Gwen Gascoyne who would bring herself into such a mess!" said Charlotte Perry.

"Um—I've a notion Netta set the ball rolling," returned Elspeth Frazer.

CHAPTER XV

STORM CLOUDS

It was only a few days after this that a letter arrived for Mr. Gascoyne which almost turned the little Parsonage upside down. Gwen could tell from Father's manner that something had happened, he seemed so unusually agitated, so perplexed, and sometimes so absent-minded that he forgot all that was going on around him. Something was wrong, argued Gwen, and as she did not like to question Father himself, she plucked up her courage and asked Beatrice.

"Well, I suppose there's no reason why you shouldn't know, so long as you don't chatter about it," said the latter. "I think you can be trusted to keep a secret?"

"If it's Dad's secret," returned Gwen.

"Well, the fact is, Dad's had a living offered to him. You needn't jump and clap your hands, for it's nothing at all out of the way—indeed he hardly knows whether to accept it or not. It's a good deal better from a money point of view than this curacy, but there are objections."

"Where is it?"

"That's one of the chief objections. It's in a very poor part of a crowded manufacturing town, a place black with huge chimneys that send out clouds of smoke, where there's hardly a blade of grass, and the very trees are all blighted with the chemicals in the air. Father knows the place well; he was curate there for a short time just after his ordination. He called it Sodom-and-Gomorrah-mixed then, and it's probably worse instead of improved, for they've built more chemical works, he hears."

"Oh!" said Gwen, her enthusiasm very much damped. "But he's surely not going to accept it?"

"I don't know. There are many things to be considered. We're a big family, and the boys have got to be educated somehow. I don't know how it's to be done here."

"There's the Stedburgh Grammar School."

"Yes, but how are we to manage the fees? Winnie can't go and teach there to equalize their school bills! If we went to Rawtenbeck, they could all three be sent to King Edward's College. It's certainly an inducement."

"And we should have to leave the Parsonage, and the garden, and everything at Skelwick!"

"Yes; that's the terrible part. Father's simply torn in two. He's done so much for Skelwick. Think what it was when he came! And now there's the Mission Room at Basingwold, and the Lads' Club, and the Library, and the Men's Class, and the Temperance Union, and all the Guilds. Perhaps, if he went, another curate might come who took no interest in them, and they would all go to pieces."

"Dad would be fearfully missed if he went."

"Yes; but there's another side even to that. He's only curate here, and if Mr. Sutton were to die, and a new rector came to North Ditton, Dad would be expected to resign. Curates always do when there's a change of incumbent; it's clerical etiquette. Mr. Sutton is such an old man that, you see, this may happen any time, so Dad can't feel really settled here."

"I wish he were rector instead of only curate!" sighed Gwen.

"Ah, so do I! But Skelwick isn't a parish by itself, it's only a part of North Ditton. If Dad accepts the living of Rawtenbeck he'll be a vicar then, and he says there's any amount of work to be done in the place. The church has been fearfully slack! He hardly knows which needs him most, Skelwick or Rawtenbeck."

"When must he make up his mind?"

"Fortunately, not immediately. The Bishop has given him six weeks to think it over before he need decide."

"Then we've six weeks' reprieve," said Gwen.

She was extremely agitated at the news. She had often thought in a vague way how nice it would be if her father were appointed to a living, but she had never anticipated such a change as this. To remove to a smoky, dirty manu-facturing town, where even the trees were blighted with chemicals! The proposition seemed intolerable. Gwen hurried out of the garden and climbed a little way up the headland at the back of the house. It was Saturday morning, and there were plenty of tasks to be done at home, but at the present she felt she must be alone with her thoughts. To leave Skelwick—to go away from all this and perhaps never see it again! She sat down on a rock, and took a long comprehensive look over the whole landscape.

There were the cliffs, and the headland, and the great wide stretch of rolling, shimmering sea, and the little red sails of the fishing smacks far out on the blue horizon; below her stretched the village, with its irregular red roofs and gay patches of flower gardens, and the shingly cove where some of the boats lay beached. She could just see the chimneys of the Parsonage, and the corner of the tennis lawn where Martin was playing with Jingles, and a scrap of the common where Winnie's hens were pecking in the coarse grass. Above the village, a conspicuous object against the sky, rose their little church of St. John the Baptist, standing on the high headland at the very edge of the bare wold, as Father often said, like a voice crying in the wilderness. Who would come there, she wondered, if Dad went? Skelwick was only a chapel-of-ease to North Ditton, and before Mr. Gascoyne's time the place had been much neglected. No resident clergyman had lived there, and though a curate had come from the Parish Church at North Ditton to take Sunday services, no attempt had been made to get hold of the rough fisher folk in the district. It had been uphill work, and with very little assistance or encouragement, for Mr. Sutton, the rector, was old and in delicate health, and quite unable to take any active part; indeed, for many years he had never visited Skelwick or the neighbouring hamlets.

"Everything worth having here is owing to Dad," thought Gwen. "I don't know how he'd ever bear to leave it."

She could not contemplate the idea of the smoky Vicarage at Rawtenbeck. Though she sometimes dreamt of how she would go out into the world and do things when she grew up, she had always imagined the Parsonage as a place that would still be there for her to come home to whenever she wished, even from the wilds of Canada. She loved every inch of the dear little house, and every clump of flowers in the garden was like a friend.

Angela Brazil

"As far as homes and houses go I'm a rank old Conservative. I hate being uprooted," said Gwen to herself.

She felt so unsettled she could not go back at present. Her preparation must wait, and she would take a walk higher up on the wold to try and recover her equanimity. The fresher air of the headland always calmed her when she was annoyed or irritable.

For some time she strolled on rather aimlessly among the heather and the gorse bushes, watching the birds or the grasshoppers, and sitting down every now and then to drink in a fuller enjoyment of the scene. She was quite alone, and to-day at any rate Gwen loved solitude. No—after all she had not the moor entirely to herself. Over a ridge of bracken loomed a funny little black figure, which seemed to be moving in her direction. As it came nearer she could make out that it was a little old gentleman, very small and thin and wizened, with a face as yellow as parchment, and a long, hooked nose, and eyes set in a mass of wrinkles. His clothes did not fit him particularly well, and were ill cut, and his hat was decidedly shabby. He walked along peering through his glasses as if he were shortsighted, and occasionally even feeling his way with a cane which he carried. When he saw Gwen he hastened towards her with an appearance of relief.

"I'm so glad to find somebody in this wild place," he began, in a funny little cracked voice that matched his face and figure. "Can you tell me if I am very far away from the village of Skelwick?"

"About two miles," replied Gwen, wondering who the stranger could be.

"Indeed! And in which direction may the place lie? I'm afraid I am rather out of my reckoning;" and he pulled a road map from his pocket and held it within two inches of his eyes.

"It's down there to the left, but the path's a little hard to find. You have to be careful you don't go through the wrong gap and walk over the edge of the cliff."

"Tut-tut-tut! Such spots ought to be marked 'Dangerous' on the maps. I shall write to the publishers and tell them so. As far as I understand now I am standing exactly here?" and he handed the rather dilapidated sheet to Gwen for verification.

"What a queer old crank!" she thought; but she answered civilly, and tried to identify the particular spot, as he seemed so anxious about it.

"Thank you! If you will put a cross at the point where you consider there is a dangerous gap I shall be obliged, and will endeavour to avoid the place," he remarked.

"I am going back to Skelwick myself, and I could show you the way if you like," returned Gwen, moved with a sudden compassion for the frail little figure, a whole head shorter than her stalwart self.

"If it will not be incommoding you, I shall be glad to avail myself of your offer. I am a trifle shortsighted, and these moorland paths are confusing."

"Yes, you can easily go miles out of your way," agreed Gwen, wondering again who the stranger could be.

He did not look like an ordinary tourist, and as they walked together over the wold he began to make a number of enquiries about Skelwick and the people who lived there. He was an artful questioner, and Gwen, almost before she realized what she was doing, gave him a full and detailed history of the neighbourhood, including what it had been before Father came, and what it was now.

"Of course some of them still drink, but they're better than they were," she said. "Six years ago most of the fishermen wouldn't go near a service, and spent all Sunday with bottles of whisky in that little cabin on the shore, the very one Dad's made into a newsroom now. I don't know what the place would do without him if he really—" but here she stopped in great distress, remembering she was letting out the secret which Beatrice had strictly enjoined her to keep.

The blinking, shortsighted eyes did not seem to take any notice of her confusion. The old gentleman twitched his mouth hard, and then merely remarked:

"It's well to be a favourite in one's parish."

"I wish it were Dad's parish!" said Gwen, following up her private train of thought. "If Skelwick were a separate living of its own, quite apart from North Ditton, he could do so much more. It's fearfully hampering to be under another church that's such a long way off. It doesn't give Dad a free hand at all."

"Yes—yes—yes; exactly so," commented the stranger, wrinkling up his forehead into thick lines.

He was very silent after this, as if he were turning something over in his mind, and Gwen, who began to think she had chattered too much, walked along trying to remember what she had said. They had almost reached the village by now; the sun was glaring on the red roofs below them and on the white highroad which led to North Ditton.

"This is my short cut back to the Parsonage," said Gwen,

stopping at a stile; "but if you want the 'King's Arms' you must go along that footpath to the right."

"Thank you! I shall get some lunch there, and then go on to North Ditton. By the by, what time is your evening service on Sunday?"

"Half-past six," replied Gwen, wondering as she turned away why a stranger who was evidently only passing through Skelwick should ask such a question.

"Mere curiosity, I suppose," she thought. "He seems an inquisitive old fellow."

She told her experiences to Beatrice and Winnie, but they had no more idea than herself of the identity of the little old gentleman.

"Some tourist on a walking tour, I expect," said Beatrice. "You were quite right to show him the way; but you really must be careful, Gwen, and not talk so freely to chance people whom you meet. I'd rather you didn't go on the moors quite alone. Take one of the boys next time."

"Stumps is a far worse blabber than I am!" laughed Gwen. "He'd have given the most intimate details of our household arrangements, and what we were going to have for dinner to-day. Perhaps have added an invitation!"

"Which would surely not have been accepted."

"I don't know! Such an eccentric old fellow might be capable of anything. I shall look out for him in church to-morrow evening."

And much to Gwen's surprise he was actually there. He

turned up rather late—during the singing of the first Psalm, in fact—and left in the middle of the hymn after the sermon. He sat on one of the benches close to the door, and Gwen would hardly have known of his presence had she not recognized the peculiar way in which he cleared his throat, which attracted her attention to him.

"Who was that stranger, Robert?" she asked the clerk afterwards.

"Don't know at all, Miss Gwen. I never see him in my life before. Funny old chap, weren't he? But he put a half-crown in the plate before he left! We don't get many half-crowns at Skelwick; it's mostly pennies and threepennybits, with a few sixpences, as I collect."

"Perhaps he just came over from North Ditton for the walk; he seems to be fond of walking, and perhaps he wanted to see the village by sunset," said Gwen. "I wish he'd stayed five minutes longer and spoken to Father. He always likes to welcome strangers who come to the church."

"And those bean't a-many," returned the clerk as he locked the big door.

It was a little incident, and seemed quite unimportant at the time. Gwen dismissed it quickly from her mind, for she had very many other things to think about just then, things that seemed paramount and far more interesting and exciting than chance tourists who asked questions.

But she was to hear of the eccentric old gentleman again.

CHAPTER XVI

FIRST AID

Gwen's quarrel with Netta was so complete that the two were no longer on speaking terms. Gwen was very apprehensive lest her former chum should carry out her old threat and betray the secret of the broken china, and in the first heat of her anger Netta had been inclined to do so; on further reflection, however, she decided that the consequences might be too compromising to herself, and that it would be safer to preserve silence. She had already scored by fetching Miss Trent into the schoolroom during Gwen's conversation with Dick, and the trouble which had ensued was almost enough to satisfy her. Really Netta had been rather tired of Gwen before this, and she was not sorry to seize upon an excuse for breaking their friendship. She now took up hotly with Annie Edwards, and the pair were for the moment inseparable.

"I believe it's as I thought," said Elspeth Frazer to Charlotte Perry; "Gwen Gascoyne's quite off with Netta. Now, if she can only get into a better set she may be a different girl. I want to find out what she's really like, so I'm going to be nice to her to-morrow when we go the geological excursion."

"Perhaps we have been rather horrid to her," returned Charlotte thoughtfully.

"It was mostly her own fault for putting on airs when she first came up, and then making such friends with Netta. She couldn't expect any of us to have anything to say to her after that."

"Probably she didn't know Netta."

"I dare say not; but it shows she's a bad judge of character. All the same I've got Gwen a little on my conscience, and I'm going to try what I can do. She may improve now."

Elspeth spoke the truth when she said that she had Gwen on her conscience. It had occurred to her several times lately that perhaps she had misunderstood her schoolfellow, and that she might have done more to help her. "Am I my brother's keeper?" rose uneasily to her mind. She had an uncomfortable feeling that in happier circumstances Gwen might have made a better impression on the Form, and that she and Hilda and Edith and Louise were partly responsible for her ill reception.

"I'm very sorry if we've been Pharisees!" she thought. "Of course one wanted to keep to one's own set, and not have anything to do with the tag-end of the Form—but—Well, I mean to give Gwen Gascoyne a chance now, anyhow."

The geological excursion was rather an event of the term. The Form had been learning geology with Miss Roberts, who promised to take the girls for an afternoon to Riggness, a place a few miles away on the coast, greatly noted for its fossils, where they could have a practical demonstration to supplement the information in their textbooks. On the Friday afternoon chosen for the ramble everybody started armed with hammers of all varieties, from Miss Roberts's beautiful geological pick to stout tack hammers and even toffee hammers.

"One never knows—one might find an ichthyosaurus embedded in the cliffs!" declared Charlotte Perry, brandishing a wooden mallet and an iron wedge, as if she were prepared to clear away tons of rock in the pursuit of her researches.

"Don't I wish we could!" said Miss Roberts. "But I'm afraid a few ammonites and belemnites will have to content us; those are quite difficult enough to get out intact. We shall do very well if we can only bring back some really perfect specimens for the school museum."

Riggness was on the other side of Stedburgh from Skelwick, and Gwen had never been there before, so the excursion was new to her. It was great fun going with the whole Form; the girls had come well prepared to enjoy themselves, and Miss Roberts also was in a jolly frame of mind, and had even brought with her a box of chocolates, which she handed round impartially till the contents vanished. Three compartments seemed to overflow with Rodenhurst hats. Gwen had just been following Millicent Cooper and Minna Jennings when Elspeth Frazer gripped her by the arm.

"Come in here with us, Gwen," she said, and Gwen, too much astonished for words, complied. Why she should be invited into a carriage with Hilda Browne, Charlotte Perry, Iris Watson, Louise Mawson, and Edith Arnold, the most elect set in the Form, was beyond her comprehension, but it was a very pleasant circumstance all the same. To be sure, they did not take much notice of her, but they were not disagreeable, and Elspeth spoke to her more than once in quite a friendly fashion. It was so utterly different from their former attitude towards her that Gwen almost believed she was dreaming. Perhaps it was only because they were on a holiday this afternoon, she thought, and to-morrow they would be as usual again. Well, at any rate, she would take advantage of to-day, and make the most of her opportunities, so she chatted a little with Elspeth, and sat ruminating over this amazing change of front on the part of those girls whom Netta, in mockery, had nicknamed "The Saints". Riggness was reached in twenty minutes, the train stopped at the small wayside station, and the Rodenhurst party got out in a hurry. They were to descend to the beach, and walk along the shore to Linkthwaite Bay, a distance of about three miles, geologizing as they went. A steep zigzag path led down the side of the cliff to the sands, and when once her flock was all collected at the bottom, Miss Roberts improved the occasion by giving a short lecture on the formation of the rocks which formed the headland, then, leading the way, she showed them how to hunt about for the ammonites embedded in the face of the cliffs, or the long belemnites that could be seen in flat terraces of rocks at the water's edge.

"Miss Roberts is right—they're uncommonly difficult to get out whole," said Elspeth, tapping gingerly round a particularly fine specimen; "just when you think you've done it, they go smash."

"It's most aggravating," agreed Gwen, whose heavy hammer, borrowed from Winnie's hen-yard, had been rather too forcible in its effects. "I'd almost got the loveliest, biggest belemnite, and it broke into three pieces like a slate pencil."

"I like my toffee hammer best," said Charlotte, tenderly fingering one or two good specimens which she had managed to secure. "I mean to save up and buy a real geological one like Miss Roberts's."

Tapping the rocks was a fascinating occupation, and a fairly profitable one, for this part of the coast was rich in fossils. By the time the girls had walked a mile along the shore they had all been able to procure some souvenirs, though as yet nothing of very special importance. Miss Roberts looked about with a practised eye, and the pick end of her hammer would withdraw a specimen neatly, where clumsier blows worked havoc.

"We'll hurry on a little farther now," she said. "Those cliffs in the middle of the bay are a particularly good hunting ground, and if there's anything interesting to be found, we ought to find it there."

At the place in question the rocks were intersected by a narrow gorge, where a small stream trickled its way from the moorlands above. The shelving platforms of the cliff were here comparatively easy to climb, and the action of water and weather combined had carried down a mass of stones and debris that would be worth investigation. Miss Roberts was as active and enthusiastic as any of the girls; she jumped lightly from stone to stone, tapping likely spots with her hammer, and finally, seeing something protruding from a rock above, began to scale the face of the cliff.

"I believe I've got something here at last!" she called.

"Oh! what is it?" cried the eager girls.

"I can't tell yet till I've cleared it a little."

"Oh! Is it an ichthyosaurus, do you think?" cried Charlotte Perry.

"I'm going to send down a shower of stones—stand out of the way!" commanded Miss Roberts, and balancing herself nimbly on a narrow ledge, she swung her hammer vigorously.

Then exactly what happened nobody quite knew. Down came the stones, rattling like an avalanche, and down with them came Miss Roberts, falling with a heavy thud upon a piece of rock below. It was so utterly sudden and unexpected that the girls stood for a moment in speechless consternation, then Hilda, Elspeth, and one or two others ran to the teacher's assistance. Miss Roberts lay at first as if she were almost stunned, then she tried to rise, and fell back with a groan.

"Do you know," she said quite calmly, "I'm very much afraid I've broken my leg." And then she closed her eyes, and turned very white.

The girls stared at one another in helpless dismay. Miss Roberts, the leader and head of the expedition, who was accustomed to give orders which they promptly obeyed, to be lying there injured and half fainting! The situation was unparalleled. Hilda Browne looked at Elspeth Frazer for inspiration, and Elspeth shook her head and looked at Charlotte Perry, but Charlotte only began to cry, while Iris Watson, Louise Mawson, Edith Arnold, and Rachel Hunter stood in utter indecision. Not one of them had the least idea what to do.

Then Gwen stepped forward. Seeing the elder and more influential members of the party collected round the governess, she, the youngest girl in the Form, and the one whose opinion had been hitherto scouted, had not ventured to interfere, but as nobody seemed to be doing anything at all, she felt licensed to come to the front.

"I took the St. John's Ambulance Course last winter, and passed the examination," she said quietly. "I know how to give first aid. Perhaps I'd better try and find out where Miss Roberts is hurt. Can't any of you get some water?" and she knelt down by the mistress's side, and began very gently to feel for the extent of the injuries.

The girls were so relieved that anybody had a knowledge of what ought to be done, that they readily allowed Gwen to assume the responsibility. Louise Mawson flew to the stream, and fetched some water in her hat, while Iris helped to unbutton Miss Roberts's boot. The unfortunate teacher revived a little with the water.

"It's my left leg, below the knee—I felt it crack as I fell," she gasped painfully.

"I'm afraid it's rather a bad fracture, too," said Gwen, when she had finished examining her patient.

"Oh! what are we to do?" moaned Louise.

"Can we carry her back to Riggness?" suggested Hilda.

"We mustn't move her an inch till we've put her leg in splints," said Gwen. "I believe it's only a simple fracture, but it might become compound with the least jolt. Elspeth, will you take hold of her foot—yes, the left one, of course—and pull it very gently."

"I—I daren't touch her!" shivered Elspeth, who had turned almost as white as Miss Roberts.

"I will—I don't mind!" said Charlotte, and she did what was required under Gwen's directions.

"Now you must hold it like that till we get some splints," continued Gwen. "You see, if the muscles contract, the rough ends of the broken bone might pierce a blood vessel, or do dreadful damage. Some of you bring some sand and make a pillow under her head, then she'll be more comfortable. What we want next are the splints."

Angela Brazil

Many willing hands obeyed Gwen's orders. In less than a few minutes the sand was heaped under Miss Roberts's head and shoulders, while Louise constantly wetted her forehead and lips with water. Gwen, with a few assistants, had gone in quest of splints. She had spied some hazel bushes farther up the gorge, which she thought might suffice for her purpose. Up the steep bed of the stream the girls climbed, splashing recklessly in and out of the water, to save time being their main object.

"They'll have to be thick pieces, and long too," said Gwen. "They ought to go from above the knee to below the foot. Whose penknife is sharpest?"

Nobody's was very sharp, and the girls had to hack and hew away slowly and painfully before they could make the least impression on the tough hazel boughs. At last Gwen secured several lengths which satisfied her, and she returned to her patient.

"Now, I want all your handkerchiefs to make bandages. Thanks! Charlotte, pull her foot just a trifle more, no—her toes should be up—so! That's better. I'm sorry to hurt you so dreadfully, Miss Roberts! I shall very soon have finished. There! I think those bandages are right. Give her some more water, Louise, quick!"

Poor Miss Roberts had indeed nearly fainted again with pain, but she recovered herself, and even smiled as she thanked her helpers.

"I've spoilt the excursion!" she murmured.

"What's to be done next? Can we carry her?" asked Hilda.

"Better not try. The quieter that leg is kept the better. She ought to be lifted on a stretcher."

"There isn't even a farm near here."

"I know. I think for the present she's best where she is, while some of you go to the station at Riggness for help. Possibly they may have a railway ambulance, or at any rate they could bring a door."

"Is there a doctor there?"

"I'm afraid not, it's only a tiny village, but the stationmaster would telegraph to Stedburgh for one. Perhaps he could come by motor, if there's no train."

It was amazing what thoughtfulness and self-reliance had come to Gwen with the emergency. She made her plans and arrangements as calmly as if she were accustomed to deal every day with accidents. No one questioned her authority, and all were willing to do what she told them. Iris Watson and two others who were judged the quickest walkers volunteered to go to the station for help, and they listened attentively while Gwen gave instructions as to what they were to ask the stationmaster to send.

"It's such a comfort you know!" said Hilda. "I wish I'd learnt ambulance."

It seemed an interminable age to poor Miss Roberts and the girls before a railway porter and two labourers who had been working on the line, arrived with a stretcher, which fortunately was kept in the inspector's office at Riggness. It was a tedious slow journey along the shore, and up to the station. The patient was nearly worn out by the time they placed her in the waiting-room, and was thankful to have the cup of tea which the stationmaster's wife brought her. A doctor arrived from Stedburgh half an hour afterwards, armed with proper splints and bandages, and he carefully examined and reset the broken limb.

"I must thoroughly congratulate the young lady who contributed first aid," he said. "She managed most skilfully. This would have been a serious thing but for her prompt measures. If the bone had been jolted about before it was put in splints, the consequences might have been permanent lameness or even loss of life. I wish it were obligatory for everybody to study ambulance."

The doctor took Miss Roberts back to her home in Stedburgh in his own car, and the girls followed by the next train, all equally anxious to get away from Riggness. They were much distressed about their teacher; the excursion had been a fiasco, and the whole party felt limp and out of spirits, like sheep without a shepherd.

"I'm thankful to get the whole crew packed off safe," said the stationmaster to his wife. "My word! It was a nasty accident to happen, down there on the shore. Good thing one of those lassies had a head on her shoulders!"

"An ordinary enough looking girl, too," remarked his wife. "I wouldn't have guessed she'd be the one to come forward. But there, one never can tell!"

"There must be more in her than shows on the outside," agreed the stationmaster.

CHAPTER XVII

A PRESSING ACCOUNT

When Gwen took her place at her desk on the following Monday morning, she was aware of a subtle difference in the general attitude towards her. She had earned the respect of the Form, and though nobody gushed, she felt she was no longer regarded as an interloper and upstart. Especially was this noticeable in the case of the nicer girls, several of whom spoke to her in quite a pleasant manner, and included her in a discussion about the tennis tournament. To Gwen, who had so long been left out in the cold, it was a most welcome change; she had never expected popularity, but she had always hoped that in time she might be able to conquer the prejudice that existed against her. It was a new thing to be asked to lend her dictionary to Hilda Browne, to compare chemistry papers with Iris Watson, or to play a game of tennis with Elspeth Frazer, Edith Arnold, and Charlotte Perry. The ban which had hitherto excluded her from the better set in the Form seemed to have been suddenly removed, the girls were looking at her from a new stand-point, and were ready to allow that after all she was different from what they had previously supposed.

Naturally Miss Roberts's accident and consequent absence from her post made a great upset in the school: classes had to

Angela Brazil

be rearranged, and lessons delegated to other teachers. It was particularly awkward, because the Fifth Form was working for the Senior Oxford, and though only a few girls were actually to take the examination, the preparation was the same for everybody.

"I call it too bad," said Betty Brierley, an acknowledged slacker, "to make the whole Form grind—grind—grind—like this, all on behalf of about four candidates. They ought to have a special class to themselves."

"There's method in the madness, though," said Joan Masters. "Miss Roscoe isn't going to tell till the very last who's to go in for it, so nobody knows if she mayn't be destined as a victim for the sacrifice, and her name already entered."

"Oh! Not me!"

"Don't alarm yourself. But there are one or two others who, I expect, are on the secret list. It depends entirely on our weekly reports."

"Then I'm safe, for mine are always bad. I wouldn't go in for a public exam, for the whole world, the school ones are quite enough for me, and too much, as a rule. Who's likely, do you think?"

"I'm not quite sure. Elspeth Frazer, for one, and—yes, I shouldn't be so very much astonished if Miss Roscoe's chosen Gwen Gascoyne."

"Gwen—yes. She's been bucking up no end lately in maths."

"And in Latin too. However, it's not our business. But I think there'll be some surprises."

Gwen, whether or not with the idea of the Senior Oxford in her head, had certainly been working hard. She had not only caught up, but even overstepped most of the Form, and her reports kept a steady average of improvement. Miss Roscoe, who was generally scanty in the matter of praise, said little, but there was an air of encouragement about her which urged Gwen to her best efforts.

"I made up my mind I'd let them all see I could do the work as well as anybody, though I am the youngest," she said to herself. "They don't sneer at me now."

Her translation from the Lower School was beginning to feel quite an old remembrance. Her thoughts went back sometimes to that first day in the Fifth, the day when Netta had taken her into Miss Roscoe's private sitting-room, and she had broken the box of china. That was a recollection which always stung, and which she would thrust away uneasily into the lumber-room of her mind. So far she had heard nothing more from Parker's, but the consciousness of the debt was there, and she knew that sooner or later she would be called upon to face the difficulty.

Nor was she mistaken. One Saturday morning, when she was taking a little vigorous exercise with the lawn mower before breakfast, she saw the postman coming in at the gate, and obeying a sudden impulse, ran to receive the letters, instead of allowing him to deliver them as usual at the door. There were four circulars for Father, a postcard for Beatrice, and one thin business envelope addressed to "Miss Gwen Gascoyne, c/o Miss Goodwin, The Thorns, Manor Road, Stedburgh," and re-directed in Netta's handwriting to "Skelwick Parsonage, North Ditton". Full of apprehension Gwen turned it over, and saw the name "J. Parker & Sons" printed on the flap. So it had come at last! Without even opening it she knew perfectly well what must be inside. She wondered they had waited so long before sending in the account again. What a mercy she had intercepted the postman that morning and taken the letters herself! If Beatrice had got hold of this it would have been impossible to conceal the matter any longer. Why had Netta sent the letter on by post instead of giving it to her at school? Surely it was a piece of spite on her part. Gwen turned quite hot as she thought of what Beatrice would have said. She hastily put the postcard and circulars on the breakfast-table, and ran down the garden to a retired place in the orchard, where she could open her ill-fated envelope in privacy.

Yes, it was just what she anticipated—a bill for ten shillings, and a polite but urgent request that the amount should be paid without further delay. She crushed it angrily in her hand, then stuffed it into her pocket and stood thinking. What was she to do? What could she do? All sorts of desperate schemes came running through her mind, and she gave each its due consideration.

"If I were a girl in a magazine story," she thought, "I suppose I'd disguise myself as a pierrette and go and sing on the promenade at Stedburgh. I dare say I'd get heaps of pennies. But—oh! I wonder if girls ever really do such things out of books? Father'd rather I owed pounds than went singing for pennies. He stopped the Sunday School children going round on Christmas Eve, but then they went into the public-houses, and of course I shouldn't. No, I couldn't risk it, and besides, I'd be too shy to sing, and somebody would be sure to find out. Shall I ask Dick to lend me half a sovereign? He would in a minute. No! I've not sunk to sponging on my boy friends, at any rate. I'd rather do a day's charing than that. A good idea! Why shouldn't I turn charwoman? If Beatrice would let me clean out the schools every Saturday, instead of Mrs. Cass, and pay me the money, I'd work off the bill in time. I wonder if I dare suggest it?"

The breakfast bell ringing loudly and clamorously at that moment put an end to Gwen's meditations, and she went indoors, but she was much preoccupied during the meal, so that she never noticed how Giles was peppering her piece of bread and butter till she incautiously took a bite and choked.

"You hateful boy! You're always up to some monkey tricks!" she exclaimed indignantly.

"'For she can thoroughly enjoy
The pepper when she pleases!'"

jeered Giles, adroitly dodging the smack she designed for him.

And the rest of the family laughed—yes, laughed, in a most heartless and inconsiderate manner.

"Your wits were wool-gathering, Gwen!" said Winnie, quoting a local proverb. "Stumps did it so deliberately and openly that anybody could have caught him who wasn't absolutely dreaming. We were all watching to see if you'd notice."

"The absent-minded beggar!" piped Basil.

"I think you're all very horrid and unkind!" complained the victim, still sneezing.

"Don't be grumpy, Gwen!"

"You must learn to take a joke, childie!" said Father, pushing back his chair and going away to his study.

Father so generally stood up for her that Gwen felt aggrieved. She had always flattered herself upon her capacity for accepting "ragging" with equanimity, but this, she considered, was beyond a joke.

"It might have got into my eyes and blinded me," she declared with plaintive dignity, and leaving the peppery remains on her plate, stalked off to the garden. She had certainly been too busy thinking during breakfast to notice her plate. It had struck her that if she really wished Beatrice to allow her to do charwoman's work at the school, she must give some proof of her capacity in that direction.

"Mrs. Cass never begins till one o'clock," she thought. "I'll go down this morning and get it all done before she comes, and then I can show Beatrice."

It seemed the only possible way of earning money open to her, so stealing one of Nellie's coarse aprons and a tin of soft soap from the kitchen, she hurried off to the school. She knew where Mrs. Cass kept the bucket and scrubbing-brush which she used for her cleaning operations; they were in a cupboard at the end of the passage. Being Saturday, the place was, of course, empty, and no one would disturb her. She had brought the Parsonage key to unlock the door, and after filling her bucket at the pump in the yard, she put on the apron, tucked up her sleeves, and set to work. And it was work! Gwen had never in her life before tried to scrub a floor, and though her arms were sturdy and strong at wielding a tennis-racket or the lawn mower, they soon began to ache at the unwonted exercise which she had set herself. The room seemed most enormously large, and she was sure it was abnormally dirty. The school children's boots must have been caked with mud. She began to have a wholesome respect for Mrs. Cass. She grew stiff and cramped with kneeling, and was obliged to stand up occasionally and take a rest.

"There are the two classrooms to do yet," she thought

ruefully, "to say nothing of the passage. I'm getting rather fed up with scrubbing."

But she was only half through, so she set grimly to her self-imposed task again. She had very nearly finished the big room when the door softly opened, and who should appear but Beatrice! At the sight of Gwen and her occupation she nearly dropped the books she was carrying.

"Gwen! what's the meaning of this? You do look an object!" she exclaimed.

Gwen jumped up hastily, well aware that she thoroughly merited any aspersions on her appearance. Both her dress and the apron were soaked with water, her face had accumulated some of the dirt, her hair ribbon had fallen off, and her hair was dangling in her eyes. A more untidy young person could not have been found in the whole village. She flung back her hair with a wet, grimy hand, and finding her pocket handkerchief, tried to wipe her face.

"What freak is this, Gwen? Whatever will you do next?" continued Beatrice.

"I didn't expect you here till I'd finished," answered Gwen, sitting down exhaustedly on a form.

"You know I often come to practise the hymns, now Winnie takes the mission-room at Basingwold. That doesn't explain why you're washing the floor."

"I wanted you to see that I could do it. I thought perhaps you'd let me scrub every week, and pay me instead of Mrs. Cass," said Gwen, blurting out her scheme in the baldest outline.

Beatrice took another comprehensive glance at her sister's disreputable figure, then sat down hilariously.

"You needn't laugh so—I mean it seriously," protested Gwen. "I want the money."

"Oh! oh! You look so funny!" screamed Beatrice; then, suddenly sobering down, she changed her tone. "I couldn't help laughing," she continued, "but it was a good thing it was only I who came in and caught you in this dirty mess. What prompted you to be so silly?"

"I've told you already."

"Gwen, don't be idiotic! How could you scrub the school every week. Besides, we couldn't take the work away from Mrs. Cass. She'd be most indignant She needs the money badly, poor body, with that large family to keep."

This was an utterly new aspect of the case that had not before occurred to Gwen.

"I want money too," she groaned.

"So do I, and so does Dad, and so do we all, but we can't get it," replied Beatrice rather tartly. "We have to make up our minds to go without. You're no worse off than the rest of us."

Gwen paused. A half impulse was stirring within her to tell her sister her difficulties. If only Beatrice looked a little more sympathetic!

"How do you know I'm no worse off?" she began.

"I've no patience with you, Gwen! You're always thinking about yourself! You've done a silly, mad prank to-day, and I don't know what Mrs. Cass will say when she arrives. Really, at your age you ought to know better and remember your dignity. You're not a child now, though I'm sure you behave like one. Go and put that bucket and scrubbing-brush away, and wash your face before you walk home. I shall have to explain to Mrs. Cass, or she'll think I've been giving her work to another charwoman. It would be enough to make her leave the church! She's fearfully touchy. I wonder when you'll learn sense."

Very crestfallen, Gwen turned away. No, it was quite impossible to confide in Beatrice. Beatrice never understood, never even seemed to want to understand. In her superior, elder-sisterly position she simply condemned everything without hesitation.

"I wonder if she used to do silly things herself?" thought Gwen. "She's always been six years older, and preached to me since I can first remember. Shall I ever catch her up, or will she seem those six years ahead to the end of the chapter?"

And having performed some very necessary ablutions, she walked home, looking tired and woebegone.

Beatrice, with a sigh, opened the harmonium and chose her hymns for to-morrow's Sunday School, wondering on her part why this particular sister was so difficult to manage, and so utterly different in disposition from the rest of the family.

"I'm sure I do my best," she thought, "but Gwen has always been a trial. I can't imagine whom she takes after. If the ugly duckling's ever going to turn into a swan, it's time she began!"

All Sunday Gwen was haunted by a horrible black shadow.

Angela Brazil

She kept Parker's letter in her pocket, and the remembrance of it never left her. Gwen generally enjoyed Sundays, but this particular day was like a nightmare. How to get out of her scrape she could not imagine. The debt felt like a heavy millstone tied round her neck. In the afternoon, when the others sat reading and chatting under the trees in the garden, she mooned about the orchard by herself, too miserable even to be interested in a book. How was the affair to end? She did not dare to go to Parker's and explain that at present it was impossible to pay the bill. She supposed she would simply have to let things drift and await further developments. What steps Parker's would take next, she could not foresee. They would probably wait a week or even more before further pressing the account, and any respite was welcome. Trouble was ahead, doubtless, but it was better ten days off than to-morrow, because there was always the faint hope that some circumstance might arise at the eleventh hour to smooth over the difficulty. On Monday morning Gwen seized an opportunity to catch Netta alone.

"I say," she began, "it was awfully mean of you to send that letter of Parker's on to me by post. Why couldn't you have brought it to school instead?"

"Why should I?" retorted Netta. "I'm not going to act postman for you, I can assure you! And look here, Gwen Gascoyne, you'll please not have any more letters directed to you at our house! We don't want to receive your bills, thank you! You must give your own address to the shops. Haven't you settled that affair with Parker's yet?"

"No, and I don't want it to be found out at home. Beatrice always takes in the letters and deals them round. It was by the merest good luck she didn't get hold of mine on Saturday. Netta, do let me use your address! You might do that much for me!"

"Why should I? I've done quite enough for you, and too much already. I'm tired of the whole business. I was silly to be mixed up with it in the beginning."

"But you started it! You took me into Miss Roscoe's room, and then you suggested going to Parker's and replacing the china."

"Are you trying to throw the blame on me?" flared Netta.

"Not altogether; but I think you were partly responsible, and that you got off cheaply."

"That's uncommonly fine," sneered Netta. "No, no, my good Gwen, that little dodge won't work. This child isn't going to be burden-bearer for your sins. If you get into scrapes you must get out of them yourself. I've lost a sovereign over you already."

"And for what?" exploded Gwen angrily. "What about my beautiful essay, that you took and used as your own?"

"Wasn't worth it! It was a freak of mine just then to win that prize, but I've never looked at the book since. I'm sorry I troubled about it. I'd rather have the sov. now."

"And I'm sorry too, because it wasn't fair and square, and I've felt vile about it ever since. I hate all these underhand things."

Netta smiled sarcastically.

"Of course you hate them when they don't turn out to your advantage. Pity you didn't pursue your course of virtue a little earlier! You were ready enough to trade the essay for the sov. at the time, so what are you grumbling about now?"

Angela Brazil

"Your meanness."

"Look here, Gwen Gascoyne, I've had enough of this! I won't hear another word about your wretched affair. As I told you before, you must get out of your own scrapes, and not expect other people to act Providence for you. If you mention the subject again, I simply shan't listen."

Gwen had scarcely expected either help or consolation from Netta, though she felt indignant that her old chum should show her so little sympathy in the matter. After all, it was only in accordance with Netta's character. Grapes do not grow on thistles; and a girl so destitute of all sense of conscience was not likely to prove a stanch and faithful friend. Gwen was learning by slow and painful experience that bright amusing manners may be worthless unless allied to more sterling qualities. She had been wont to admire Netta's easy style, and even to try to copy it; now it struck her as hollow and vapid. If only she could have started quite afresh, with no guilty memories to disturb her, she felt she had the chance of getting into a better set in her Form. But what would Elspeth Frazer, Hilda Browne, Iris Watson, or any of the nicer girls think of her conduct, both in regard to the broken-china episode or the transferred essay? She knew it would not accord with their code of honour.

"I wish I had the courage to tell Miss Roscoe everything," groaned Gwen. "It would have been the straightest course if I'd gone and confessed at once when I smashed the china. It would have saved a great many complications. Dare I possibly tell now?"

She walked along the passage to the study. The door was open, so she peeped cautiously in. Miss Roscoe sat correcting papers, and nobody else was in the room. If she wished to make her confession, here was certainly her opportunity. Her heart beat and thumped, and the words seemed to freeze upon her lips. Miss Roscoe looked so stern as she sat at her desk making pencil notes on the margins of the exercises; there was a hard, uncompromising expression on her face which Gwen knew only too well, and which did not tend in the direction of tenderness towards wrongdoers. Gwen was still smarting from the scolding she had received for her conversation with Dick out of the window. If Miss Roscoe viewed that peccadillo so seriously, what would she say to the tale which her pupil had to unfold?

"I daren't! I daren't!" thought Gwen. "No, I really can't screw up the courage. I loathe myself for a deceitful wretch, and yet—oh, dear!—there's nothing in this world I dread so much as being found out!"

She ran down the passage again with a sense of relief. One voice in her heart assured her that she had escaped a danger, though another upbraided her for her cowardice.

"If Miss Roscoe hadn't looked quite so severe I might have ventured," she sighed in response to the latter. "I don't believe I'll get even so far as the study door again."

So a golden opportunity was lost, and Gwen, who might even thus late have chosen the straighter, harder path, shirked the disagreeable experience, and was left perforce to reap the harvest of her own sowing.

Angela Brazil

CHAPTER XVIII

GWEN'S BRIGHT IDEA

As Gwen went down the corridor she noticed a small crowd collected round the notice board, and, edging her way in among the crush, read an announcement which Bessie Manners, the head girl, had just pinned up.

"There will be a General Meeting of the Seniors at 2 p.m. in the Sixth Form room. Business—to consider what steps can be taken for an adequate celebration of the school anniversary. All are urged to attend."

"Hello! Whence this thusness?" exclaimed Gwen. "What have we got to do with the school anniversary? I thought Miss Roscoe engineered the whole of it!"

"So she does, ordinarily," answered Moira Thompson, one of the prefects. "But we want this to be a very special festivity; not just the usual picnic or garden party."

"But why?"

"Haven't time to explain now. Come to the meeting and we'll expound our views. I think it's a ripping notion of Bessie's myself."

"Do give me a hint!"

But Moira shook her head and passed on, leaving Gwen to curb her curiosity until two o'clock, for the prefects had not imparted their plans to anybody as yet, and none of her own Form could enlighten her.

At the hour stated nearly all the Seniors presented themselves in the Sixth Form room. Bessie Manners was voted to the chair, and at once began an explanation of why she had called the meeting.

"Girls," she said, "you all know that we're accustomed to have some kind of festivity on 1st June, the day of our school anniversary. Now it happens that this particular occasion is one of more than usual interest. Miss Roscoe has been Principal of Rodenhurst for exactly ten years, and it seems only fitting that due recognition should be made of the circumstance. The question that we have met to discuss is the shape and form in which we can adequately celebrate this event. We feel that the suggestion ought to come from the girls themselves, though we may need aid from the mistresses in carrying it out. I shall be glad if anyone who has a plan to lay before the meeting will propose it."

"I am sure," began Moira Thompson, rising in response to Bessie's nod, "that everybody would like to show Miss Roscoe how we value her as a headmistress. For my part I think there should be a testimonial, subscribed for in the school, and that we might have a public presentation of it."

"Hear! Hear!"

"What kind of a testimonial?" asked one of the girls.

"That remains to be discussed, and would, of course, depend

upon how much was collected."

"A silver tea service, or something of that kind?" enquired Natalie Preston, one of the prefects.

"Probably: we shall have to find out what Miss Roscoe would like best."

"And where would the celebrations come in?" asked Iris Watson.

"That also must be talked over. So far, Miss Roscoe has always arranged a treat for the school on anniversary day, but we think this year it ought to be the other way, and the girls arrange a treat for Miss Roscoe and the mistresses. I'm sure they'd appreciate it."

"Each Form might have a collecting book. We ought to raise quite a handsome sum," said Bessie Manners. "Then there could be a garden fete for the presentation."

"Only for the school? Or would parents and friends be allowed to come?" asked one of the Sixth.

"I don't see why they shouldn't. It would make the affair seem of more importance. We could get up an extra fund to provide afternoon tea."

"Or get it catered for, and let people pay for their own."

"Like one does at a bazaar?"

"Exactly."

"The idea is feasible. Anybody any amendments to offer?" said Bessie.

Then a sudden and brilliant suggestion came to Gwen—one of those lucky flashes of inspiration that occasionally, in our happier moments, strike us.

"May I speak?" she cried impulsively, starting up.

"By all means," nodded Chairman Bessie.

"It seems to me," said Gwen, "that if we're going to do this thing at all, it might just as easily be on a large scale as a small one. Miss Roscoe, no doubt, would be very pleased with a silver tea service, but I know something I believe she'd like far better. Don't you remember how frightfully interested she is in the new Convalescent Home? She urged us all to help it if we could. Suppose we could raise enough money to found a cot, and call it the Rodenhurst Cot, wouldn't that be a nice memorial?"

"After Miss Roscoe's own heart!" gasped Bessie.

"Ripping!" agreed most of the girls.

"But what would it cost? Is it possible?" enquired Olga Hunter.

"I believe it is. We have some papers at the Parsonage about the Convalescent Home. I was looking at them only yesterday. Any donor of L100 is to be allowed to name a cot, and nominate the special children who occupy it. Now in this big school we ought to be able to raise L100."

"A large order," said Natalie Preston.

"Not if it's undertaken systematically. As it's for a charitable object we can ask subscriptions from outsiders."

"I see your point," said Bessie. "Yes, we could beg for the Convalescent Home when we couldn't ask for contributions for a personal testimonial to Miss Roscoe. But this would please her far more. A Rodenhurst Cot! She'd love it!"

"If each girl in the school could collect five shillings," continued Gwen, "that would be over seventy-five pounds. Then suppose on anniversary day we had a grand gymkhana, and charged a shilling admission. Surely every girl could persuade two people to come, which would make at least six hundred guests. Six hundred shillings mean thirty pounds, so there you are!"

"We could have tea extra and perhaps sell flowers," added Olga Hunter, as an amendment "I'm willing to second the proposal."

"It certainly sounds feasible on these lines. We might even raise more than the hundred pounds," said Bessie.

"In that case we could add a personal testimonial to Miss Roscoe."

"Hear! Hear!" shouted several.

"Put the motion in due form, Gwen."

"I beg to propose that in order to celebrate the tenth year of Miss Roscoe's headmistress-ship, and the seventeenth anniversary of the school, we should endeavour to collect L100 to found a Rodenhurst cot in the Convalescent Home," proclaimed Gwen.

"And I beg to second that proposal," said Olga Hunter enthusiastically.

"All in favour please signify!" murmured Chairman Bessie.

Such a chorus of "Aye!" came in response that the motion was carried unanimously, and nothing remained but to discuss details.

"We shall have to let the Juniors know about it, and start them collecting," said Natalie Preston.

"We'd better each collect as much as possible in our own district or parish," suggested Gwen. "Lesbia and I, for instance, can undertake Skelwick. I'm sure some of the people there would give towards a cot."

"Then we'll have cards or books to enter the amounts?"

"Of course."

"What about the gymkhana?"

"We must appoint a special committee to arrange a programme and competitions, and ask people if they'll offer prizes."

"I vote we appoint the prefects, then, as a committee."

"Right-o!"

Gwen came away from the meeting with flying colours. She had certainly made a proposition which nobody else had thought of, but which all acknowledged was exactly the most fitting to meet the circumstances. For the first time in her experience she found her remarks receiving the attention not only of her own Form, but even of the Sixth. The prefects, mindful of their dignity, generally held themselves aloof, so it was indeed a triumph for Gwen to be seized upon, after the

Angela Brazil

meeting was over, by Bessie Manners, and consulted upon the general working of the scheme. To walk down the corridor linked arm in arm with the head girl was a distinction that fell to few, and Gwen, though she accepted the honour with apparent unconsciousness, knew perfectly well that it would make an enormous difference to her position in the school. For the moment she was talked about. Her plan for the cot was called "Gwen Gascoyne's scheme", and to her was given the entire credit for originating it. The more the idea was discussed, the more everybody liked it. The mistresses sympathized heartily, and the Juniors promised earnest co-operation. Gwen, for once, was appreciated to her heart's content. It was wonderful how gracious the prefects were towards her, and how the members of her own Form suddenly treated her with respect. After so long a period of unpopularity it was very sweet to find general opinion had thus veered round, and Gwen enjoyed her new character of organizer to the full. She threw herself heart and soul into the working of her scheme, and thanks partly to her parish experience at Skelwick, and partly to a practical element in her composition, she was able to give really good and helpful advice, both as to the collecting of the fund, and the arranging of the gymkhana. There was very little time before the day of the anniversary, so those in authority were obliged to push matters as fast as they could. Each girl in the school begged in her own circle most assiduously, and from the reports that began to be circulated the result seemed most encouraging.

"I believe we're going to get the L100 just by collecting, and that the gymkhana will be extra," said Bessie Manners exultingly. "By the by, Miss Roscoe wishes it to be known that she would much prefer not to be offered a private testimonial, but that everything should go towards the cot."

"Oh, we wanted to give her some remembrance, though," cried several of the girls, rather disappointed.

"I'd set my heart on her having a silver teapot at least," said Iris Watson.

"It's just like Miss Roscoe not to want anything personal," said Gwen. "I must say I admire her for it. She always reminds me of an ancient Roman—the State first and foremost in her estimation, and herself nowhere."

"Yes, she'd sacrifice a good deal for the sake of the school," agreed Bessie Manners.

It was decided to turn the anniversary into a kind of floral fete, to be held in the large cricket field. There were to be morris dances, a maypole dance, a procession of decorated bicycles, and numerous athletic competitions. Tea, coffee, and lemonade would be served at tables on the ground, and flowers and sweets could be carried round in baskets and sold during the afternoon. It was wonderful when once the ball had been set rolling how quickly offers of help flowed in. The girls' parents and friends approved of the idea of a "Rodenhurst" cot for the Convalescent Home, and were most kind in their contributions. Enough cakes were promised to provide amply for afternoon tea. Bessie Manners's mother undertook to send a supply of ices, and a generous store of sweets and flowers seemed forthcoming. To have such an excellent mutual object to work for seemed to unite all the members of the school, and especially to break down the barrier between Seniors and Juniors which had hitherto existed. While before it had hardly been considered etiquette for the Sixth and Fifth to talk to those in the Lower Forms, they might now be seen conferring on quite pleasant terms about the gymkhana, comparing notes on subscriptions, and making arrangements for flower selling and sweet vending.

Considering the large amount of home preparation that was expected from her in view of the forthcoming examinations,

Gwen found she had set herself a task in undertaking any more work, but by arranging her time very carefully, she managed to perform one set of duties without neglecting another. She and Lesbia collected fifteen and ninepence for the cot among their friends in Skelwick, and wrote down the various items with much satisfaction in a notebook supplied for the purpose. The Gascoynes did not possess bicycles, so could not join the cycle parade, but Lesbia was to sing in one of the glees, and Gwen meant to enter for certain of the athletic sports. Her long arms and legs would, she hoped, stand her in good stead in a contest of running or jumping, and even if she did not win a prize, it was worth competing for the mere fun of the thing. Giles and Basil were scarcely less excited, for the Boys' Preparatory Department was to have its share in the celebrations, and they looked forward to showing their prowess in public. They spent much of their spare time in training for various Olympic games, an occupation of which Beatrice heartily approved.

"It keeps them out of mischief for the whole evening," she declared. "I bless the gymkhana."

"It's wonderful how it's drawn everyone together at school," observed Gwen. "Even Miss Roscoe isn't nearly as starchy as usual, and Miss Trent was quite jolly when we were talking over the programme. As for Upper and Lower School, we just ignore any distinction between the two when it's a question of the fete."

"I'm glad to hear it," said Beatrice, "I always thought the Seniors at Rodenhurst were much too stand-off. It will do them a world of good to forget their dignity for once, and mix freely with the rest of the school."

"Yes, it's quite a comfort to be able to talk to Lesbia in the gym. now," agreed Gwen.

"Do you mean to say you couldn't before?" exclaimed Beatrice. "Things weren't so bad as that when I was there."

"Etiquette's been getting stricter and stricter since you left. The prefects of about two years ago started the notion that Seniors must keep to themselves, and not have anything to do with Juniors, and you know when an idea like that gets broached how everybody takes it up and sticks to it. It's impossible to defy a rule of that kind just 'on one's own'."

"I know; rules the girls make for themselves are generally better kept than those made at headquarters. I agree that you couldn't break through the etiquette of your Form. Still, I'm glad the barrier is down at last, and hope it will never be raised again."

"I shan't be the one to plant a stake in the fence of division!" laughed Gwen.

Practising for the various items of the fete proceeded briskly at Rodenhurst. The younger girls, during the winter course of dancing lessons, had learned to plait the maypole, and to execute some lively morris dances. Though Miss Robins, their teacher, was not in Stedburgh during the summer, they remembered their steps quite well enough to enable them to give a performance, with the aid of a little supervision from some of their elders. Various members of the Seniors, who understood morris dancing, undertook to superintend rehearsals, and drill the small girls in any details they had forgotten. It was thought that this portion of the entertainment would form a great attraction of the fete, and give it somewhat the character of a May Day celebration. The Juniors who were fortunate enough to be taking part were immensely important, and keenly anxious to make their contribution to the programme a complete success. They turned up loyally for rehearsals, and were unwearied in practising any difficult bits where there was a likelihood of a hitch occurring.

One afternoon, about two o'clock, Gwen, with her Virgil in her hand, sauntered down the Rodenhurst garden into the playing field which lay at the back of the school. She was anxious to seize the half-hour for preparation, as she knew she would have scant time in the evening for all she was obliged to finish, and she hoped to find a quiet corner in the open air, where she might study in peace. As she walked along, seeking a shady spot, she was attracted by the sound of angry voices, and peeping over the hedge that divided the small playing field from the larger hockey and cricket field, she saw a selection of Second Form girls collected for a rehearsal. Netta Goodwin was the Senior in command, and with Netta these Juniors were evidently having an excited altercation.

"But Moira Thompson didn't do that!" shrieked an indignant voice.

"Do as I tell you!" ordered Netta tartly. "You lot go over there, and begin your dance, and Ida Bridge and Peggie Weston stop here and hold this rope."

"But I'm the leader!" wailed Ida. "They can't get on without me!"

"They'll have to, for once."

"But it's not fair! You've come to help us to practise—not for us to help you!"

"That's as I like to arrange it!"

"Oh, you are a beast!"

"Apologize for that word, or I'll spiflicate you! Where are your manners?"

"If you're not fair, we shan't mind manners, so there!"

"Ida Bridge, do you intend to hold this rope?"

"Shan't! I'd rather tell Miss Trent first."

"You miserable little sneak!"

"I'm not a sneak! It's your fault! Why can't you take our rehearsal properly, like the others did? We're wasting time."

"So we are! Get to business, you kids over there. Why don't you begin your precious dance?"

"We can't without Ida and Peggie—specially Ida!" fumed the performers.

"Well, I've told you I want them myself, and you'll just have to manage as best you can. Now then, off you go—one—two—three! Bother the lot of you! What are you waiting for?"

"For Ida Bridge."

"You won't get her!"

"Then the rehearsal's off!"

"No, it's not off, you lazy little wretches! You can manage all right if you like; I know perfectly well you can! It's just a piece of obstinacy. Pig policy doesn't pay with me, I assure you! I've been put in authority for this afternoon, and I mean to have my own way, so I give you warning. Start that dance

Angela Brazil

instantly, and Ida and Peggie hold this rope."

Instead of obeying, the Juniors crowded round Netta uttering protests and reproaches in a perfect chorus of mutiny. Gwen, who could not quite grasp the cause of the quarrel, made her way through a gap in the hedge and entered the large field.

"What's all the shindy about?" she enquired. "You're like a set of wild Irishmen at a fair. I thought you were supposed to be rehearsing?"

"How can we rehearse by ourselves?"

"And without our leader?"

"Netta won't conduct!"

"She told us to go and dance by ourselves, while she practised her own jumping."

"And she wanted to make Ida and Peggie hold the rope for her."

"How can we do our morris dance without Ida and Peggie? It spoils the figures."

"Netta!" gasped Gwen. "Did you actually mean to practise jumping instead of taking this rehearsal?"

Netta shrugged her shoulders easily.

"The kids know their steps so well, they can do the thing perfectly," she replied. "What was the good of wasting my time drilling them? I thought I'd make them of some use, and let them hold a rope for me. They're an ungrateful little set of sneaks—won't do a thing for their seniors!"

"Why, I should think not, in this case, when you'd been specially told off by the Committee to superintend their dance. I sympathize with the kids. They've right on their side. It's you who are the sneak."

"Oh! Am I indeed, Miss Gwen Gascoyne? Thank you for nothing. It's a pretty name to have called me, and I shan't forget it."

"But it's true!" returned Gwen with warmth. "It's simply abominable behaviour to pretend to act dancing mistress and use the time for your own purposes. Why should these kids hold a rope for you?"

"And why should you take me to task, I'd like to know? You're not a prefect."

"I only wish I were."

"No doubt you do!" sneered Netta. "You've been so stuck up since your Cot scheme was adopted, that you seem to imagine yourself as good as the head of the school."

"Gwen, you take our rehearsal instead—we've wasted ten minutes or more over wrangling!" pleaded one of the Juniors.

"I will, if Netta will let me."

"Oh, I yield my place with pleasure to the all-important, all-necessary Gwen Gascoyne!" retorted Netta. "We humbler members of the Fifth don't get a look-in nowadays. But just let me give you one word of good advice, my lofty Pharaoh—pride occasionally comes before a fall!"

CHAPTER XIX

A SCHOOL GYMKHANA

Thanks to the vigorous efforts of the Committee and of the various organizers of the entertainment programme, every-thing was in good training by the first of June, and anniversary day seemed likely to prove a huge success. It was decided that the gymkhana should begin at three o'clock, and be held in the large cricket field, admission being either by ticket or gate money. There was a little discussion about the arrangements in that respect, some members considering the printing of the tickets an unnecessary expense, and others their sale beforehand an essential feature.

"It's far better to sell them in advance," urged Bessie Manners, "because people will often buy them, even if they're not certain of going. If it were a showery afternoon many might stay away—then if they hadn't taken tickets it would be so much loss to the funds."

"We'll accept money at the gate, though?" queried Olga Hunter.

"Yes, we must have a gatekeeper, and provide her with shilling and sixpenny checks. I think children ought to be half-price. So many of us have little brothers and sisters who would like to come, and a shilling seems too much to pay for a child."

"Right you are! Who'll be gatekeeper?"

"Oh, some sturdy Fifth Form girl. I propose Gwen Gascoyne."

"Yes, Gwen would do splendidly. She deserves some post of honour for evolving the scheme. Besides, she's got a head on her shoulders. She'd keep the gate like Horatio kept the bridge."

"One could trust Gwen, I know. Now Rachel Hunter or Edith Arnold would make mistakes in the change, and lose their presence of mind, and perhaps let half a dozen people push in free while they were reckoning up the sixpences."

"Gwen it shall be, then. I'll ask her to-day if she'll undertake it."

Gwen was only too proud to be invited to assume such a responsible position. She felt much flattered that it should have been offered to her instead of to Elspeth Frazer, Hilda Browne, Iris Watson, or other of the older members of the Form.

"I'm the youngest of all, and yet I'm to be trusted the most!" she said to herself with a sigh of gratification. "Gwen Gascoyne, I congratulate you! You're coming on!"

There was great excitement at Skelwick Parsonage on the day of the fete. Beatrice had made several boxes of sweets to be sold on the ground, and Winnie picked the very choicest flowers in the garden for the same object. Mr. Gascoyne, Beatrice, and Martin were to come to the gymkhana, and had promised to clap their loudest at Giles' and Basil's performances in the sports. Those two heroes kept examining the muscular development of their young arms like a pair of practised Roman gladiators, and ate quite a double allowance of breakfast on the strength of the trials that were in store for them. They were so eager to start for school, that for once Beatrice had no need to urge them to hurry, and they departed in excellent spirits, vaulting, for practice, over the orchard hurdles instead of going out through the front gate.

Morning school was held as usual at Rodenhurst, but ceased at twelve, so as to give time for preliminary arrangements to be completed. The classrooms were to be used as dressing-rooms for some of the performers, and the gymnasium was turned into a repository for the parcels of sweets, cakes, and flowers which kept arriving from the generous friends who had promised such gifts. To unpack these and apportion them to different tea tables or vendors' baskets was a task which needed all the energies of the members of the Committee, who were kept so busy at the work that they had scarcely more than ten minutes to spare for dinner. As a rule, unpunctuality at this meal was visited with direst penalties, but to-day Miss Roscoe only smiled as the prefects rushed in very late, hastily bolted their meat course, and fled minus the pudding. Their zeal and virtuous example had the desired effect. Everybody upon whom any responsibility devolved made an extra effort, so that by half-past two everything was in perfect order and readiness.

"Thank our lucky, lucky stars it's a decent day!" said Gwen, gazing up at a sky which, if not blue all over, held only clouds of an apparently harmless character. "I don't believe it intends to rain at all, and I expect everybody will come, and the audience be 'large and appreciative', as the newspapers say. If I don't clear a good sum of gate money, I shall be amazed."

"Are you ready, Gwen, to act Horatio?" said Bessie Manners, bustling up in a hurry. "You understand the business, don't you? Those with tickets you of course let in free. Everybody else must pay a shilling, or children under ten sixpence. Here are two rolls of checks, sixpenny and shilling ones. You must hand checks to all comers for the amount they have paid you, and they will present the checks at the entrance to the big field. You will stand at the gate that leads from the garden to the smaller field."

"I understand all right!" laughed Gwen. "I've brought a satchel to hold the money, and I'll undertake not a soul gets in without paying. It will have to be 'over my body' if they do!"

"Moira will be at the second gate, and she won't allow anyone through without handing her a ticket or a check, so I think we shan't lose anything there," replied Bessie, turning away satisfied.

Gwen took up her station at once, for visitors were already beginning to arrive at the school, and she was soon fully occupied in receiving coins and tearing off checks. She rather enjoyed being at the receipt of custom, and was particularly gratified at the amount that went into her satchel. The fine afternoon had tempted people to come to the gymkhana, old Rodenhurst girls and their friends had turned up, as well as parents and relations of present pupils, so the gathering was quite considerable. The many pretty summer dresses and bright parasols gave a most festive appearance to the ground, even before the performers arrived on the scenes. Various girls, furnished with tasteful baskets, had been chosen to sell sweets and floral buttonholes, and soon began to find customers for their wares, while the lemonade and ice-cream stalls were already doing a roaring trade.

Lesbia had been selected as a flower vendor, and looked

absolutely charming in a white China-silk dress and Tuscan hat trimmed with daisies, which, by her usual good luck, she had received from Aunt Violet only the week before. Pretty Lesbia, with her pink cheeks and her lovely flaxen hair, really made quite a picture as she carried round her basket, and many people bought flowers from her, just because they could not resist the entreaty in her blue eyes, and the soft little voice that pleaded the cause of the Rodenhurst Cot.

"She's just twice as good at selling as I should have been," thought Gwen, watching her sister rather wistfully. "There's a fascination about Lesbia which I don't possess in the very least. She must be making a little fortune with those posies. Well, never mind. I'm keeping the gate. That's more important still. To business. Here's someone else coming. Hello! Why, Dick! This is awfully good of you!"

It was Dick Chambers who presented himself and paid his shilling. "I hardly knew whether I dared come," he grinned, "after the row I got you into that afternoon when you fished out of the window for sweets. Will any of the teachers seize upon me and turn me out as a pernicious character? I shall demand the return of my money if they do!"

"They're too busy," laughed Gwen, "and besides, I don't think anyone would recognize you. Miss Trent didn't see you, you know; she only caught me leaning out of the window."

"Then you think I may venture without fear of consequences? I feel rather like Romeo going into the Capulet mansion. Can you give me a watchword to use if I get into difficulties?"

"The Rodenhurst Cot and Coin of the Realm are our two watchwords this afternoon. Stick to those and you can't go wrong, even if you beard Miss Roscoe herself. She is over there if you'd like to shake hands with her."

"No, thanks! I've no wish to risk such an ordeal. In fact I'll give her as wide a berth as possible. Should you be allowed to negotiate an ice if I brought you one?"

"Not while I'm on duty. Look here: 'You are requested not to speak to the Woman at the wheel'. Here's a fresh batch of people arriving."

"Mayn't I tear off the checks?"

"Certainly not. Go along and buy some of Lesbia's flowers, if she has any left by now. If you don't scoot quick, I'll report you for impeding me in the performance of my work. Then they'd turn you out, with a vengeance."

"I'll be good," chuckled Dick, as he moved on to find Lesbia, and invest in her wares.

The cycle parade was about to begin, and those who meant to take part in it were wheeling their machines through a private door which led from the stable yard into the field. Not only had the competitors decorated their bicycles, but they themselves had donned fancy costumes, many of which were of quite an elaborate description. There was a Dutch maiden with white sleeves, velvet bodice, starched cap and wooden sabots, a sweet little Miss Jap-Jap-Jappy in gay kimono, a flower tucked into her dark hair, an Indian squaw with bead-embroidered garments and fringed leggings, several pierrettes, a Red Riding Hood, a Goody Two Shoes, and other characters of nursery fame or fairy-tale lore. But the best of all, so everyone agreed, was Rachel Hunter, who came arrayed as a cat. Her costume, cut on the pattern of a child's sleeping suit, was most cleverly contrived out of brown plushette, painted in bold bars to represent the stripes of a tabby. She wore a cat's mask on her head, and made such an excellent representation of a gigantic specimen of the feline race that the effect was quite appalling. The younger children squealed when she appeared on the field, especially as, to keep up her character, she made an occasional claw at one of them as she passed, or gave vent to a tremendous "Miau!" or "Fuff!" She had decorated her bicycle with chocolate mice, and halted now and then to eat one with great apparent gusto, hugely to the delight of the juvenile portion of the audience, who clapped her again and again. But the real triumph of her costume was her tail, a splendid appendage fully a yard in length. By a most ingenious contrivance of a strong wire spring, worked with a piece of elastic, she was able to curl and uncurl it, or to lash it to and fro in the most diverting fashion. Altogether Puss was a huge attraction, she acted her part capitally, and when on reaching the judge's stand she purred loudly, and pretended to wash her face with her tawny paw, the general cheering easily secured for her the first prize.

The second prize was won by a classmate of Basil's from the Boys' Preparatory Department, who came attired as a golliwog, with blackened face, fuzzy hair, and a selection of Dutch jointed dolls slung from his bicycle. His laurels were closely contested by a dainty Miss Butterfly and a picturesque Cavalier, but on the whole the funny costumes seemed to find greater favour with the majority.

Everybody voted the cycle parade an entire success, and the audience looked quite regretful as the long line of troubadours, Dolly Vardens, brigands, fairies snow queens, Italian peasants, Kate Greenaway rustics, and other interesting characters took their departure through the gate. But there were further items on the programme, and all eyes turned eagerly to the band of quaintly dressed little maidens who now ran out joyously hand in hand to perform the ancient ceremony of plaiting the Maypole. The children had been well drilled, and had practised assiduously, so each took her ribbon with confidence, and started off at the sound of the music, to tread the intricate steps required for the due twisting and combination of the colours. The affair went without a hitch, the maypole was plaited and unplaited, and the effect was so pretty that the audience encored the performance. Feeling that they had covered themselves with glory, the May-maidens retired to make room for the morris dancers, who were waiting anxiously to have their turn. The oldfashioned costumes, with their decorations of flowers, ribbons, and bells looked well with the green field for a setting, and when the band struck up, and the dancers began their lively yet graceful motions, everyone felt transported back to mediaeval days, when the world was young and joyous, and our country merited its title of "Merrie England". The Second Form girls, to whom had been assigned this portion of the programme, contrived admirably to convey the original spirit of the dance; their steps seemed so fresh and spontaneous and gay, their actions so prompt and appropriate, and all went in such excellent time to the music that the approving spectators accorded them an encore, much to their satisfaction, for they were anxious not to be beaten by their rivals the maypole plaiters.

After the dancing was finished there was an interval for refreshments before the sports began. Tea and coffee were served on tables which had been carried out from the school, the ices were much in demand, and lemonade and ginger beer bottles maintained a brisk series of pops. Gwen, whose duties had kept her by the entrance gate, had only been able to view the festivities from a distance, and she could not yet desert her post as late comers were still arriving.

"I've brought you a cup of tea, Gwen, if you can manage to drink it, and a slice of cake. It's rather hard you have to act sentry all the afternoon," said Iris Watson.

"I don't mind. It's prime fun taking the tolls. I feel like an ancient turnpike man. Thanks immensely for the tea! I'm more thirsty than hungry, but I shan't despise the cake. Isn't it a piece of the one your mother sent?"

"Sweets, sixpence a box! Peppermint creams! Chocolate caramels! Almond toffee! All home made! The best value for the money in all Stedburgh! Perfectly delicious! Buy a box and taste them!" called a well-known voice, and Lesbia marched up, smiling at her own eloquence.

"Why, you young Cheap Jack, I thought you were selling flowers!" exclaimed Gwen.

"So I was, but I completely cleared out my stock, and Miss Trent set me up in the confectionery line instead. I'm doing equally well, or even better. By the by, can you give me change for a two-shilling piece? Miss Douglas has just bought sixpenny-worth, and she has nothing but a florin. I've this moment handed my money to Miss Trent to take care of. I've no pocket in this dress, and I gave my bag to Miss Barton with the proceeds of the flowers in it. Here's the florin—I want a shilling and two sixpences for it, or else four sixpences."

"Right-o!" said Gwen, opening her satchel. "Oh, bother! Here are some more people arriving! You'll have to wait!"

"Do give it me, quick! Miss Douglas is in a hurry," pleaded Lesbia.

"Then take it out of my satchel yourself. Be sure you put in the florin."

Lesbia hastily complied and ran off, for Miss Douglas was beckoning to her impatiently, and teachers may not lightly be kept waiting.

"Have you managed to get change? That's right—give me three sixpences," said Miss Douglas, hurriedly putting the money in her purse. "I have to rush indoors now and help to dress the 'Elizabethan' girls for the final madrigal. The whole affair's going very well. We may all congratulate ourselves on what we're making."

"Hurrah for the Cot!" sang Lesbia, tripping away with a step that was meant to be in imitation of the morris dancers.

The athletic sports, open to all comers, were naturally a great feature of the afternoon. The prizes had been given by various friends who had responded so generously to the appeal made to them that the Committee had been able to place a large number of competitions upon the programme. The proceedings led off with a boys' flat race, in which Giles and Basil took part with great credit, though neither was fortunate enough to outstrip the winner, a fleet-footed little brother of Charlotte Perry. The obstacle races were voted immense fun, the humorous feature being the performance of such feminine tasks as needle threading or button stitching by the boys, and rapid bean sorting by the girls. Giles and Basil were successful in a three-legged race, and Martin, to his huge delight, won the sack race for visitors under seven. He bore away his prize—an indiarubber ball—with great pride to show to Beatrice. Long jumping and high jumping proved equally popular both with boys and girls, some of the records being excellent. Linda Browne a younger sister of Hilda Browne, particularly distinguished herself in this respect, and won laurels for the Lower Third. Vaulting over hurdles of varying heights made a graceful competition, and one in which Elspeth Frazer came off a victor. She was an athletic girl, and possessed a wonderful power of spring that caused her to clear the bars like a bird.

"Our Form hasn't done badly," said Iris Watson, running to Gwen to tell her of Elspeth's triumph. "Must you stick at this gate all the time? Can't you leave it and compete for the dart-throwing contest? It's always ripping. Surely nobody else will come now?"

"Don't suppose they will, and I'd love to try the darts. But what am I to do with this satchel? It contains solid wealth."

"I'd give it to Miss Roscoe if I were you and ask her to take charge of it. Can you lock it?"

"Yes, I have the key in my pocket. I'll put the unused checks inside with the cash. There! That's safely locked up. The bag is quite heavy! The gate has made a splendid contribution towards the cot I feel so jubilant I want to 'cock-a-doodle'!"

Miss Roscoe readily took charge of the precious satchel, leaving Gwen free to enter for any of the remainder of the sports in which she might care to try her skill. The dart-throwing contest was just about to take place, so she promptly joined the ranks of the competitors. Each in turn had to throw six darts at a target, the one obtaining the highest score securing the prize. It was a task that needed a true eye and a firm hand, and proved far more difficult than most of the girls anticipated. Some of them failed altogether to hit the target, and others only achieved a chance dart in the outside rings. One or two of the Sixth Form did fairly well, but did not secure a bull's-eye.

"They've fixed the distance too far. It's impossible to shy properly when one's such a long way off," declared Charlotte Perry, retiring disconsolately after a series of bad shots. "It's your turn now, Gwen. I wish you better luck than I've had."

Gwen took her six darts and advanced to the white circle which was marked on the grass as the throwing place. It was a game which she had played frequently at the Parsonage, where she had often matched her skill against that of her father and Beatrice. She had a strong arm and a very true aim, two great essentials for success, and though the number of paces was certainly greater than that to which she was accustomed at home the increased distance did not seem an insuperable difficulty.

"I must throw a little higher and harder, that's all," she said to herself. "Fortunately there's no wind blowing to speak of."

Gwen's first shot went wide, but her second lodged in the outer ring of the target. Profiting by the experience she regulated her aim, and sent her third dart into the second ring. Her fourth and fifth were nearer the centre still and the spectators began to cheer. Only one dart remained; it was the best feathered of the six, and she had purposely kept it until the last. She poised it carefully, calculated for the slight breeze, then with a neat turn of her wrist hurled it as swiftly as possible at the target. It whistled rapidly through the air and lodged full in the bull's-eye. A storm of clapping greeted her achievement. She was the last on the list of competitors, so she had gained a full and complete victory over her rivals in the contest. She beamed with satisfaction as she went up to receive her prize—a pretty little silver brooch.

She had no further good fortune, though she tried her luck in the potato race and the ball-catching competition, which concluded the sports. It was now after five o'clock, and a procession of girls in Elizabethan costume came on to the field to sing the final madrigal which was to wind up the fete. As the last strains died away and the band began "God

Save the King", everybody joined in the National Anthem and gave three hearty cheers for the Rodenhurst Cot.

"It has been a splendid afternoon," said Miss Roscoe, as the crowd began to disperse and the sweet vendors and flower sellers came to hand over their gains. "I'm sure we shall have realized quite a large sum. It's too late to count our proceeds this afternoon. You must all go home now, but if you have each labelled your own bag I will lock them up in my safe until to-morrow. I think we may congratulate ourselves on the success of our anniversary. It has more than answered our expectations."

Gwen went home in high glee. She had enjoyed her part of the celebrations thoroughly, and the consciousness that she had originated the cot scheme gave an added degree of pleasure to the general sense of prosperous termination of the affair. As she walked with Lesbia round the orchard that evening she indulged in a little self-congratulation.

"It is nice to have engineered all this!" she admitted. "Miss Roscoe's pleased about it, I'm sure. She was so gracious to me when I took her my satchel. She actually called me 'dear'!—a thing she's never done in her life before. It's been a ripping day. School will seem quite flat again after it. I wish there were another fete to look forward to!"

"There's the tennis tournament," suggested Lesbia.

"Yes; but I shan't have much chance for that with my wretched old racket!" sighed Gwen.

"Suppose I'd a new one, and could lend it to you?" said Lesbia quickly. "A lovely half-guinea one!"

"You don't possess half a guinea to buy one, my child!"

"But I do! I've got the money, and I'm going to get the racket I shall go to Graham's to-morrow for it."

"I thought your savings box was empty again? How in the name of wonder did you come by ten and sixpence?"

"Never you mind—I've got it, and that's the main point," replied Lesbia, turning very pink.

"But how?"

"I shan't tell you! Leave me alone, Gwen! You've no right to pry into my affairs. I never bother about yours. Let go my arm!" and Lesbia, blushing even more furiously, wrenched herself free and fled towards the house.

Lesbia seldom had secrets, so her conduct was the more astonishing. Gwen gazed after her in great surprise, half inclined to follow her and press the point; but remembering that her Latin for the next day was still unprepared, she fetched her books instead, and buried the remembrance of her sister's strange behaviour in Virgil and a dictionary.

Angela Brazil

CHAPTER XX

A DAY OF RECKONING

Gwen went to school next morning in the jauntiest of spirits. She was satisfied with the part she had played both in organizing the fete and in helping to make it a success, and she fully expected approval from headquarters.

"This will set me all right with Miss Roscoe now," she thought. "She'll quite forgive me that business about Dick and the sweets on the strength of a 'Rodenhurst Cot'. I think I've scored considerably."

When at eleven o'clock, therefore, Gwen received a summons from the Principal, she was not at all dismayed, and presented herself in the study with a smiling face. To her surprise, however, she was hardly welcomed with the enthusiasm she expected. Miss Roscoe looked grave and annoyed, and greeted her more as if she were a culprit than a praiseworthy collector of money.

"Sit down, Gwen," she said coldly, motioning her pupil to a chair near her desk. "You can unlock your satchel and go over your accounts with me; then there is another matter that I wish to talk to you about afterwards."

Feeling decidedly chilled, Gwen produced her key. Miss Roscoe emptied the contents of the bag on to a tray, and proceeded to count the various coins. She reckoned them twice over, frowned, consulted a paper, then turned to Gwen.

"See how much you make it!" she said abruptly.

Gwen carefully went over the piles of half-crowns, florins, shillings, and sixpences, and added them together.

"I get thirteen pounds seven and six," was her conclusion.

"So do I, so we must both be correct," returned Miss Roscoe. "Now the checks that Moira Thompson received at the second gate register thirteen pounds seventeen shillings. How is it you are nine and sixpence short?"

"Am I that much short?" cried Gwen. "It can't possibly be!"

"Look for yourself," said Miss Roscoe. "The checks are all numbered. There are two hundred and fifty-one shilling admissions and fifty-two sixpenny ones. Examine the numbers on the rolls of checks left in your satchel; you will see they begin at Nos. 252 and 53. That means that you certainly issued 251 checks at a shilling and 52 at sixpence. The right amount ought to have been in your bag."

"Is there nothing left stuck in the corners?" asked Gwen, utterly dumbfounded at the defalcation.

"Nothing whatever. Look and satisfy yourself."

Gwen seized the satchel, and almost turned it inside out in her eagerness, but there was no remaining coin to be found.

"Did you give any people checks without receiving the

money in return?" enquired Miss Roscoe.

"No, certainly not. I was most particular. I didn't let anybody in without paying. If they had no tickets I sold them checks. I don't see how I can be all that amount wrong."

"Unfortunately both our reckonings show the same deficit. What I want to know, Gwen, is what has become of this missing nine and sixpence?"

"I can't imagine."

"But it is your duty to account for it. You alone are responsible; and it is my duty to enquire where it has gone."

"Miss Roscoe! You surely don't think I've pocketed it?" broke out Gwen, the drift of the Principal's remarks suddenly dawning upon her.

"I say nothing except that it is a very strange circumstance that you cannot produce it. Was the satchel in your own possession the whole of the afternoon?"

"Yes—at least—yes, it was!" stammered Gwen, looking very red and confused. The remembrance had just struck her that she had allowed Lesbia to take some change from her bag, and at the same instant Lesbia's extraordinary behaviour of the evening before flashed across her mind. Could there possibly be any connection between the two incidents? The idea was so horrible that she blushed at entertaining it even for a moment.

Miss Roscoe glanced at her keenly.

"Do you assume the full responsibility for this?" she asked in a strained voice.

"Absolutely. Nobody except myself had anything to do with the gate money."

The Principal's face, which had been grave before, took a yet sterner expression.

"I am sorry, Gwen. Very sorry and most concerned. I thought I could have trusted you entirely. It pains me beyond measure to find you have betrayed my confidence."

"But I didn't take that nine and six! I didn't, indeed! I don't know where it has gone; but I haven't got it! How can you accuse me of such a dreadful thing?" blurted out Gwen indignantly.

"You can't deny the deficit," returned Miss Roscoe icily. "There is the evidence of the checks and the cash to prove it. As you are not able to account for it, I can only draw my own conclusions. As it happens, I was this very morning made aware of the reason which must have prompted your most dishonourable act."

"What do you mean?" cried Gwen with a choke in her voice.

For answer Miss Roscoe handed her a folded piece of paper. She opened it nervously. It was a bill from Messrs. Parker & Sons, Glass and China Merchants, to Miss Gwen Gascoyne, for ten shillings "to account rendered", and written at the bottom were the words: "Your immediate settlement will oblige". It seemed such a bolt from the blue that Gwen turned all colours, and her hand trembled till she nearly dropped the paper.

"Ah, you may well look conscious, Gwen! I have just learnt the full history of this most deceitful business. I have had a letter from Mrs. Goodwin, telling me that her daughter had confessed her share of it, and as another bill for the broken china had arrived for you, directed under cover to Netta, she considered it best to forward it on to me, with an account of what had occurred, as it was only right that I should know about it. She is most pained that her daughter should have been even slightly implicated in such an affair, and Netta herself seems truly to regret countenancing the deception and screening you. I had a talk with her before school this morning. I cannot exonerate her, but she is at least sorry for her conduct. With this knowledge of your debt, Gwen, and your reasons for concealing it, of course I realize plainly enough why you have been foolish and wicked enough to take some of the gate money. No doubt you yielded to a desperate temptation; you had much better make a clean breast of it."

Gwen was trembling so greatly that she could hardly utter a reply. Several times her white lips framed the words before she gasped out:

"I did break the china, and I owe the ten shillings for it, but I never took a penny from the satchel. I may be naughty, but I'm no thief!"

Miss Roscoe shook her head sadly.

"What's the use of persisting in denying a fact that's absolutely palpable?"

"But I didn't! Oh, I didn't!"

"It's little use arguing the matter at present, Gwen, if you take up this stubborn attitude. If you think things over, you will see it is much better to confess. I have probably startled you by springing the news upon you that I was aware of your substitution of my china tea service. When you are calmer you will be more ready to acknowledge what you have done. Go to the little music room at the head of the stairs—it is not in use this morning—and stay there until I come or send for you. Reflect seriously upon what I have said, and make up your mind to be brave enough to tell me everything."

With feet like lead, and a head that throbbed and burned, Gwen walked upstairs. The little music room was unoccupied. It only contained a piano, a stool, and a chair, and on the last-named piece of furniture she sank down wearily. Her thoughts flew so rapidly through her brain that she could scarcely regulate them. She felt as if a net had been spread for her, and had entangled her unawares. First and foremost was the sense that Netta had betrayed her. Netta, who had promised at all costs to keep her secret, had basely revealed it. She saw how cleverly her old chum had managed to whitewash herself by making a confession and feigning penitence, and how much darker this act caused Gwen's own share in the matter to appear by comparison. Naturally Miss Roscoe viewed Netta as the one with the tender conscience, and Gwen as the unrepentant sinner.

"Why didn't I tell her myself that day I meant to, and got as far as the study?" wailed the unfortunate culprit. "Then I should have been spared all this!"

Why, indeed? How many of us mourn over our past follies and cowardices, bitterly regretting the wasted moment or the lost opportunity? Gwen's fault was indeed being visited heavily upon her shoulders. She had sown the wind and reaped the whirlwind. She felt keen resentment against Netta. It was a dastardly trick to have played upon her. Netta might at least have warned her that the bill was to be sent on to Miss Roscoe—then she could have been prepared for the worst. It was surely mere spite on the part of her friend, who, having quarrelled with her, was anxious to find some means of annoying her. Netta had been jealous of her new-found appreciation in the Form, and had taken this opportunity of trying to humble her. The deficit in the gate fund filled Gwen with surprise. There seemed only one way of accounting for it, and that was so painful that she shrank from facing it. Lesbia had taken change out of the satchel, and that same evening Lesbia had acknowledged the possession of ten shillings, but had refused to reveal how she came by the money.

Gwen groaned as she remembered her sister's conscious looks and evasive replies. Could it actually be possible that Lesbia had abstracted this money? She was rather silly, flighty, and irresponsible, but she had always been truthful and honourable. No, it was surely absolutely foreign to her character! Then where had she obtained half a guinea to buy a new tennis racket? And what was the reason of her extreme embarrassment? Gwen abandoned the question in despair.

"If she really did take it, I must shield her at any cost," she decided. "She'd get into such frightful trouble, and scolding Lesbia is like breaking a butterfly. I can bear things better than she can. But—oh, dear! What am I to say to Dad if he asks me? I can stand Miss Roscoe's wrath, but I can't face making Dad look sorry."

The Principal left Gwen until one o'clock to reflect upon her sins, then summoned her again to the study, and urged her in strong terms to confess.

"I will forgive you if you only acknowledge it, but if you persist in denying it, I shall have to go more deeply into the matter," she said sternly. "I cannot allow such things to happen at Rodenhurst. It is a very grave fault, Gwen. Do you wish me to send for your father?"

"No, no!" cried Gwen hastily.

"Then will you confess?"

"I can't! I didn't do it! Oh, I don't understand!" responded Gwen, torn in two between the desire to defend herself and the fear of involving Lesbia. She did not dare to tell Miss Roscoe that her sister had taken change from the satchel, yet by that circumstance only could she account for the loss.

"Miss Douglas is as distressed as I am," continued the Principal. "I was obliged to tell her, in order to explain your absence from your classes. Here she comes now. Perhaps she will be able to persuade you better than I."

"Oh, Miss Roscoe," exclaimed Miss Douglas, entering the study with a hurried step and a heightened colour, "I have just made the most astounding discovery! I happened to look in my purse, and to my amazement and consternation I found half a sovereign which certainly ought not to be there. I am sure I know how I came by it. Yesterday, just before I went into the house to dress the girls who were to sing the Elizabethan madrigal, I bought a box of sweets from Lesbia Gascoyne. I gave her a two-shilling piece, and as she had no sixpences, she ran to Gwen to ask change for my florin. She came hurrying back, and handed me, as we both imagined, three sixpences. I put them in my purse without looking at them. Now I am quite sure that one of these supposed sixpences must in reality have been half a sovereign, given by mistake. I undoubtedly had no ten-shilling piece in my purse. The difference of giving half a sovereign in lieu of sixpence would be exactly the nine-and-six that was missing from Gwen's satchel. Let us exchange the two coins, and the deficit will be made up."

It was such a natural, simple, and self-evident explanation of the situation that its truth could not be doubted. Miss Roscoe heaved a sigh of intense relief.

"I am grateful to you beyond words, Miss Douglas," she returned. "Gwen, I am most delighted that your honour is cleared, and regret I harboured so unjust a suspicion against you. I confess it was the affair of the broken china that prejudiced me in your disfavour. It supplied so strong a motive. Why didn't you come and tell me about that right away when if happened instead of trying to settle it in such a crooked fashion? It wasn't straight and square, was it? Have I heard the whole story?"

Gwen, who had not shed a tear before, was crying bitterly now. Miss Roscoe's present kindly tone hurt more than her former severity. Almost in spite of herself the girl began to blurt put her version of how she had accidentally broken the tea service, had intended to pay for it at once, and how Emma had absconded with the money. The housemaid's part in the drama was news to Miss Roscoe, and she hastened to ask for particulars.

"This must be investigated immediately," she declared. "I shall send for Emma Dalton this afternoon. I happen to know that she has a place as parlour-maid at a house not far away. If I had heard of this I could not have given her a character. Indeed she deserves to be prosecuted for theft. I must write a note to her present mistress."

Miss Roscoe never let the grass grow under her feet. In this case she acted with her usual promptitude, and by two o'clock Emma, in much alarm, and weeping like a water-spout, was ushered into the study and confronted with Gwen and Netta, who were both summoned for the occasion.

"Now, Emma, this is a serious charge. Have you anything to

say for yourself?" enquired Miss Roscoe, seating herself at her desk with the air of a magistrate about to try a case.

"I didn't pay the money at Parker's, and I don't deny it," sobbed Emma. "I meant to, but I saw a coat and skirt I wanted, so I thought I'd borrow it, and the bill might just wait for a bit. I've intended to go and settle every month when I got my wages, but it's never seemed the right time. I didn't know Parker's were pressing for it. Oh, dear, I've been a bad girl!"

"You have indeed," said Miss Roscoe. "It was wrong of Miss Gascoyne to ask you to help her to deceive me, but worse for you to defraud her."

"It wasn't Miss Gascoyne that suggested sending back the broken china to Parker's and saying nothing about it; it was Miss Goodwin," declared Emma, pointing at Netta. "She planned the whole thing! Yes, I can tell you she did. She's a deeper one than the other. It was half her fault, I'll be bound!"

Netta's face was a study, especially as Miss Roscoe looked at her keenly, though she made no remark.

"I've brought the money with me," continued Emma, still sobbing, "if Miss Gascoyne will please take it and forgive me."

"You don't deserve any consideration, Emma," said Miss Roscoe.

"For the sake of my mother!" pleaded Emma. "Oh, don't prosecute me! It would brand me for life!"

"Don't send her to prison, please!" interposed Gwen.

"Well, we don't want to be too hard on you and ruin your life. Let it be a warning to you to be honest in future. I am sure Miss Gascoyne has no wish to prosecute you. I shall be obliged to let your mistress know about this, however. I gave you so good a character to her, that it is not fair she should remain in ignorance of so serious a slip. She must be the judge whether she keeps you in her service or not."

"I'll go home to my mother and work at dressmaking," snivelled Emma as she prepared to depart. "Here's the money, Miss Gascoyne; I'm sorry I took it, and thank you kindly for not prosecuting."

Netta fled from the study the moment Miss Roscoe gave her leave to go. She was anxious not to have to speak to Gwen, for she knew she had not behaved well towards her. Emma's unexpected accusation had given rather an awkward turn to the affair, and she had hardly come out of it with the credit she expected. Gwen lingered behind. She felt she could not leave without offering the apology which for seven long months she had wished to make.

"Please, Miss Roscoe, I'm most dreadfully sorry about all this. I know I ought to have come and told you at once when I knocked over the box of china," she blurted out abruptly. "I've been miserable the whole time about it."

"Well, Gwen, it's a lesson to keep square, isn't it? One little step from the straight road often sends us farther out of our way than we have any intention of going. I don't think you will descend to anything so underhand again, will you?"

"Never in all my life!" protested Gwen with energy.

"Then we'll say no more about it."

The news that Gwen had been suspected of appropriating some of the gate money had leaked out, as news always leaks out, and was received with great indignation by the rest of the Fifth.

"Gwen Gascoyne simply isn't capable of doing such an abominable thing!" declared Elspeth Frazer.

"No. Gwen's gauche and brusque, but she's unimpeachable," agreed Hilda Browne.

"I'd rather suspect myself!" said Charlotte Perry.

Much satisfaction was expressed in the Form when the report of the mistake in Miss Douglas's change was circulated, and Gwen's complete acquittal secured. Everybody congratulated her heartily when she returned to the classroom.

"You're the heroine of the hour," said Louise Mawson. "It was an uncommonly disagreeable thing to happen. But in a bag full of change it's very easy to confuse a half-sovereign and a sixpence. By the by, has Miss Roscoe added up all the accounts yet? How much have we made?"

"One hundred and fifty-three pounds altogether," replied Gwen. "We got a hundred and nine pounds by collecting, and the gymkhana has made forty-four."

"Hooray! Then the cot is an accomplished fact."

"We shall all have to pay a visit to the Convalescent Home and see it, as soon as the name is painted up over it," said Hilda Browne.

"Won't it look scrumptious to see 'Rodenhurst Cot' in black and white?" chuckled Charlotte Perry.

"We shall have to publish reports of our special convalescents in every number of the school magazine," suggested Iris Watson. "It will be so interesting to read about them."

At four o'clock, by Winnie's express permission, Gwen went to Parker & Sons and made a final settlement of their account. The relief of being free from her load of debt was very great, and she came out of the shop happier than she had been since the day she first entered it. As Emma had refunded the one pound two and sixpence in full, Gwen had twelve and sixpence in hand, and, in consequence, felt rich beyond the dreams of avarice. The vision of a new tennis racket began to dawn on her horizon. That evening she managed to cajole Father for a short stroll on the moor. It was seldom she could secure such a *tete-a-tete* walk, but she was longing so much to unburden her mind that she gave him no peace until she had got him all to herself. Once they were seated on the heather, with the wold behind and the sea in front, Gwen began to pour out the story in her usual abrupt, jerky fashion, not omitting the matter of the prize essay which she had sold to Netta.

"Why didn't you tell me all this before, Gwen?" asked Mr. Gascoyne when she had finished.

"Because—oh, Dad, I thought it would worry you! Beatrice said you were so dreadfully hard up."

"It would have worried me far more to feel that you owed money. How much did Netta Goodwin lend you?"

"A sovereign."

"Then I will make up your twelve and six to twenty shillings, and you shall pay her back. I don't like that transaction about the essay at all."

"Netta doesn't deserve it!" exclaimed Gwen.

"I dare say not, but your conscience demands it. Honour forbids you to expose Netta, but the affair was so discreditable that I want your part at least to be set straight. That sovereign was ill-gotten gains, Gwen!"

"Oh, Dad! Are you very angry with me?"

"No, not angry, but I wish you'd trusted me. The whole business, childie, hasn't been on the square."

"I knew it wasn't, all the time," confessed Gwen, scrubbing her eyes. "But—oh, Dad, it was so hard! Why do such hard places come into one's life?"

"To give one the opportunity to get strong. If everything were always pleasant and smooth and easy, we should be poor sort of creatures in the end, with no character worth having. I feel that every day myself, and give thanks for the hard things, and I've had my share of them."

Gwen looked at Father, and a sudden perception of his meaning swept over her. Young as she was, she knew something of the struggles and disappointments, the lack of appreciation, the mistrust, the misconstructions, the slights which had met him in his parish work, and the burden of poverty which he carried so bravely and uncomplainingly— somewhat, too, perhaps, she divined of the hopes he had left behind. Her own little struggles faded into nothingness in the shadow of his.

"Yes, you've had a hard life, Dad," she repeated slowly.

"Sentry duty. That's all! A hard life is the soldier's post of honour," said Father.

Angela Brazil

He looked far out over the sea as he spoke, and it almost seemed to Gwen as if his face shone.

There was still one point which Gwen was anxious to elucidate, and that was the reason of Lesbia's peculiar conduct in the orchard on the evening of the gymkhana, and where she had obtained the ten and sixpence of which she had spoken. Lesbia seemed very unwilling to discuss the subject, but when the two girls were in their bedroom that night, Gwen held her to the point.

"Oh, Gwen, you've got me in a corner!" protested Lesbia. "I didn't mean to tell a soul about it, except Kitty Macpherson! Well, if you must know, this is what happened. One day Kitty brought a copy of *The Gentlewoman's World* to school. It had a beauty competition in it, and she urged me to try my luck, so I sent up my photo—that one which Aunt Violet had taken of me when I was staying at Greylands. It actually won a prize, and the magazine sent me a postal order for ten and sixpence. I didn't dare to tell any of you at home, because I knew you'd all think me so terribly vain and conceited. Beatrice is fearfully down on me for that kind of thing, and I knew the boys would tease, and call me 'Proudie' and 'Madam Conceit'."

Gwen laughed long and heartily. She did not tell her little sister of the unjust suspicion she had for a short time harboured against her. The whole affair was so exactly like Lesbia, from the competing for a beauty prize to the careless taking of wrong change.

"How will you explain your new tennis racket?" she enquired. "Beatrice will ask where you got the money to buy it."

"I never thought of that. I suppose I shall have to confess, then, and be labelled 'Miss Vanity'," sighed Lesbia. "It's a ripping racket, Gwen. It's exactly the same that Kitty Macpherson has. I'll lend it to you whenever you want it. Are you cross with me for not telling you before?"

"No, dear; it wasn't such a fearful crime after all," returned Gwen, half sighing, for Lesbia's secret seemed so much more innocent a one than her own had been.

CHAPTER XXI

RETRIBUTION

Gwen took back the sovereign next morning to Netta, who received it with amazing coolness.

"An unexpected blessing," she remarked. "I'd put that sov. down as a bad debt. Better late than never. We're quits now, Gwen Gascoyne."

"Not altogether," returned Gwen. "I've set my part straight, but you've still got the credit for my essay. You haven't put that to rights."

"Catch me telling!" laughed Netta. "No, my good Gwen, that's a little too much to ask. Don't expect more than you're likely to get, and then you won't be disappointed. I'm afraid I must still consider Mr. Thomas Carlyle my special property. You really can't eat your cake and have it."

"That's exactly what you're doing," retorted Gwen. "You took my essay, and now you've got the sovereign as well."

"But I helped you out of a temporary difficulty. You forget that, and don't show as much gratitude as you might."

"Not much cause for gratitude," grunted Gwen.

"This is what comes of being too philanthropic. I won't help anybody out of scrapes again. One never gets thanked for it."

"Not when you give your help on such terms."

It was no use arguing with Netta, so Gwen turned away, glad to have closed the transaction, even though she had been decidedly the loser. There were plenty of other matters to occupy her mind, as this afternoon the tennis trials were to take place as a preliminary to playing for the Form trophy, and later for the County shield. Gwen had given in her name to Moira Thompson, the head of the games committee, and expected that she would be accepted at least for the trials. Nor was she mistaken, for when, at two o'clock, Moira pinned her paper on the notice board, the fourth couple down for singles were Gwen Gascoyne against Geraldine French. All the school was assembled to watch the play, since on this afternoon's victories would largely depend the future choice of champions.

"Here's my new racket. Do use it—it's a perfect beauty," whispered Lesbia, edging through the crowd, and pushing her treasured possession into her sister's hand. "It will just make all the difference to your play."

Gwen accepted the loan thankfully. Her old racket had been her greatest impediment, and she had not liked to borrow often from her classmates. As Lesbia had prophesied, it made all the difference to her serves, and she played up in a way that astonished everybody. Geraldine French, who was considered almost invincible by the Sixth, had not taken Gwen seriously, and was therefore most electrified and disgusted to find herself beaten by a Fifth Form girl of no particular reputation in the world of tennis. The Fifth were in a state of immense delight.

"Gwen's serves to-day were unique," declared Iris Watson. "If she can keep this up our Form may have a chance for the trophy."

"I'd no idea Gwen could do so well," agreed Elspeth Frazer. "She's suddenly developed into quite a crack player."

"And she's such long legs and arms, she seems all over the court, and scarcely misses a ball."

"She's shown up in a new light this afternoon. We shall have to think her over for a championship."

The match for the Form trophy was to be played in a week's time. At present the beautiful silver cup was in the possession of the Sixth, but the Fifth were not without hopes of winning it, and transferring it to the chimney piece of their own classroom. It was an old-established custom at Rodenhurst that after the trials had taken place each Form competing for the trophy should vote its own champions. The election was naturally a highly exciting event; all the points of the various candidates' play were carefully discussed, and the two who were considered the most likely to do credit to the Form were returned. On this occasion five girls appeared of such equal merit that the running between them would be very close. Hilda Browne and Charlotte Perry were last year's champions, and were steady players, though many thought that Charlotte had gone off a little in her serves. Betty Brierley was brilliant but unreliable, sometimes making more splendid scores than anybody in the school, and sometimes playing love games. Netta Goodwin had a special reputation for back work, in which she excelled, and this circumstance might very possibly cause her to be chosen in conjunction with a good net champion. Gwen's unexpected prowess had been a complete surprise to the Form, and had made such a favourable impression that many were inclined to vote for her. To none of the five girls did the vision of a championship appear more attractive than to Netta. She loved to shine, and it was a sore point with her that she was not more popular in her Form. Here, at any rate, seemed a chance to gain the applause of her schoolfellows. She was conscious of playing well, and though she was not a general favourite, she knew the girls did not allow individual preferences, as a rule, to bias their judgment when it was a question of winning or losing the trophy. She canvassed diligently, put any pressure she could bring to bear upon her particular friends, and began carefully to reckon up how many votes she could reasonably count upon. The result was not altogether reassuring. Both Hilda Browne and Gwen seemed powerful rivals to her pretensions, and the chances were that the election would return Hilda for first champion, and either Gwen or Charlotte Perry for second. The prospect of being beaten in an affair upon which she had set her heart filled Netta with dismay.

The voting was by ballot, and took place in the classroom immediately after morning school. When the bell rang the girls did not immediately leave their desks as usual, but sat still while Miss Douglas distributed to each a half sheet of notepaper and an envelope. All that was required was to write down the names of two champions, fold the paper and put it in the envelope. No signatures were allowed, so that even Miss Roscoe should not know who had voted for which candidate. The whole affair did not take more than a few minutes. The girls hastily scribbled the names of their favourites, many of them in feigned handwritings, fastened their envelopes, and then returning them to Miss Douglas, left the classroom.

"I wonder how soon we shall know the result!" said Netta, as the Form trooped downstairs.

"It depends upon how soon Miss Roscoe has time to count them," replied Iris Watson. "She may be in her study now, or she may be too busy to look at them until four o'clock."

"Too bad to leave us in suspense."

"I'm not going to think about it," said Charlotte Perry. "It will be time enough to rejoice or moan when one knows."

"Oh, bother the election!" said Betty Brierley. "Come and see if we can get a court and have a set before dinner."

Netta did not follow the others to the tennis grounds. She was much more anxious about the result of the ballot than they, and had no heart at present for playing. Instead, she walked into school again, and finding the door of Miss Roscoe's study open, she peeped in. The room was empty, and on the desk lay the nineteen envelopes, each marked solely with a large V, that represented the voting of the Fifth Form. Netta looked at them wistfully. How she longed to open them and learn their contents! Such a proceeding was, of course, impossible, and she turned away with a sigh. As her glance wandered round the room, she noticed a large parcel of stationery which had just been unpacked, and lay spread upon a side table. Miss Roscoe had evidently opened it to get the paper and envelopes needed for the election, and had not yet had time to put it away in the drawers of her secretaire. Then suddenly an idea occurred to Netta—an idea so original and daring that she almost laughed at her audacity in entertaining it. It was a scheme which no other girl in the Form would have dreamt of for a moment, but Netta was troubled with few scruples of conscience, and was never deterred by a question of honour from attaining her wishes. Very quickly she abstracted nineteen envelopes and ten sheets of notepaper, and fled with her spoil to her own classroom. She bolted along the passage and upstairs in such a tremendous hurry that she did not notice the impish face of Ida Bridge peering from the Second Form room as she passed.

"Oho, Miss Netta Goodwin! What's the matter with you?" thought Ida. "You have an uncommonly guilty look about you, almost as if you were committing a crime. What's up, I wonder? I think I'm just going to track you and see."

Since the stormy episode on the day when the Second Form girls were rehearsing for their morris dance, Ida Bridge had detested Netta. She felt she owed her a grudge, which she was most anxious to pay if a reasonable opportunity could only be found. She followed now post haste, and adopting the tactics of a scout, waited till Netta was safely inside the Fifth Form room, then peeped cautiously round the door. What she saw did not particularly enlighten her. Netta was busily tearing sheets of notepaper in half, was scribbling something on them, blotting them and putting them into envelopes. No one else was in the room, and there was nothing to suggest an explanation of this rather mysterious employment.

"I'm sure she's up to something, though," murmured Ida to herself, still keeping a watchful eye on the enemy's movements. Netta wrote away, and kept folding her pieces of paper with record speed; there was a complacent look on her face, and she chuckled occasionally, as if with deep satisfaction. At the sound of the dinner bell she started, and hurriedly swept her correspondence into her desk. Ida, with admirable presence of mind, bolted into the empty Sixth Form room opposite, and having seen Netta depart down the corridor, took the liberty of going to make an inspection of what she had been doing.

Angela Brazil

"Um—indeed! What have we here?" said Ida, opening the desk. "Envelopes marked with a V, and sheets of paper with names on. Let's take a look at them. 'Hilda Browne—Netta Goodwin.' 'Netta Goodwin—Gwen Gascoyne.' 'Betty Brierley—Netta Goodwin.' 'Charlotte Perry—Netta Goodwin.' All in such different styles of writing, too! I believe I begin to see daylight. Now, shall I go and call Miss Douglas at once to look at this? No—it's incriminating, but not sufficient evidence to convict. I must let things develop a little further first. I think I'd better have a witness, too. Miss Netta Goodwin, I believe you're going to be rather too clever for once, and that you'll find yourself outwitted by one of the despised Juniors."

Ida Bridge was late for dinner that day, but she took Miss Roscoe's reproof with a sangfroid at which her Form marvelled.

"I don't care if I have to write fifty lines as a punishment," she murmured to her neighbour and chum, Peggy Weston. "What I've just discovered is worth a thousand lines. I can't explain why now, but the moment dinner is over you and I must stalk Netta Goodwin, and, without letting her know it, never take our eyes off her till afternoon school begins."

Quite unconscious that two small spies had resolved to keep her movements under surveillance, Netta slipped away from her friends after dinner, and returned to the classroom. It did not take her long to finish her task; she had soon fastened her nineteen envelopes, then, concealing them in an exercise-book cover, she hurried downstairs. Miss Roscoe's study was still empty, and nobody seemed about, for Netta never noticed the cautious pair who were dodging and watching in her rear as cleverly as a couple of young detectives. After a hasty glance round the room she advanced to the Principal's desk, and deeming herself quite unobserved, rapidly exchanged the pile of envelopes there for those which she had brought with her. She gave one look of satisfaction at the substituted set—they were such an excellent imitation—and bore off the genuine ballot to the Fifth Form room. Ida and Peggie, with breathless interest, followed, and saw her putting the stolen goods into her desk; then, having witnessed as much as they considered necessary, they flew in hot haste to lodge the information with their own Form mistress. Miss Broughton, amazed at what they told her, sought Miss Roscoe, who summoned Ida and Peggie, and listened attentively to their story.

"This must be enquired into promptly," she declared. "Come with me at once to the Fifth Form."

The girls had just assembled for afternoon school when the Principal entered, bearing the substituted pile of envelopes, and accompanied by Ida and Peggie.

For Miss Roscoe to arrive at such a time was an absolutely unprecedented occurrence. A dead silence at once reigned. Everybody wondered what had happened, and why Miss Roscoe should have brought the two children with her. The headmistress walked straight up to Netta's seat.

"Netta Goodwin," she said, "such an extraordinary incident has just been reported to me that I feel it is my duty to investigate it immediately. I wish to see what you have here," and, throwing up the lid, she began to investigate the contents of the desk.

Netta gave a gasp as if an earthquake had opened at her feet, and turned deathly white. She did not venture to say a word. All in the room waited in mute suspense, realizing that the matter must be of vital importance. With a sad face Miss Roscoe drew out the nineteen envelopes and compared them with those which she held in her hand.

"I have a very serious charge against you, Netta Goodwin," she said sternly. "You were observed in the act of taking these letters from my study, and substituting a similar set which you had yourself written. Ida Bridge and Peggie Weston can testify that they themselves witnessed your deed. I have a strong suspicion of your motive, and I am going to open the envelopes to ascertain if I am correct."

Putting each pile separately, Miss Roscoe rapidly tore open the two ballot sets, and glanced over them.

"It is a peculiar circumstance," she remarked icily, "that in the original voting papers your name occurs only nine times, and in the substituted papers eighteen times."

A wave of indignation passed round the Form. The girls at last understood the point, and realized the full significance of Netta's action. The excitement was intense, though awe for the headmistress forbade anybody to speak.

"To make absolutely certain," continued Miss Roscoe, "we will take the voting again. Miss Douglas, will you kindly deal a sheet of exercise paper to each desk? Now I put everyone on her honour to repeat the names of the two candidates that she wrote this morning."

For a moment the girls scribbled, then folded the papers and handed them to Miss Douglas, who went round the room to collect them. Miss Roscoe examined them attentively, and compared them with some figures she had jotted down.

"They correspond absolutely with the papers which I have just found in your desk, Netta Goodwin! Ida Bridge, come here! It is only fair that Netta should hear your accusation.

Tell me again, in her presence, exactly what you witnessed."

"Please, Miss Roscoe," began Ida in her high-pitched voice, "I saw Netta come out of your study before dinner, and come here. I peeped round the door, and she was writing something on half-sheets of paper, and putting them inside envelopes. Then I told Peggie, and afterwards we watched her go into your study again and put her pile of envelopes on your table, and take yours away and pop them into her desk."

"Do you endorse this statement, Peggie Weston?"

"Yes, Miss Roscoe, it's quite true," murmured Peggie nervously.

"Netta Goodwin, have you anything to answer in reply to this charge?"

But Netta kept her eyes on the ground, and did not reply. Miss Roscoe, who was still standing beside the open desk, began to turn over some of the loose pieces of exercise paper which it contained, and shook her head as she noticed the names of various candidates scrawled in different hand-writings, evidently for practice. Determined to investigate the affair thoroughly, she pulled out yet more papers, and among them a small roll fastened by a brass clip. At this she glanced with attention, then with marked surprise. "Netta Goodwin," she continued, "this is an entirely different matter, but one which I should like explained nevertheless. Last term you gained a prize for an essay on Thomas Carlyle. How is it that there is a manuscript of this essay in your desk, signed 'Gwen Gascoyne'? Yes, and in Gwen's handwriting, too, which I know well."

Netta glanced hastily at Gwen, who had turned as red as fire. Perhaps feeling that she had already been so entirely exposed that an added circumstance would make little difference, and wishing to get Gwen also into trouble, Netta suddenly resolved to make a full confession.

"I suppose I may as well tell everything," she volunteered sulkily. "Yes—I did want to get the tennis championship, and I altered the names because I didn't think I had a chance otherwise. About that essay, it was Gwen Gascoyne's. She wrote it, but she sold it to me for a sovereign."

"And you passed it off as your own?"

"I'd paid for it, so I just copied it. I couldn't see where the harm came in!" said Netta doggedly.

"Netta Goodwin, have you absolutely no sense of right and wrong, or any vestige of conscience?"

"I can't see that I'm worse than some other people," replied Netta, with a spiteful glance at Gwen.

"Gwen Gascoyne, did you sell this essay to Netta?"

"Yes, Miss Roscoe," gulped Gwen, covered with shame, and too much embarrassed to offer any explanation.

"I shall have a word with you later on. Netta, by your own confession you admit appropriating a schoolfellow's work last term, and altering the voting papers this afternoon. Forgery is a very ugly word and one which I am sorry to use, but there is no other name for what you have done. In all the years of my headmistress-ship here such a thing has not occurred before. I have had unruly and disobedient girls occasionally, but in the whole of my experience never a girl so deliberately bad as you. It is well for the school that this has occurred, and that I have discovered your true character;

your influence must have been most pernicious, and I can only hope that it has not already done harm. It is, of course, impossible for me to allow you to remain at Rodenhurst. It is the first time I have been obliged to expel a pupil, and I much regret the necessity, but I feel that to keep you would be to retain a source of moral infection. You will go home at once. Your books and any other articles belonging to you will be sent after you, and I shall write to your parents, informing them of the circumstances under which you have been sent away. I am grieved for the sorrow which I know it will cause them. Go!"

Miss Roscoe pointed peremptorily to the door, and Netta, all her jaunty, self-confident airs gone for once, with downcast eyes that did not dare to meet the scorn of her schoolfellows, and white lips that quivered with passion, slunk ignominiously from the room. The Principal waited a few minutes to allow her time to go downstairs, then she ordered Ida and Peggie back to their own classroom, and turned with a sigh to Gwen.

"You will come with me to the study," she said briefly. Gwen followed in a state of abject misery. Was she never to finish reaping that harvest of tares, the sowing of which she had already so bitterly repented. One initial slip had indeed plunged her into undreamt-of trouble.

"Well, Gwen, you had better tell me all about this unhappy business," said Miss Roscoe as soon as they were alone. "Let us get to the bottom of everything this time, and leave nothing concealed."

Hard though it was to make confession, Gwen was almost glad to have the opportunity of doing so, and of at last setting straight the last threads of the tangled web she had woven. She felt that she would have told before about the essay if

Netta had not been implicated, but her father had agreed that she could not in honour expose her schoolfellow. By skilful cross-questioning Miss Roscoe soon gathered the facts of the case.

"I understand," she said thoughtfully; "I am glad you paid back that sovereign, Gwen! It gives me a higher opinion of you than I should otherwise have had. I judge that your own conscience and your father's disapproval have punished you so severely that I can add little more in the way of reproof. I can trust you not to do such a thing again. Do I now know absolutely the whole of that transaction?"

"Every scrap!"

"Then we will consider the slate wiped clean."

"Thank you just a thousand times!" said Gwen, as Miss Roscoe with a nod dismissed her from the study.

CHAPTER XXII

THE TENNIS TOURNAMENT

Netta's expulsion naturally made a great sensation in the school. To prevent misconceptions Gwen told her classmates the entire story both of the breaking of the china and the selling of her essay. They already knew so much, that she felt it was better for them to learn the whole; they could then form their own judgment of the case, and decide upon what terms they would receive her back amongst them.

"I'm fearfully sorry about it," she said in conclusion; "I know I don't deserve you to be decent to me."

"I'm extremely glad you've told us," said Hilda Browne, acting mouthpiece for the rest. "It explains so very much. We never could understand why you were friends with Netta, and it made us think badly of you that you seemed so chummy with such a girl. But of course this accounts for it. I won't whitewash you, but since you're sorry, I vote we all agree to drop the thing."

"Yes, anyone who refers to it will be a sneak," agreed Elspeth Frazer. "Gwen's made a fresh start, and it's not fair that any old scores should be raked up against her. Netta's gone, of which I'm heartily glad, and I hope now there'll be a better tone altogether throughout the whole Form."

Elspeth mentioned no names, but she looked meaningly at Annie Edwards, Millicent Cooper, and Minna Jennings, and the three reddened beneath her glance. They were not bad girls, but they were weak, and under Netta's sway they had been very silly, and sometimes dishonourable.

"We must all try and help each other to keep rules," said Hilda Browne quickly and tactfully. "I'm sure none of us like cheating, and that we'd every one be willing to promise to be absolutely square in our work, and in games and everything. Shout 'Aye!' those who agree."

Eighteen voices were raised in unison, Annie's, Millicent's, and Minna's among the heartiest.

"Carried unanimously!" said Hilda, with a sigh of satisfaction.

"Now the matter's thrashed out, let's talk about tennis," said Edith Arnold. "Do you know, Gwen Gascoyne, that you were elected one of our Form champions?"

"Oh! oh!" gasped Gwen.

"Yes, you and Hilda Browne were the pair chosen, and we look to you both to win the trophy."

"You take net, then, Hilda, and I'll take back," suggested Gwen.

"Netta was certainly very good at back-balls," began Minna Jennings, but Elspeth Frazer struck in immediately:

"Let us please agree that Netta Goodwin's name is not

mentioned again in this Form. She's best forgotten. I think Hilda and Gwen will work together splendidly. They must practise as much as they can before Friday."

Thus forgiven and reinstated both by Miss Roscoe and the Form, Gwen felt she had at last started quite anew, with her bygones to be remembered only as danger signals for the future. Her elevation to the proud position of Form champion half elated and half weighed her down. It was an enormous responsibility to have to compete for the trophy, and she hoped her play would justify the girls' choice. Friday afternoon was to be given up to the match, the Forms allowed to take part being the Sixth, the Fifth, the Upper, Middle, and Lower Fourth, handicaps, of course, being arranged by the Committee. The event was one of the chief excitements of the term, and when Friday arrived the whole school turned out to act audience. The Fifth was drawn to play first with the Lower Fourth, and in spite of a heavy handicap scored an easy victory.

"Not much triumph in beating those kids," remarked Gwen. "They're simply not in the running."

"Our trials are all to come," agreed Hilda. "We're against the Upper Fourth now, and if we beat them, then we may expect our tussle with the Sixth."

"I'm shaking in my shoes already!"

"Don't make too sure; the Upper Fourth are better than the Lower, and need taking seriously. We may lose on this."

"I think the handicap's too big," grumbled Gwen.

As Hilda had prophesied, the Upper Fourth proved adversaries worthy of their skill. Eve Dawkins and Myra Johnson were both as old and nearly as tall as Gwen, and they played up with grim determination. At first the score went against the Fifth, and the spectators watched with keenest interest, but in the end Gwen's swift serving told, and Eve and Myra retired vanquished. The Middle Fourth had already been beaten by the Sixth, so it was now the Final between Sixth and Fifth.

"When Greek meets Greek, then comes the tug-of-war!" said Hilda.

"I found a four-leaved clover this morning on the wold, and I've pinned it on to my dress as a mascot," returned Gwen.

"May it bring us luck! though I believe in play more than in mascots. Keep as cool as you can, Gwen, and remember Olga's nasty balls."

"I'll do my best, though I'm afraid you'll all rue choosing me for a champion," said Gwen, as she took her place.

Geraldine French and Olga Hunter, their two opponents, were renowned players in the school, and very few of the lookers-on expected the Fifth to have any chance at all.

"I'm afraid we'll lose!" sighed Edith Arnold.

"Oh, we won't give up too soon!" declared Elspeth Frazer. "Geraldine is in form to-day, certainly, and Olga is serving swifter than I've ever known her before, but we haven't proved yet what Hilda and Gwen are capable of."

It was Olga's serve. She sent one of her famous invincible balls, which hardly rose from the ground, and Gwen missed it. A suppressed cheer rose from the adherents of the Sixth. Gwen clenched her teeth hard, and watched for the next ball with the expression of a Red Indian. It skimmed over the net as swiftly as its predecessor, but Gwen was prepared this time, and returned it.

"Well played!" cried the Fifth ecstatically.

All four champions were on their mettle, and the fight that ensued was of the keenest. Gwen was not a graceful player, but, as her friends observed, she seemed capable of being everywhere at once, she was so extremely lithe and quick.

"Very good! Excellent!" were the remarks that passed round at certain of the strokes.

"I'd no idea Gwen had it in her!" commented Miss Trent.

In spite of Gwen's exertions the first game fell to the Sixth. They were heartily clapped, and the Fifth began to look rather blue. Each side now played with extreme caution. They had taken one another's measure, and knew what they had to expect. Hilda Browne kept her nerve well, and her serves were acknowledged to be what the girls called "clinchers". As for Gwen, her arms seemed elastic. This time the Sixth were beaten, and the Fifth began to breathe.

"It would be just too ripping if we really won!" exclaimed Betty Brierley.

"We mustn't crow too soon, we're not out of the wood yet," returned Irene Platt.

The excitement had risen to high-water mark. Some of the school were for the Sixth, and some for the Fifth, and their rival claims were discussed eagerly.

"Try and think you don't mind, and then you'll be far less

nervous," whispered Hilda to Gwen.

Gwen nodded. She had almost passed the stage of nervousness.

"We can't do better than our best," she replied.

Perhaps Olga and Geraldine were nervous too; they made one or two bad strokes which seemed to put them out considerably. Gwen, on the contrary, surpassed herself. Never in her life before had she played so well. She seemed able to take every ball in whatever awkward spot it landed. Thanks largely to her ubiquity, the set ended in the triumph of the Fifth. A tremendous clapping and cheering ensued. For three years the Sixth had held the trophy, so it was indeed an honour to have won it from their possession. Gwen and Hilda were absolutely feted by their Form, and even the vanquished Sixth had the magnanimity to praise their play.

"Gwen Gascoyne is simply A1," was the general verdict. "She's a perfect surprise. We didn't know we'd anyone so good in the school."

"Look here, Gwen, you and Olga will have to enter for the shield. You and she have proved yourselves far and away the best champions this afternoon," said Bessie Manners.

"Compete for the shield!" cried Gwen, turning hot with pleasure at the bare idea.

She and Hilda were called up then to receive the trophy, and bore away the silver cup with much pride. All the Form marched into the school to see it put in its place upon the mantelpiece of their classroom.

"Well done, the old Fifth!" said Betty Brierley.

"And hurrah for its champions!" added Rachel Hunter.

To Gwen, though the winning of the trophy had been a wild delight, Bessie's hint was a cause of even greater excitement. Rodenhurst belonged to the County United Schools' Tennis League, which every year played a big tournament in Stedburgh. Ten different schools were in the league, four being from Stedburgh and the others from various places in the neighbourhood. Each sent their two best champions; the prize, a large brass shield mounted on oak, becoming for the year the property of the winners. Though Rodenhurst usually did fairly well, it had not been able to compete with some of the boarding schools in the district, and at each successive tournament had been obliged to see others bearing away the coveted honours. Last time the Radcaster High School had come off victorious, a circumstance particularly annoying to Rodenhurst, as they felt they had been beaten by day girls like themselves.

"Boarding schools get more time to practise, and have always more courts in proportion than we have," so they grumbled. "One expects a boarding school to have an advantage, but we mustn't let the Radcaster High score over us again."

The tournament always occupied a whole Saturday, and was held at the Stedburgh Pavilion Gardens, an excellent place for the purpose, for not only could the best-kept courts in the county be hired, but there was plenty of accommodation for spectators, and refreshments could be obtained at the restaurant, a consideration for those schools which came from a distance. It was necessary for entries to be sent in at once, and when, as Bessie Manners had suggested, Olga Hunter and Gwen Gascoyne were appointed champions, all Rodenhurst joined in approval of the choice.

"But it's to-morrow week!" quavered Gwen.

"You'll just have to practise like billy-ho!" said Betty Brierley, who was addicted to slang.

Nobody dared to indulge in any very particular hopes. It was one thing to gain a Form trophy, but quite another to win the shield of the league.

"I hear Miss Crawford's girls are in good form this year," said Rachel Hunter, who had a cousin at a school at the other side of Stedburgh. "Nell says they're pretty confident."

"They won't beat those twins from Appleton House. Their serves were ripping," returned Betty. "I forget their names, but I sometimes see them on the Parade."

"Unless they've gone off in their play."

"Yes, of course—people occasionally do. One can never tell from year to year. Do you remember Freda Harmon? She swept everything before her, and then she grew too fat and was a dismal failure."

"Would you like me to bant in case of accidents?" laughed Gwen. "You'd better weigh me daily, like they do jockeys."

"There's a great deal in luck," said Charlotte Perry. "If you draw the crack school you may be done for straight away."

Gwen practised her utmost during the brief week before the tournament, and congratulated herself that her play improved. She had her choice of rackets, for everyone was not only willing but anxious to lend her the best obtainable. She tried a selection, until she found the one that suited her best. It was the property of Natalie Preston, who gladly relinquished it in her favour.

"If it wins the tournament I shall be proud!" declared Natalie.

"'If' is sometimes an important word!" answered Gwen, with a dubious shake of her head.

On the eventful Saturday every member of the Fifth and Sixth and numbers of the Juniors turned up at the Pavilion Gardens to watch the contest. Miss Roscoe and most of the mistresses were there, and many friends who were interested in the fortunes of Rodenhurst. Most of the other schools were equally well represented, so that the audience was a large one. Olga Hunter, who was a pretty girl with chestnut hair, looked charming in a white dress, and large ribbon knots of pink and light blue—the Rodenhurst colours—pinned beside her badge. Gwen, in plain serge skirt and low-necked muslin blouse looked prepared for business, if not so ornamental as her companion. Winnie had made her a little bouquet of roses and forget-me-nots to match her colours, and Beatrice had lent her a pale-blue belt for the occasion.

"I haven't got a hobble skirt, at any rate!" laughed Gwen. "Do you remember that girl from Ravensfield last year, and how fearfully hampered she was?"

Gwen was most tremendously excited at the greatness thrust upon her. To represent Rodenhurst at the tournament seemed honour enough even if she were vanquished in the very beginning.

"I wish Dad could have been here!" she sighed.

But neither Mr. Gascoyne nor Beatrice could spare the time on this particular Saturday, so Winnie and Lesbia were the only members of the family present.

Rodenhurst had been drawn against Hetherby College for the first set, much to their relief, for Hetherby had no particular reputation. Gwen and Olga played carefully nevertheless, for, as Olga justly remarked, "You can never tell beforehand how a school may have improved." The Collegians were better, certainly, than last year, but their game was not up to much, and they were easily beaten. At the conclusion of the first round, Rodenhurst, being among the winning couples, drew again, and this time was matched against Appleton House. The twins of whom Betty Brierley had spoken were again champions, and proved no mean rivals. Gwen had an anxious moment or two when she thought the credit of Rodenhurst trembled in the balance, but by frantic efforts on her part and Olga's, the set was secured, and the twins conquered.

"You're getting on splendidly!" said Bessie Manners at lunchtime, plying the so-far victorious pair with ham sandwiches and lemonade. "Everybody says Rodenhurst is looking up. I feel so proud of you!"

"Too soon to rejoice! We haven't tackled Miss Crawford's girls yet, and then there'd be Radcaster," replied Gwen.

"It makes one wildly hungry!" declared Olga.

"You mustn't have more than four sandwiches and a bun, or it'll spoil your play," interposed Bessie, who considered herself in the light of a trainer for her special champions, and enforced her rules with Spartan severity.

Olga sighed humorously, but obeyed.

"There was a rumour that Ravensfield lost the shield one year on buns," she remarked. "I don't wish a like fate to befall Rodenhurst."

It was immensely encouraging to hear that their play had attracted notice; they felt braced up for the next contest, and went back to the fray in quite good spirits.

"One wants to strike the happy medium between faint heart and over confidence," said Olga.

"I prefer to strike the ball!" laughed Gwen.

There was no doubt that Rodenhurst was this year increasing its reputation by leaps and bounds. Instead of falling out among the early sets it had kept steadily on, and spectators began to speak of it as likely to carry off the prize. Radcaster had also done excellently, so when it came to a final struggle between those two rivals, the excitement of their respective adherents knew no bounds. The Rodenhurst girls could hardly keep still, and each held a handkerchief ready to wave in case of victory. That it would be a tremendous battle Gwen and Olga knew only too well. The Radcaster champions were the same girls who had won the tournament the year before, and many people deemed them invincible. They seemed inclined to hold that opinion themselves, for they glanced at their opponents with a rather superior and almost pitying smile. That look put Gwen on her mettle. "They shan't have it this time!" she murmured grimly as she took her place. Whether Gwen really excelled herself, or whether the Radcaster girls were a little tired or too secure of victory was a debatable point, but at the end of a splendidly played set Rodenhurst stood as the winner. The two successful champions turned to each other almost incredulously. The shield was theirs! A perfect storm of applause came from the crowd. The Rodenhurst girls were beside themselves with joy, and clapped and waved and hurrahed till they were hoarse.

"Well done! This is indeed a triumph!" said Miss Roscoe,

who hurried up to congratulate her victorious pair, looking as pleased as any of her pupils. This afternoon's success would wipe away the former reproach of the school, and lift it to a point of importance in the tennis league.

"The shield will hang in the lecture hall!" rejoiced Bessie Manners. "It will be sent to us as soon as our name is engraved upon it."

"I wish we could erase Radcaster!" said Gwen.

"Oh! I like to see the names of the other schools upon it. It gives me all the more joy of present possession."

"Gwen, you were just splendid!" declared Olga. "How you managed it I can't imagine, but you seemed to jump at the balls and catch them."

"I'm a spread-eagle player, I know; not nearly so graceful as you," laughed Gwen. "Well, I've 'done my possible', as the French say. Now I shall have to drop tennis and grind, for Miss Douglas has been grumbling most horribly, and declares she'd have stopped my being champion if she'd known how my prep. was going to suffer. It's been Latin and maths. versus tennis this last week."

"She'll forgive you when she sees the shield!" chuckled Bessie Manners.

CHAPTER XXIII

GWEN TO THE RESCUE

It was now the middle of June, and the weather, even at Skelwick, was hot and enervating. There was thunder about, and frequent rain. It was trying for everybody. The constant heavy showers necessitated carrying mackintoshes to school, as if it were winter; the lawn was too wet and sopping for tennis, and most outdoor plans had to be abandoned. The boys, overflowing with high spirits, chafed at confinement to the house, and their noise was a serious impediment to Gwen, whose evening preparation was a matter of vital importance at present. It was impossible to get out of earshot in the little Parsonage, and though she retired to her bedroom and stuffed her fingers in her ears, Latin translation and mathematical problems were sadly disturbed by the din below. Gwen was working tremendously hard just now. Miss Roscoe had not yet announced the names of those who were to take the Senior Oxford. It was rather a curious notion of hers to preserve silence on the subject, for she was obliged to send in the entry forms for her candidates early in May, and must therefore already have made her decision. Her motive was to spur on the whole of the Fifth to equal effort. Her past experience had shown her that when a few top girls only were taking an examination, the rest of the Form was apt to slack and lose interest, and she considered there were several

Angela Brazil

who, though not actually candidates, would benefit by the special preparation, and would make efforts on the chance of having been selected. Gwen did not, of course, know whether her name was on Miss Roscoe's private list, but she secretly cherished the possibility. She knew her work had improved; indeed that it was equal to that of anyone in the Fifth. There was no age limit for the Senior Oxford, and though she was the youngest in her Form, her fifteenth birthday would fall on the first day of the examination. Gwen was very ambitious; to be chosen as a candidate, and to pass with distinction, seemed a goal worth all the hard work of the school year. It brought visions of other and higher examinations in years to come; honours and scholarships which were waiting for those who had the pluck and the ability to win them, a rosy dream of college and university success on a distant horizon.

"I'm going to be Gwen Gascoyne, B.A., somehow before I've finished," she thought. "I've made up my mind to that!"

It was just at this crisis that Beatrice caught a severe chill. She—the wisest at health precautions where others were concerned—did a series of exceedingly rash and foolish things, with the result that she was obliged most reluctantly to give in, and allow Dr. Chambers to be sent for. Though Beatrice tried to make light of her own illness, the doctor took a different view of the case, and greatly to her consternation ordered her promptly to bed.

"I can't stop in bed! It's impossible!" she protested indignantly. "What's to become of the household? Nellie can't do everything; besides, she's no head, and she'd forget to feed the chickens, or she'd burn the bread, and let Martin tumble down the well if nobody was there to look after her."

"Then one of your sisters must stop at home, for you've got

to stay in bed!" commanded Dr. Chambers. "Yes, I insist, and if you won't obey me, I shall send for a hospital nurse to make you!"

At this awful threat Beatrice subsided into unwilling obedience, only stipulating that her enforced retirement should be as brief as possible, and that she might be allowed to direct domestic affairs from her bedroom.

"I suppose I can't stop you worrying over the household, but you're not to stir out of bed till I give you permission, and I'll probably keep you there for a fortnight. The rest will do you all the good in the world," replied the doctor. "As for managing without you, they'll just have to manage!"

Dr. Chambers's autocratic orders were, of course, to be followed to the letter, everybody realized that; the only difficulty was how it was going to be done. The family held an immediate conclave on the subject in the invalid's room.

"I suppose I shall have to stay at home," said Winnie, "though I hardly dare suggest it to Miss Roscoe. With Miss Roberts still away, it makes things doubly difficult. I'm already taking four extra classes, and who's to teach those, and my own as well? It's enough to disorganize the school."

"Miss Roscoe would be furious if you stopped away!" said Gwen. "I don't see how you can."

"I'll write to Cousin Edith, and ask if she can help us," suggested Mr. Gascoyne.

"No, don't!" groaned Beatrice. "If Cousin Edith comes, I shall get straight out of bed, in spite of Dr. Chambers. I warn you I will! She and I don't get on."

Nobody was anxious for Cousin Edith's presence, so the suggestion dropped.

"A charwoman wouldn't meet the want," sighed Winnie. "It must be somebody who knows all the ropes of the household, or she'd be no use. Lesbia's too young; but how about Gwen? She ought to be able to manage."

Gwen did not wait to hear Beatrice's reply, but bolted straightway to her own bedroom. The proposal was as unwelcome as it was unexpected. To stop at home now, for a whole fortnight, just when every moment at school was of such great importance! Why, such a proceeding might wreck every chance she had for the exam.! Of course she was not sure whether she was really a candidate, but she had a shrewd suspicion that she was one of the selected number. She wished Miss Roscoe had openly given out the names, then she would have known exactly what to do in the circumstances. Could anything be more exasperating? It was impracticable for Winnie to fill the breach; with one teacher short, Miss Roscoe could not possibly spare her, especially at such a busy time as the end of the term. Gwen realized that perfectly. Lesbia—little, childish Lesbia—would be about as much use as Stumps or Basil—why, she would be playing with Martin in the orchard while the fowls went hungry and Nellie burnt the bread. As for Cousin Edith, she was not a favourite with the Gascoynes, and the fact of her presence would be hardly conducive to the invalid's recovery.

"I verily believe Bee would get up if she knew Cousin Edith were poking about downstairs," thought Gwen. "I know I ought to stay—but I can't, I can't! It means so much to pass that exam. It would be horrid to stop at home, too, with Bee in bed directing everything. If she were going away, and would leave me to it, I shouldn't mind. It's not the work I'm dreading. But I know Bee only too well. She'll ring a bell and have me up to her room every five minutes to ask how things are getting on, and what I've done and what I haven't done, and she'll worry, worry, worry, and scold, scold, scold the whole time. There'll be no credit in my slaving, not the least. No, I don't think it can be expected from me. It's too hard."

Gwen made the last remark aloud, and she repeated it again emphatically, because she just happened to catch sight of the New Year motto that hung over her dressing table.

> "Oh do not pray for easy lives. Pray to be stronger men. Do not pray for tasks equal to your powers. Pray for powers equal to your tasks. Then the doing of your work shall be no miracle. But you shall be a miracle. Every day you shall wonder at yourself, at the richness of life which has come to you by the grace of God."

"I thought it meant school work," she said to herself. "But after all I suppose it means home work as well, or any kind of work that comes uppermost. I wonder if I could. Look here, Gwen Gascoyne, it's rather a big sacrifice, but you've got to make it for once. With four daughters, Dad has a right to expect somebody to keep the house comfortable, and just at this critical moment you're the only one available. It's hard, but it'll have to be. Your little ambition, my dear, must take a back seat for the present, while you go and 'wash dishes and feed the swine'. You'd better make the plunge and get it over!"

Father and Winnie had adjourned to the garden, so Gwen hurried downstairs before she repented her resolution.

"Dad! I believe I can manage, if Bee will let me try," she blurted out, for Gwen generally did things abruptly.

Winnie drew a sigh of relief.

"I believe you could, too," she said hastily, "and I've been telling Beatrice so. Miss Roscoe will think I'm playing her a very nasty trick if I stop away. She'd never forgive me. You're strong, Gwen, and you know all about the hens and the pigs, and you can keep an eye on Nellie."

"Yes, try, childie. It will be a good practice for you—and there's nobody else," agreed Father.

Thus it came about that Gwen entered upon an entirely new experience. She had, of course, helped in the house before, but only under Beatrice's personal supervision; it was quite a different matter to have to take the responsibility of the whole establishment.

"Bother your sister as little as you can, I want her to have a complete rest," said Dr. Chambers. "You mustn't let her worry about what's going on downstairs."

It was easy enough for the doctor to give orders, thought Gwen, but a difficult matter to carry them out. She was determined, however, to do her best, and she made a most heroic effort to be patient with the invalid. The fact was that poor Beatrice, who never spared herself, was overworked, and the hot, damp weather had affected her nerves. Dr. Chambers knew his patient when he prescribed a fortnight in bed, and was well aware that it was the only way of persuading her to take the rest she needed. At first Gwen's anticipations of a trying time were literally fulfilled. Beatrice's bell was ringing constantly, and she had to keep running up and down stairs and listening to endless and minute directions, and to answer a perfect catechism of questions as to how affairs were progressing in the kitchen. Nellie also was in a grumpy mood, and difficult to conciliate. She did not like having instructions sent to her through Gwen, and showed her resentment by clattering about the kitchen and banging doors. It required more tact than Gwen had ever made use of in her life before to keep the peace. Then Martin was no slight anxiety, for the little scamp thought he could take advantage of Beatrice's absence to get into as much mischief as a magpie, and Gwen hardly dared trust him five minutes out of her sight. Between Martin, household tasks, and certain parish duties which could not be omitted, there was plenty to be done, and the days seemed full from morning till night.

Gwen had never before realized how very much lay in Beatrice's hands, and she began slowly to appreciate how heavy a burden her sister carried year in and year out, with scarcely ever a holiday to relieve the tension.

"It's far worse than any amount of lessons," she thought. "Going back to school will be quite a holiday after this."

One resolve Gwen had made, and stuck to with grim determination—to spend a certain time every day over mathematics and one or two other subjects in which she feared she was weak. She got Lesbia to bring her books from school, and every night, long after the latter was asleep, she would sit up in their joint bedroom studying. It was impossible to snatch five minutes during the day, but when the house was still and quiet it was easier to concentrate her thoughts, and she was surprised sometimes what progress she was able to make. Night after night she heard the clock strike twelve before she put out her lamp, and once even the early midsummer dawn stole in and caught her unawares. None of the family knew that she sat up working so late, or probably Father would have forbidden it, for it was certainly burning the candle at both ends. It was very difficult to rise at six o'clock and help to prepare breakfast when she seemed only to have had a few hours' sleep, and it was often a great temptation to ignore the alarum and turn over on her pillow.

But having accepted the household drudgery, Gwen had enough grit to carry out her duties thoroughly, however unwelcome some of them might be, and to secure breakfast in time was a cardinal virtue at the Parsonage. To her credit she never once let the others start late for school, or forgot to place their packets of lunch ready, and Beatrice herself could not have been more solicitous about drying wet boots and stockings.

"You're getting quite grandmotherly, Gwen," laughed Basil. "You never used to care about damp feet before. You're nearly as big a fusser as Bee. You made my cricket flannels look no end, though. I will say that for you."

"I like Gwen's housekeeping, she puts so much jam in the tarts!" remarked Giles approvingly.

"Gwen lets me feed the chickens my own self," said Martin with a satisfied chuckle. "And she mended my kite, too."

"I wish you'd mend my blue print dress, Gwen," said Lesbia. "I tore it again at school yesterday. That last darn of yours was uncommonly neat."

"Are they really getting to appreciate me more now I do more for them?" Gwen asked herself. "I never thought they cared an atom about me before. I was always the odd one at home. It's hard work, and a fearful trouble to do all those extra things, but oh!—it is nice to feel one's wanted."

At the end of a fortnight Beatrice was decidedly better, but Dr. Chambers was still unwilling to allow her to come downstairs.

"Best complete the cure while we're about it, and take another week in your room," he decreed. "If you begin to bustle round the house too soon, it may undo all the good of this enforced rest.

"I feel such a slacker," groaned the invalid.

After the doctor had gone the family held another conference in Beatrice's room.

"I had a letter from Cousin Edith this morning," said Mr. Gascoyne. "She offers to come and take full charge, both of you and the household. What do you think, Bee? Had we better let her come for a while, just until you're fit to be about again?"

"It isn't worth it for a week—and I mean to be down then, doctor or no doctor!" announced Beatrice, with characteristic firmness. "In the meantime I'd rather have Gwen than anybody, if she doesn't mind staying at home a few days longer. She's a kind little nurse, and she's kept things going wonderfully. I'd never have believed she'd manage so well."

Gwen's eyes filled with tears. Beatrice, of all people in the world, to yield her so high a tribute of praise! Beatrice, who had been so captious and hard to please as she lay in bed giving elaborate directions, and whose fidgety ways had needed so much patience!

"I'm glad if I've been of any use," she faltered.

"Use! You've been a jewel. I don't know whatever we should have done without you," said Beatrice, catching Gwen's hand, and squeezing it hard. "Can you spare another week as general slavey? Miss Roscoe would quite understand."

"I'll do anything you like, Bee," said Gwen, returning the squeeze.

Angela Brazil

CHAPTER XXIV

THE SENIOR OXFORD

Gwen went back to school after three weeks' absence, fearing that every chance of the Senior Oxford must have faded into thin air. She had worked as well as she could at home, but it had not been the same as studying with a mistress, and she felt her deficiencies painfully.

"There's no time to make things up now, either," she thought. "The exam. begins on the sixteenth, and that's actually next Monday. Oh dear! If only I were better up in maths! I know the chemistry'll stump me too. That's to say if I'm even allowed to go in at all!"

On this last point her doubts were soon dispelled. At eleven o'clock she received a summons to the headmistress's study.

"Well, Gwen," said Miss Roscoe. "It has been very unfortunate that you were obliged to stay away so long, but you must do your best, notwithstanding. I entered your name as a candidate for the Senior Oxford, so you will, of course, take the examination. Miss Trent has arranged to give you some extra coaching in the dinner hour every day this week, and I think you ought to be able at least to secure a pass. You're fairly certain all round."

"Except in maths.," said Gwen.

"Well, you must give all the time you can spare to that. But don't overdo the cramming. It's sometimes a fatal mistake to work early and late till your brain's utterly exhausted. I did that once myself and missed a scholarship through it. Take an hour at tennis every evening before you go to bed. Exercise is an absolute necessity if you're to be in form for next week. You're looking pale, and you mustn't break down before Monday. Tell your father to buy you a tonic."

Miss Roscoe spoke kindly, more sympathetically indeed than Gwen ever remembered to have heard her before. She had a wide experience with girls, and could estimate their capacities to a nicety. She had chosen her candidates carefully, and would ensure that they were sent in well prepared. So far she had had few failures in public examinations, and every pass brought extra credit to the school.

Five members of the Form were to take the Senior Oxford; Elspeth Frazer, Edith Arnold, Louise Mawson, and Betty Brierly, being the other four, all of them considerably older than Gwen.

"We call you the five victims!" said Charlotte Perry. "I'm glad I'm out of it. I sang a jubilee last week when Miss Roscoe read the list and my name wasn't on it."

"There were eight girls sent in last year," said Hilda Browne.

"Yes, and two failed—Majorie Stevens and Daisy Wilson. I don't think Miss Roscoe has forgiven them yet."

"Oh, dear! I'm afraid she'll be very down on me then," wailed Gwen. "I'm a doubtful quantity!"

"You? Oh, you'll be all right! She'd never let you try if you weren't—trust her!" said Charlotte Perry, and the rest agreed.

In spite of her schoolmates' assurances Gwen did not feel at all certain of success, and it was in very blue spirits and a state of woeful apprehension that she betook herself on the fateful sixteenth of July to the Stedburgh Town Hall, which was the local centre for the examination. It was her fifteenth birthday, and it seemed a funny way of celebrating the day. She had been so agitated that morning that she had scarcely been able to realize her presents, except the fountain pen which Father and Beatrice and Winnie had clubbed together to give her, and which she had brought with her to the exam. room.

At her first paper, however, she cheered up a little. It was easier than she had expected, and though one or two questions were beyond her, the rest were well within her capacity. Her new pen flew over the sheets of foolscap, and if she was too nervous to do herself full justice she at least acquitted herself with credit. The time-table only allowed an hour between one and two o'clock for lunch, which was provided for the candidates in a room at the Town Hall. Gwen anxiously compared notes with Elspeth, Edith, Louise, and Betty, as they hastily demolished plates of beef sandwiches and drank tumblers of lemonade. On the whole she had done as well or even better than they, and she began to cherish hopes.

As the week went on, Gwen, though not daring to be too sanguine, could not help feeling that her papers had reached a fair standard even in her weakest subjects. She had grown so accustomed to the examination room that she was no longer nervous and was able to express the facts she knew at their best advantage.

"There!" she said, when she had at last handed in her final sheets. "It's a toss-up whether I'm through or not. I expect it depends on the temper of the examiner who reads my papers. I'll hope he'll get his dinner before he tackles them!"

"Your writing's clear at any rate," said Elspeth. "Mine's such a scrawl I'm afraid that will be against me. Aren't you thankful the thing's over?"

"Thankful hardly expresses my state of bliss."

"It's rather sickening to have school exams, next week, after all this!" said Louise.

"They'll seem a mere trifle compared with the Oxford!" declared Gwen.

After the ordeal they had passed through in common the candidates were on terms of good comradeship, and with Elspeth Frazer Gwen felt there was a prospect of permanent friendship.

The last days of the term passed rapidly away. To Gwen the great event of the school year was over. Though she did her best at them, Rodenhurst examinations were a matter of quite minor importance. She welcomed the breaking-up with intense relief. After the strain of the past few weeks the holidays seemed an imperative necessity. It was delightful to have a complete rest, to idle about in the garden or on the shore, or take long invigorating walks on the moors. It would be five or six weeks before she could hear the result of the Senior Oxford, so she was obliged to endure the suspense as best she could.

In the meantime something happened—something so very unexpected and extraordinary that for a time it almost put even her examinations in the shade. It was Beatrice who told her the good news. Lately Beatrice had begun to treat Gwen as one of the grown-up members of the household, and to include her in their discussions of family affairs.

"It seems almost too wonderful to believe," said Beatrice. "Old Mr. Sutton has resigned his incumbency of North Ditton, and do you know the living is to be divided, and Skelwick, Basingwold, Hethersedge, and Rigby are all to be one big new parish by themselves. And who's to be Vicar, do you think?"

"Not Dad?" gasped Gwen incredulously.

"Yes. It has been formally offered to him, and he's going to accept it. Oh! and, Gwen, the funny part is, do you know, that queer old gentleman you met upon the wold turns out to be Sir Benjamin Hazlett, the patron of the living."

"He didn't look like a Sir Anything!" exclaimed Gwen. "He was the oddest, shabbiest, crankiest old fellow, and so inquisitive!"

"I hear he's very eccentric, and of course one sees now why he asked so many questions. He'd actually never been at Skelwick before, although he's the patron, and nobody here in the village knew him. He told the bishop you'd suggested dividing the parish!"

"I!" shrieked Gwen, "I wouldn't have dared to suggest such a thing. I only said it would be nice."

"Well, you put it into his head, anyway. He said the idea had never occurred to him before, and he saw at once its extreme advisability. He talked it over with the bishop, and they both agreed it ought to be done. I suppose he came to church that evening to hear Dad preach, and judge for himself what he was capable of."

"He evidently liked him. But who wouldn't?" returned Gwen. "Then Dad has refused Rawtenbeck?"

"Yes; thank goodness we needn't go and live amongst chemical works and factory chimneys! The Diocesan Society's going to build an extra bedroom on to the Parsonage. Isn't that lovely?"

"It will be the Vicarage now, if you please!" declared Gwen, rubbing her hands with satisfaction.

That her father's hard work should be recognized and rewarded at last was indeed a triumph, and the thought that she had perhaps had an unconscious share in bringing this about added a special element of joy.

"It was like entertaining an angel unawares!" she chuckled. "Though anybody less angelic-looking than poor old Sir Benjamin one couldn't imagine! I'm glad I took that solitary walk on the wold, Bee!"

"So am I, as it happens, though it's the exception that proves my rule."

The appointment to the new parish was indeed an important event for Mr. Gascoyne in more ways than one. It not only gave him a better position and larger opportunities of carrying on the work he had begun, but it meant also pecuniary benefit. The living of Skelwick was to be worth treble his curate's stipend, and though he was an unworldly man, his children's future was a necessary consideration. He would not be opulent, but he would now at any rate be free from money troubles, and the family could carry out many precious schemes which before had seemed mere dreams. The boys could be educated in course of time at Stedburgh Grammar School, Lesbia could take music lessons, and Gwen's visions of college might actually some day see fulfilment. Winnie could give up the teaching she hated and become housekeeper at home, that her elder sister might be free to take her training at a great London hospital, for Beatrice's heart was still set on entering the nursing profession.

"You'll see me a matron yet!" she announced. "I warn you that I'm ambitious, and mean to get on!"

"I'll be a B.A. by then, and we'll shake hands over our mutual success!" laughed Gwen.

"Don't forget you promised to be a lady doctor and study at college with me!" put in Dick, who had become almost one of the family at the Parsonage.

"You'll have to look out then, or I'll get ahead of you!"

"You won't do that, madam! I'm going back to school next term, remember."

Dick was fortunately quite strong again. The specialist who had examined him before declared he had outgrown his temporary delicacy, and even gave him permission to play football when the season began, as well as to recommence his work at Stedburgh.

"I shall be sorry to lose my pupil," said Mr. Gascoyne. "The children will miss you here on Saturdays."

"I'll see them all every day in the bus," returned Dick cheerfully.

As the holidays wore on and it grew nearer and nearer to the time when she might expect to hear the result of the Senior Oxford, Gwen waxed impatient. The suspense was hard to bear, and seemed harder the longer she waited.

"I want to be put out of my misery," she declared. "If I've failed I'd like to know and have done with it."

"But you thought you'd done pretty well," said Winnie.

"How can I tell? Every day I think of something more that I left out in my papers, and it makes me less and less hopeful. I've borrowed one of Dad's big pocket handkerchiefs all ready to weep into! I warn you I shall cry gallons if I've not passed."

Miss Roscoe had arranged that a telegram should be sent to each of the candidates announcing the lists, and on the day when the news was likely to arrive the Gascoyne family haunted the rampart on the wall, watching eagerly for the advent of the telegraph boy. It was Basil who spied him first, and Giles who got to the gate quickest to meet him, and Beatrice who tore open the yellow envelope and read the message to the excited audience.

"'First-class Honours, and Geographical Society's Silver Medal!'"

Gwen nearly dropped on the grass.

"Let me look at it!" she quavered. "Are you sure you haven't made a mistake, Bee?"

"Here it is in black and white. Look at it yourself, then, you sceptic, and be convinced! I do congratulate you!"

Angela Brazil

"Hip, hip, hooray!" yelled the boys with such vigour that their shouts aroused curiosity in the village, and several parishioners came to enquire the cause of the rejoicings.

Gwen had known that the Royal Geographical Society offered two medals, one of silver and one of bronze, to the two Senior candidates who gave the best answers to the geography papers, but in her wildest visions she had never contemplated winning one of them. To come out first in all England in geography seemed an honour almost above the flights of ambition.

"Miss Roscoe will be so rejoiced!" said Winnie. "She always thought you'd do well, Gwen. Why, you'll be a credit to the school. She'll boast about this silver medal for evermore. I expect it will go down in the prospectuses! You'll get coached up for a scholarship next, you'll see."

"I still can't quite, quite believe it—it's too absolutely, perfectly, deliriously scrumpshus!" bleated Gwen hysterically.

"Dad's big pocket handkerchief won't be wanted after all to dry your tears," laughed Lesbia. "Oh, there's Dad coming up the road now—go and meet him, Gwen, and tell him your own self!"

The next prize-giving at Rodenhurst was a more than usually special occasion, for not only had four girls matriculated, but five had passed the Senior Oxford, two of them in the Honours Division. Gwen's medal was acknowledged the triumph of the school, and both pupils and mistresses spoke of her as likely to win more laurels in the future.

"She's one of the best workers we have," said Miss Roscoe to the Mayor, who was acting chairman; "a very clever girl. I believe she has a career before her."

As Gwen went up to receive her prizes and certificate the girls clapped and clapped till, not content even with the noise they were making, they broke into ringing cheers. Half-dizzy with emotion, Gwen returned to her place—these were the very same schoolfellows who, only one short year ago, had allowed her to walk down the hall without a sign of recognition or appreciation. From being the outcast of her Form she had risen to the height of popularity.

"I always said, childie, that if you only bided your time and worked your very hardest, the girls would be proud of you in the end!" declared Father when the celebrations were over and the Gascoynes had returned to the Parsonage.

"Oh, it was ripping to hear them all clapping and cheering, Gwen! And after last year, too—it's like a miracle!" exclaimed Lesbia rapturously.

"Yes, that's just what it is—a miracle," said Gwen, thinking of the motto that hung on her bedroom wall.

* * * * *

Choose from Thousands of 1stWorldLibrary Classics By

A. M. Barnard
Ada Leverson
Adolphus William Ward
Aesop
Agatha Christie
Alexander Aaronsohn
Alexander Kielland
Alexandre Dumas
Alfred Gatty
Alfred Ollivant
Alice Duer Miller
Alice Turner Curtis
Alice Dunbar
Allen Chapman
Alleyne Ireland
Ambrose Bierce
Amelia E. Barr
Amory H. Bradford
Andrew Lang
Andrew McFarland Davis
Andy Adams
Angela Brazil
Anna Alice Chapin
Anna Sewell
Annie Besant
Annie Hamilton Donnell
Annie Payson Call
Annie Roe Carr
Annonaymous
Anton Chekhov
Archibald Lee Fletcher
Arnold Bennett
Arthur C. Benson
Arthur Conan Doyle
Arthur M. Winfield
Arthur Ransome
Arthur Schnitzler
Arthur Train
Atticus
B.H. Baden-Powell
B. M. Bower
B. C. Chatterjee
Baroness Emmuska Orczy
Baroness Orczy
Basil King
Bayard Taylor
Ben Macomber
Bertha Muzzy Bower
Bjornstjerne Bjornson

Booth Tarkington
Boyd Cable
Bram Stoker
C. Collodi
C. E. Orr
C. M. Ingleby
Carolyn Wells
Catherine Parr Traill
Charles A. Eastman
Charles Amory Beach
Charles Dickens
Charles Dudley Warner
Charles Farrar Browne
Charles Ives
Charles Kingsley
Charles Klein
Charles Hanson Towne
Charles Lathrop Pack
Charles Romyn Dake
Charles Whibley
Charles Willing Beale
Charlotte M. Braeme
Charlotte M. Yonge
Charlotte Perkins Stetson
Clair W. Hayes
Clarence Day Jr.
Clarence E. Mulford
Clemence Housman
Confucius
Coningsby Dawson
Cornelis DeWitt Wilcox
Cyril Burleigh
D. H. Lawrence
Daniel Defoe
David Garnett
Dinah Craik
Don Carlos Janes
Donald Keyhoe
Dorothy Kilner
Dougan Clark
Douglas Fairbanks
E. Nesbit
E. P. Roe
E. Phillips Oppenheim
E. S. Brooks
Earl Barnes
Edgar Rice Burroughs
Edith Van Dyne
Edith Wharton

Edward Everett Hale
Edward J. O'Biren
Edward S. Ellis
Edwin L. Arnold
Eleanor Atkins
Eleanor Hallowell Abbott
Eliot Gregory
Elizabeth Gaskell
Elizabeth McCracken
Elizabeth Von Arnim
Ellem Key
Emerson Hough
Emilie F. Carlen
Emily Bronte
Emily Dickinson
Enid Bagnold
Enilor Macartney Lane
Erasmus W. Jones
Ernie Howard Pie
Ethel May Dell
Ethel Turner
Ethel Watts Mumford
Eugene Sue
Eugenie Foa
Eugene Wood
Eustace Hale Ball
Evelyn Everett-green
Everard Cotes
F. H. Cheley
F. J. Cross
F. Marion Crawford
Fannie E. Newberry
Federick Austin Ogg
Ferdinand Ossendowski
Fergus Hume
Florence A. Kilpatrick
Fremont B. Deering
Francis Bacon
Francis Darwin
Frances Hodgson Burnett
Frances Parkinson Keyes
Frank Gee Patchin
Frank Harris
Frank Jewett Mather
Frank L. Packard
Frank V. Webster
Frederic Stewart Isham
Frederick Trevor Hill
Frederick Winslow Taylor

Friedrich Kerst
Friedrich Nietzsche
Fyodor Dostoyevsky
G.A. Henty
G.K. Chesterton
Gabrielle E. Jackson
Garrett P. Serviss
Gaston Leroux
George A. Warren
George Ade
Geroge Bernard Shaw
George Cary Eggleston
George Durston
George Ebers
George Eliot
George Gissing
George MacDonald
George Meredith
George Orwell
George Sylvester Viereck
George Tucker
George W. Cable
George Wharton James
Gertrude Atherton
Gordon Casserly
Grace E. King
Grace Gallatin
Grace Greenwood
Grant Allen
Guillermo A. Sherwell
Gulielma Zollinger
Gustav Flaubert
H. A. Cody
H. B. Irving
H.C. Bailey
H. G. Wells
H. H. Munro
H. Irving Hancock
H. R. Naylor
H. Rider Haggard
H. W. C. Davis
Haldeman Julius
Hall Caine
Hamilton Wright Mabie
Hans Christian Andersen
Harold Avery
Harold McGrath
Harriet Beecher Stowe
Harry Castlemon
Harry Coghill
Harry Houidini

Hayden Carruth
Helent Hunt Jackson
Helen Nicolay
Hendrik Conscience
Hendy David Thoreau
Henri Barbusse
Henrik Ibsen
Henry Adams
Henry Ford
Henry Frost
Henry James
Henry Jones Ford
Henry Seton Merriman
Henry W Longfellow
Herbert A. Giles
Herbert Carter
Herbert N. Casson
Herman Hesse
Hildegard G. Frey
Homer
Honore De Balzac
Horace B. Day
Horace Walpole
Horatio Alger Jr.
Howard Pyle
Howard R. Garis
Hugh Lofting
Hugh Walpole
Humphry Ward
Ian Maclaren
Inez Haynes Gillmore
Irving Bacheller
Isabel Cecilia Williams
Isabel Hornibrook
Israel Abrahams
Ivan Turgenev
J.G.Austin
J. Henri Fabre
J. M. Barrie
J. M. Walsh
J. Macdonald Oxley
J. R. Miller
J. S. Fletcher
J. S. Knowles
J. Storer Clouston
J. W. Duffield
Jack London
Jacob Abbott
James Allen
James Andrews
James Baldwin

James Branch Cabell
James DeMille
James Joyce
James Lane Allen
James Lane Allen
James Oliver Curwood
James Oppenheim
James Otis
James R. Driscoll
Jane Abbott
Jane Austen
Jane L. Stewart
Janet Aldridge
Jens Peter Jacobsen
Jerome K. Jerome
Jessie Graham Flower
John Buchan
John Burroughs
John Cournos
John F. Kennedy
John Gay
John Glasworthy
John Habberton
John Joy Bell
John Kendrick Bangs
John Milton
John Philip Sousa
John Taintor Foote
Jonas Lauritz Idemil Lie
Jonathan Swift
Joseph A. Altsheler
Joseph Carey
Joseph Conrad
Joseph E. Badger Jr
Joseph Hergesheimer
Joseph Jacobs
Jules Vernes
Julian Hawthrone
Julie A Lippmann
Justin Huntly McCarthy
Kakuzo Okakura
Karle Wilson Baker
Kate Chopin
Kenneth Grahame
Kenneth McGaffey
Kate Langley Bosher
Kate Langley Bosher
Katherine Cecil Thurston
Katherine Stokes
L. A. Abbot
L. T. Meade

L. Frank Baum
Latta Griswold
Laura Dent Crane
Laura Lee Hope
Laurence Housman
Lawrence Beasley
Leo Tolstoy
Leonid Andreyev
Lewis Carroll
Lewis Sperry Chafer
Lilian Bell
Lloyd Osbourne
Louis Hughes
Louis Joseph Vance
Louis Tracy
Louisa May Alcott
Lucy Fitch Perkins
Lucy Maud Montgomery
Luther Benson
Lydia Miller Middleton
Lyndon Orr
M. Corvus
M. H. Adams
Margaret E. Sangster
Margret Howth
Margaret Vandercook
Margaret W. Hungerford
Margret Penrose
Maria Edgeworth
Maria Thompson Daviess
Mariano Azuela
Marion Polk Angellotti
Mark Overton
Mark Twain
Mary Austin
Mary Catherine Crowley
Mary Cole
Mary Hastings Bradley
Mary Roberts Rinehart
Mary Rowlandson
M. Wollstonecraft Shelley
Maud Lindsay
Max Beerbohm
Myra Kelly
Nathaniel Hawthrone
Nicolo Machiavelli
O. F. Walton
Oscar Wilde

Owen Johnson
P.G. Wodehouse
Paul and Mabel Thorne
Paul G. Tomlinson
Paul Severing
Percy Brebner
Percy Keese Fitzhugh
Peter B. Kyne
Plato
Quincy Allen
R. Derby Holmes
R. L. Stevenson
R. S. Ball
Rabindranath Tagore
Rahul Alvares
Ralph Bonehill
Ralph Henry Barbour
Ralph Victor
Ralph Waldo Emmerson
Rene Descartes
Ray Cummings
Rex Beach
Rex E. Beach
Richard Harding Davis
Richard Jefferies
Richard Le Gallienne
Robert Barr
Robert Frost
Robert Gordon Anderson
Robert L. Drake
Robert Lansing
Robert Lynd
Robert Michael Ballantyne
Robert W. Chambers
Rosa Nouchette Carey
Rudyard Kipling
Saint Augustine
Samuel B. Allison
Samuel Hopkins Adams
Sarah Bernhardt
Sarah C. Hallowell
Selma Lagerlof
Sherwood Anderson
Sigmund Freud
Standish O'Grady
Stanley Weyman
Stella Benson
Stella M. Francis

Stephen Crane
Stewart Edward White
Stijn Streuvels
Swami Abhedananda
Swami Parmananda
T. S. Ackland
T. S. Arthur
The Princess Der Ling
Thomas A. Janvier
Thomas A Kempis
Thomas Anderton
Thomas Bailey Aldrich
Thomas Bulfinch
Thomas De Quincey
Thomas Dixon
Thomas H. Huxley
Thomas Hardy
Thomas More
Thornton W. Burgess
U. S. Grant
Upton Sinclair
Valentine Williams
Various Authors
Vaughan Kester
Victor Appleton
Victor G. Durham
Victoria Cross
Virginia Woolf
Wadsworth Camp
Walter Camp
Walter Scott
Washington Irving
Wilbur Lawton
Wilkie Collins
Willa Cather
Willard F. Baker
William Dean Howells
William le Queux
W. Makepeace Thackeray
William W. Walter
William Shakespeare
Winston Churchill
Yei Theodora Ozaki
Yogi Ramacharaka
Young E. Allison
Zane Grey